CLASS MATES

Male Student Culture and the

Making of a Political Class

in Nineteenth-Century Brazil

ANDREW J. KIRKENDALL

University of Nebraska Press

LINCOLN & LONDON

Portions of this manuscript have been
previously published as "Orators and Poets:
Language and Elite Male Identity at the São Paulo
Law School, 1850–1880," *South Eastern
Latin Americanist* 38, no. 4 (spring 1995): 43–48,
and "From 'Liberty and Order' to 'Order and
Progress': Republican Discourse among
São Paulo Law Students, 1878–1889,"
SECOLAS *Annals* 27 (March 1996): 91–96.
They are used here with permission.

LIBRARY OF CONGRESS
CATALOGING-IN-PUBLICATION DATA
Kirkendall, Andrew J.
Class mates : male student culture
and the making of a political class in nineteenth-
century Brazil / Andrew J. Kirkendall.
p.   cm.—(Engendering Latin America)
Includes bibliographical references and index.
ISBN 0-8032-2748-5 (cloth : alk. paper)—
ISBN 0-8032-7804-7 (pbk. : alk. paper)
1. Law students—Brazil—History.
2. Young men—Brazil—Intellectual life—History.
3. Political leadership—Brazil—History.
I. Title. II. Series.
KHD196 .K57 2002 340′.092′2—dc21
2001052237

CLASS MATES

Engendering Latin America
VOLUME 6

EDITORS

Donna J. Guy
University of Arizona

Mary Karasch
Oakland University

Asunción Lavrin
Arizona State University

CONTENTS

ACKNOWLEDGMENTS

This book would not have been possible without the help of many people. Any project in preparation as long as this one is, unfortunately, often prone to make its author forget even some of our most serious debts. For those generous individuals I have neglected to mention here I hope that you will conclude that I am just forgetful and not ungrateful.

This book began as a doctoral dissertation at the University of North Carolina at Chapel Hill. Without a number of grants made available through the Duke-UNC Program in Latin American Studies, however, there would have been no dissertation. I am grateful for grants from the Tinker Foundation and a grant from the U.S. Department of Education Foreign Language Area Studies Program, as well as for two small Mowry research and writing awards from the UNC history department. The Texas A&M University history department has given me a place to teach and has encouraged me in my research and writing. Judy Mattson and Jude Swank helped me enormously when computer problems threatened to keep me from making an important deadline. The university's Program to Enhance Scholarly and Creative Activities enabled me to turn a dissertation into a book.

As a college student at Wesleyan University bent on becoming an ethnomusicologist, I veered off into more familiar terrain and rediscovered history. This was in large part because of two gifted teachers, Peter Dobkin Hall (who helped me understand the importance of examining education critically and historically) and Henry Abelove (who taught me how to read carefully). In my graduate career I accumulated quite a number of debts, far too many of which, I am sure, I have forgotten. Don Mathews, John Kasson, and Gil Joseph let me know that I had something to offer at a time when I could find little in myself to give. Gil introduced me to Latin American history; he even introduced me to the academic study of Brazil, and for that, and for many subsequent favors, I am thankful. Members of my doctoral dissertation committee (including Sarah Chambers, Peter Filene, John French, and Jim Leloudis) inspired me in many and various ways. My greatest intellectual debt is to John Charles Chasteen, a creative thinker, a tireless researcher, and a beautiful writer — in short, the ideal mentor as well as a dear friend. He was always willing to read whatever I had and able to inspire me to give him more to read.

Numerous people have offered me encouragement, even when I have not always followed their advice. I think particularly of Jeremy Adelman, Roderick Barman, Stephen Frank, Charles Hale, and Iván Jaksić. Peter Beattie and an anonymous reviewer for the University of Nebraska Press also offered advice that I hope has made the following clearer. Whatever errors remain are mine and no less dear to me for being wrongheaded.

Anyone who spends much time overseas inevitably relies on the aid of many, some of whom remain total strangers. Brazilian archivists and librarians were always professional in their dealings with me; I am particularly grateful to the staff of the Biblioteca Nacional for microfilming thousands of pages of student newspapers for me. But I am also conscious of the help I received from taxi drivers, hotel desk clerks, and doormen. To stand for all these others, I must express my appreciation for a man who, in 1993 at least, was employed in the last-named occupation: Ricardo César Soares da Silva Barrozo.

Long before I decided to become a historian and all along the way since, Brazilian friends, few of them academics, have opened up their homes and their hearts, in particular, Manuel Serpa and Angela Colognesi, Martha Sales Costa and her family, and Josué Modesto dos Passos Subrinho.

Nothing in my life would have been possible without the help of my mother, Joan Carol Nelson Kirkendall (who taught me to love books), and my father, Richard Stewart Kirkendall (who taught me to love libraries). I will never be able to repay what I owe to my in-laws, Major Paul Raymond Reynard, U.S. Air Force (retired), and Kathy Dundas Reynard.

My greatest personal debt is to my wife and best friend, Meg Reynard, who taught me how to live in the present. The life we have made together and the lives we have made together (Panalin Reynard Kirkendall, Booker Reynard Kirkendall, and Eli Reynard Kirkendall) are the proofs I offer that miracles exist.

INTRODUCTION

A Brazilian writer in the early twentieth century recalled of his father, a magistrate and politician: "For him, Brazil only existed because of the law school in São Paulo." From that school emanated the "integration of the national spirit in the political and juridical order."[1] To understand Brazil's distinctive development as an independent nation, one has to look at this school and its sister institution in the northeastern province of Pernambuco as well as the complex process of political class formation that took place in these two locations during the imperial period (1822–89). Although Brazil clearly did not exist solely because of these institutions, the young men who passed through the law schools' doors left an indelible mark on the country's political culture and structures of power. They were the victors in the postcolonial struggle for authority that characterized much of nineteenth-century Latin American political life. I wrote this book to explain the intertwining of education and power in nineteenth-century Brazil and how a small group of men were socialized, and socialized themselves, until they developed a sense of common identity as the legitimate leaders of their society.

In the decades following independence from Spain and Portugal, the new Latin American nations sought to create functional state governments and bureaucracies. Few were successful. The complex and convoluted process of independence in most of the former Spanish colonies resulted in the establishment of new political norms and paths to power. Political violence and personalistic rule hindered the development of the state in much of Spanish America. Those individuals seeking to establish civilian supremacy over political institutions found themselves struggling with other heroes of the independence movement who derived their legitimacy from achievements on the battlefield. Many colonial administrators had themselves been military men. They shared the experience of soldiering not only with the conquistadors of the early years of conquest and settlement, but also with the captains-general, whose powers were strengthened following the centralizing reforms of the eighteenth-century Bourbon rulers. Elites born in Spanish America found status and privilege in the colonial militias as well and, in some cases, received training that served them well in the wars of independence.[2]

Legal training, too, had provided an avenue for civilian advancement after the conquest, as the Spanish Crown sought to provide a formal structure for the colonies. *Letrados* (men with a university degree) had a privileged status in Spain and in the New World that took effect when they began their studies. They became accustomed to special privileges from their time at the university (they were generally immune from prosecution, for example), and after they received their diplomas they were, like the nobility, exempt from direct taxation. A university education, particularly in the law, became increasingly important for those young men interested in serving as agents of the Spanish Crown during the colonial period.[3]

With independence, the contest between the pen and the sword became more intense. Throughout most of Spanish America in the nineteenth century, *letrados* vied with *caudillos*, men whose authority was defined by land ownership and power over those who worked the land or by proof of military valor.[4] In Mexico, for example, it has been said that of all the nineteenth-century politicians who were old enough to fight, 80 percent fought in one or more of the century's three major military conflicts.[5] In some Spanish-speaking countries, "the military and associated militias virtually created the states."[6] But men with training in the law sought to build on the historical status they gained from their service to the Crown; they attempted to create an enhanced authority of their own that, theoretically, could now be derived from republican notions of popular sovereignty.[7] This was the case in the new nation of Colombia, for example.

In many Spanish-speaking nations in the Western Hemisphere, the *letrados*'s triumph over their competitors was neither immediate nor sustainable. Furthermore, university-trained men found that they could no longer inspire the deference they had come to expect during the colonial period. And if the task of constructing a functional state was often arduous, the achievement of a sense of national identity was often obstructed by even more tenacious loyalties to region, patron, or political party.[8]

Brazil was far more successful than any other Latin American country in achieving political stability and civilian supremacy. The Portuguese royal family's escape in late 1807 from the forces of Napoleon Bonaparte to the safety of their colony in South America enabled that colony to avoid the uncertainty and conflict that overtook Spanish America after the French emperor's removal of Ferdinand VII the following year. The resettlement of the royal family in Rio de Janeiro made it possible, ultimately, for an impulsive Portuguese prince to establish Brazil as an independent nation and become its first emperor in 1822. With his traditionally legitimate, genetically derived source of authority, Dom Pedro I was able to establish a monarchical system in Brazil that lasted for much of the rest of the nineteenth century. Although Dom Pedro I himself only ruled Brazil until 1831, when he (once again impulsively) abdicated and returned to Portugal, his son, Dom Pedro II, would rule for almost fifty years, by far the most successful example of a New World monarchy. Brazil was not immune from regional revolts and slave rebellions, particularly in the turbulent period of the Regency from 1831 to 1840 when Dom Pedro II was too young to assume power. Nonetheless, Brazil achieved a level of political stability unmatched by most of its Spanish American neighbors.

The Brazilian path to independence had not legitimized the armed path to power or created new "heroes on horseback."[9] Central to Brazilian stability was not only the political institution of a constitutional monarchy, but also a cohesive, plantation-owning economic elite and a political class, the members of which were often one and the same.[10] The key institutions in which the political class was formed were the two state-run law schools, founded in 1827 and located in the provinces of São Paulo in the south and Pernambuco on the northeast coast. Graduates of the schools staffed the centrally appointed imperial bureaucracy as magistrates and provincial presidents and served in the bicameral Congress, the foreign service, and the imperial ministries. Brazil may have had the most highly developed system of elite recruitment in the Western Hemisphere.[11]

In establishing the law schools in the late 1820s, Brazil's legislators followed the Portuguese model for the proper functioning of universities in a monarchy and "empire." The Brazilians had been ill served by their Portuguese rulers, for they had failed to establish, and even actively prohibited the creation of, institutions of higher education. While the Spaniards founded the first universities in the New World, the Portuguese Crown assumed that their subjects in the far-flung reaches of a global empire could return to the mother country and study at the University of Coimbra, the training ground of officials and magistrates since 1308. The university flourished as the Portuguese trading empire expanded into Asia, Africa, and America in the fifteenth and sixteenth centuries. Those Brazilians trained in Portugal, of course, were expected to be loyal to the Crown. The only significant educational institutions that were allowed to develop in the Portuguese American colony were closely tied to the Roman Catholic Church and particularly to its most prominent representatives in Brazil, the Society of Jesus. The Jesuits, however, were expelled in 1759 because of pressures from colonists who resented the Jesuit order's role as protector of Brazil's indigenous population and also because of a general drive for more centralized control.[12] As a result, Brazil's educational system all but collapsed.

Most of Brazil's political leaders of the 1820s had attended the University of Coimbra. The political class trained there played a significant part in enabling Portuguese America to remain united while Spanish America fragmented into seventeen different and largely unstable countries after independence.[13] Under the colonial system, Brazilian-born Coimbra graduates had served the Crown primarily as magistrates. With independence came the opportunity to become professional politicians, as well, by serving on local, provincial, and national levels. For these men, mastery of the language of liberalism would be a defining characteristic.

The dominance of a legally trained elite had deep roots in Portuguese history, yet it is clear that alternative patterns could have developed. As already suggested, the monarchical framework inhibited Brazilian *caudilhos* (in the Portuguese spelling) from achieving national power. At the same time, it enhanced the authority of the Brazilian *letrados* or *bacharéis* (literally, anyone with a bachelor's degree) and helped justify their hegemony over society. The early Brazilian legislators rejected the idea of founding a university. Other than the medical schools in Rio de Janeiro and Salvador, the law schools were the only significant institutions of higher learning in the imperial period. Although the debate over establishing a Brazilian university continued throughout the nineteenth century, most argued that Brazil lacked the economic and intellectual resources for a university.[14]

The failure to establish universities guaranteed that there would be little chance for alternative elites with diverse academic and professional backgrounds to challenge the law school graduates. Medical schools predated the law schools, but they provided little in the way of scientific learning until late in the imperial period. Since by this period medical doctors could still provide little reliable proof that their treatments would heal more than harm, their social status and cultural authority were not high. Military academies remained subordinate in stature since the armed forces were deprived of prestige and resources. The training in engineering that the military schools provided would prove attractive late in the imperial period, but engineers themselves received little acclaim in imperial Brazil's agrarian society. Few plantation owners would have welcomed a son's choice of engineering as a profession. (Only one Brazilian-born engineer was ever granted a title of nobility for his achievements in the field.)[15]

The professions, as a whole, developed slowly. Lawyers found it difficult to make a living, even in the imperial capital of Rio de Janeiro. Moreover, the time and energy they devoted to private practice were often limited to the years after graduation before they could find employment as agents of the state or win election to public office.[16] Given the attractions of state employment, it should not be surprising that the independence associated with the professions in the Anglo-American world also developed slowly.[17] It is because of the direct relation between legal education, state employment, and public life that the law maintained its preeminence throughout the imperial period (and well into the twentieth century).[18]

The clergy, another possible competitor for cultural authority, had been subordinated to the Crown since the colonial period through the "system of royal patronage" (*padroado real*). This system had evolved from the special privileges the Pope had granted the Catholic kings to encourage the conversion of the indigenous peoples to Christianity. The Crown's attempt to further enhance its power in the eighteenth century included an attack on the Church, and particularly the Society of Jesus, which had led the missionary effort in the New World. By the time of independence in 1822, the Church was a much weaker institution in Brazil than in most of Spanish America, despite the fact that Catholicism remained the official religion. The *padroado real* was maintained. Although some clergymen took part in politics in the early postindependence years, notably the priest and regent Diogo Antônio Feijó in the 1830s, as with the military they found themselves increasingly on the sidelines. The clergy's social and cultural authority remained limited throughout the imperial period. Dom Pedro II and the Brazilian parliament kept a tight rein on the Church, providing only limited support for seminaries and deliberately keeping the number of dioceses small.[19]

For most of the nineteenth century, Brazil was defined, politically, by the monarchy and a complex system of limited political representation and socially by the institution of slavery. At the time of Brazil's independence in 1822, roughly one-third of its population was enslaved. Slaves worked on the declining sugar plantations of the northeast coast, where Brazilian civilization was born. Men and women of African descent labored in the burgeoning coffee plantations of the south; in the Paraíba River Valley near Rio de Janeiro, the capital of the empire; and in the eastern parts of São Paulo province. Slaves also provided much of the manpower for the gold and diamond mines of Minas Gerais and the cattle ranches of Rio Grande do Sul, the empire's southernmost province. In the cities as well, slave labor was employed in domestic service, on the docks, and in selling goods on the streets. Slavery was an inescapable fact of Brazilian life, for some a reason for the nation's economic development so far and, for others, the cause of its backwardness.

While many Brazilians had reason to bemoan the relative lack of economic progress, members of Brazil's ruling class found comfort in the deep continuities of their social and political life. Like slave owners in other societies, they feared change and disorder. The transitions in Brazilian social and political life were often slow and hesitant. This was especially true of the transition to free labor, which was not completed until 1888, thus making Brazil the last country in the Western Hemisphere to abolish slavery.

Colonial Brazil was not only a slave society; it was also a patriarchy, in which the power of men and of fathers was assumed. This aspect of nineteenth-century society was nowhere better described than in the works of Gilberto Freyre (perhaps because he so thoroughly identified with it). Many who have done research on the Brazilian family have had good reason to question the applicability of Freyre's model to the Brazil that lay outside of the northeast and to the nonelite sectors of society. Nevertheless, his work remains rich in insight, particularly as it relates to the lives of the members of the political class who are the object of my study. Freyre's work is important not least of all because it seeks to explain the slow but significant transitions in Brazilian social life and to demonstrate that Brazil's patriarchy was far from a static institution. One of the largely forgotten insights of Freyre's neglected book *The Mansions and the Shanties* is that nineteenth-century society was metamorphosing from "patriarchalism" to "individualism." In a century in which the colonial patriarchy was decaying, new conflicts arose between fathers and sons. In Freyre's somewhat schematic presentation, the urbanized law students were in league with the modernizing emperor Dom Pedro II. This led to conflict with their plantation-owning fathers, as new models of masculinity competed with traditional ones.[20] Luís Martins developed Freyre's idea of the split between fathers and sons in a neo-Freudian interpretation of the growing divisions between the emperor and the young *bacharéis* in the waning days of the empire. Martins was struck by what he interpreted as a widespread sense of guilt among those who had committed a symbolic patricide by helping force Dom Pedro II into exile in late 1889. Only those republicans who were inclined toward positivism were free from these guilt feelings because they had substituted Auguste Comte as a surrogate father figure for Dom Pedro II.[21]

The arguments of both Freyre and Martins can be faulted for some obvious weak points. Martins's thesis is unnecessarily complicated. A simpler explanation for the positivists' lack of despair was that they had a program and clear ideas about what to do once they gained control of the government. Freyre, for his part, overstates the degree to which the patriarchy had broken down. Throughout the imperial period, a *bacharel*'s success continued to be closely tied to his father's position. Moreover, Freyre not only overstates the degree to which Brazil had become urbanized in the nineteenth century but also the extent to which the interests of urban and rural elites diverged. Urban elites inevitably had family and commercial ties to rural elites; one could hardly expect it to be otherwise in an economy still largely based on plantation agriculture.

Nevertheless, both men pointed out important themes that I will develop further. An understanding of Brazil's patriarchal system is crucial to an understanding of the young men of the law schools, and relations between fathers and sons will be a recurring theme in this book. Martins, for his part, correctly identified that a strong sense of nostalgia for the imperial order was particularly marked among men whose fathers had been successful politicians under the empire. And his work showed a clear grasp of the importance of Dom Pedro II as man and symbol, one that recent works have finally begun to address more fully.[22] Both Freyre and Martins grasp the intensity of the feeling, if they exaggerate the hostility, between planters and *bacharéis*.[23] While I do not reduce this conflict to a generational one between uneducated fathers and *bacharéis*, I find this ambivalent relationship to be central to the formation of student identity during their law school years.[24]

Building upon Freyre, Raymundo Faoro argued that the division between state and society was the central dynamic in Luso-Brazilian history. Faoro's *bacharel* lost "his identity of origin" and joined the enemies of his plantation-owning father (representing society) "to realize the mission of exalting the state."[25] Faoro's sweeping interpretation still has its adherents, not least of all Eul-Soo Pang, who has argued that "two nobilities — the economic and the political" existed during the imperial period.[26] In response, Richard Graham has forcefully argued that the two were hardly so distinct. State agents were never free from a sense of responsibility to kin and patrons; Graham considers Faoro guilty of "reifying" the state.[27] While Graham is convincing on this and other points, he misses something that the state-versus-society scholars understand, if at times only implicitly. The *bacharel* considered himself to be fundamentally different from the landowner. While the plantation owners were not universally uneducated, as Freyre suggested, the *bacharel* nevertheless saw himself as the representative of civilization and progress, at times in opposition to the plantation owners. Those who argue that the *bacharel* was merely the mouthpiece of the landowning class miss the complexity of his own central ambivalence. By shifting the focus of the argument somewhat to questions of identity formation, as I do in this book, I may not resolve this issue. However, I do provide an understanding of the lived experience of young men in transition from family life to a career as an agent of the state within a patriarchal, slave society.

As the basic structures of Brazilian society resisted change, the Brazilian political class formed and reformed over time. Patronage defined the daily exchanges of nineteenth-century political life and guaranteed political stability while they also limited access to political power. For the students at the law schools, patronage was as inescapable a part of the social fabric as the institution of slavery. Brazilian elite males in their youth felt most keenly the ways in which this patron-client system created opportunities and imposed restrictions.[28] An ambitious young Brazilian male who lacked a patron found it difficult to gain access to the political class. Access to higher education in the imperial period virtually defined access to political power; the law schools had a central role to play in patronage networks as well as in the imperial political system as a whole.

For the most part, the ruling class thought that higher education should help produce and reproduce a small political class. Some seven thousand men graduated from the law schools from the 1830s to the 1880s, and they dominated the imperial political system. No matter how much the Brazilian elite admired Europe and European culture, few of those trained in Europe (except for Coimbra graduates in the early postindependence period) could hope to prosper politically.[29]

It is the process of production and reproduction of a political class that forms the focus of this book. I analyze this process from within, by looking at how students formed their identities as members of a political class while in law school. My focus is on a group all too frequently ignored by historians: students. Sérgio Adorno and Alberto Venâncio Filho have argued convincingly that the law schools must be understood as more than just centers of political indoctrination. Both argued that the "extracurriculum" should be the primary focus of attention, and I have developed their insight at length in this study.[30] Insights from the anthropology of education are crucial for an understanding of how identities are formed in the school years. Recent work on schooling has suggested the need to go beyond what R. W. Connell has called the "black box" theory of education. Too often scholars strangely conflate what is taught with what is learned. Ethnographers of education have turned away from a focus on the ideology of education to an examination of daily practices in the school and among students, not only peer group dynamics but also the "systems of meaning" these practices constitute.

While the central place of the law school graduates in the imperial system has long been recognized, this process by which a political class was produced and then reproduced over time has gone largely unexamined. It is the central concern of this book. It is undoubtedly true, as a number of scholars have argued, that a certain amount of political indoctrination took place at institutions that were, after all, created and administered by the state. But indoctrination, for reasons I discuss in chapter 4, was not the primary, or even the major, achievement of these schools. The profound state of disorganization at the law schools and the restiveness of the young males themselves made simple inculcation of dominant ideologies difficult.

When I began this project, moreover, I was puzzled by the anomaly of state agents who were in training to serve a monarchy and maintain a hierarchical slave society spending much of their time organizing republican and abolitionist organizations. Existing understandings of schooling and society seemed inadequate to explain the dynamics at work in the Brazilian law schools. I became convinced that I had to look at the subjects of my inquiry not as fully formed adults but as young males making the difficult transition from boyhood to manhood. (Entering law students had to be at least fifteen years old.) I realized that I needed to look at how these law students viewed themselves and their role in society as they undertook the larger process of socialization into adult roles. I sought to understand what to me seemed increasingly to be a complex process of identity formation in a distinct phase of life — youth, which in these young males' minds constituted the five years they spent in law school.[31]

My initial reading of graduates' memoirs had made clear that what they remembered best and what mattered to them most were the literary and political associations they formed during their school years as well as the affective ties they developed. Student identities were formed even more outside than inside of the classroom. I was struck by the degree of autonomy these law students possessed, which was far greater than in most other societies and times, even for elite males. Here was another indication of the transformation of the patriarchy during the nineteenth century. That they used their time outside of the classroom to write poetry rather than study law suggested avenues of investigation toward an understanding of their own mentalities. As I read more deeply in a large collection of student writings spanning the course of the imperial period, I began to see that student identities were not static, that they evolved in response to a slowly changing social and political context. "Generations" did not come and go mathematically according to a particular length of time but in response to changing historical contexts and transformations in the students' understandings of themselves. Moreover, I began to see how these identities were shaped not only by common experiences in group living arrangements and in literary and political organizations but also within the larger communities they inhabited in Olinda (and after 1854 in neighboring Recife) and São Paulo. An important part of their development came from relations with older males. This meant their teachers, of course (as I explore in chapter 4), but also the politically active men who lived in these cities. Throughout the imperial period identities often were formed in conflict with family members and patrons as well.

This book explores the ways in which these young men forged common bonds, not always evenly or straightforwardly but in the end successfully, to create a cohesive elite. Drawn from many corners of the Brazilian empire, these young men developed national as well as regional ties, as I discuss most fully in chapter 3. Their rites of passage were undoubtedly important, but no more so than the total rite of institution of the law school experience itself, which, as Pierre Bourdieu would say, separated them ineluctably from other young men and women who would never under any circumstances undergo the same experience.[32] In this time of opportunity and experimentation, students looked to each other more than to their fathers and teachers for their values and attitudes. They discovered themselves through their extremely active extracurricular peer culture.[33] They chafed at the boundaries of a society that theoretically valued age over youth as it prized masculinity over femininity. Two individualistic ideologies, Romanticism and liberalism, helped them define themselves outside of family identities and, paradoxically, defined their group identity as well.

Students tested the limits of behavior and discourse even as they enjoyed the privileges of their class and gender. And in testing social and political boundaries they sought to establish themselves as the political leaders of the future. As youth in transition to manhood, they sought both recognition of the independence that would define them as men and assurance that their political futures would be bright ones (in part, because of the very patronage structures that sustained and nagged at them). Frequently sons and grandsons of prominent politicians (further proof of the deep continuities in Brazilian political life), they sought to be more than just their father's and grandfather's progeny. The political utility of their connections was no less troublesome for being ready-made.

This study is based largely on primary research I conducted in a rich collection of student newspapers microfilmed for me by the Biblioteca Nacional as well as in the official records of the law schools in the Arquivo Nacional (both in Rio de Janeiro). Through it, I sought to locate student culture and identity formation within a changing social and political context from the 1820s through the 1880s. Ethnographers typically interview their subjects at a particular moment in time and therefore can pay relatively little attention to questions of historical process. I have been fortunate that the documentation that exists for a historical study of nineteenth-century student life is unparalleled because the student press had an importance in imperial Brazil that it rarely has had in any culture. Most of the works in this field also have primarily been concerned with examining the life of subordinate members of society, whether working-class "lads" (Paul Willis) or women (Dorothy C. Holland and Margaret A. Eisenhart). In my case, my subjects are the elite, and my questions have necessarily been different ones. So many of the student newspapers have been preserved, largely because they represent the earliest writings of some of the most significant political figures and authors of the nineteenth century. Thus, I have had an opportunity to examine how a national political class was formed over time, in large and small ways, and how an incipient political class understood itself and its claims to legitimate authority. Information on the question of identity formation and the quest for cultural authority is abundant because the imperial political class was so committed to oral and verbal expression that it left extensive documentation behind, material that has only rarely been exploited by historians.

An intensive study of the student newspapers makes clear the extent to which these young males were engaged in a quest for cultural authority.[34] Each new crop of future leaders had to find its own way, not merely to maintain the social and political structures as they found them, but to provide a reason why their leadership should supplant (or at least complement) the previous generation's. A political class in formation needs to strike a balance between continuity and change. Without continuity, too many could take part in the race for political power. Without change, there would be no reason to pass the baton to a new generation. Although much in the process of identity formation remained constant, the claim to political legitimacy, even relevance, was subject to much change. Each new generation had to redefine itself, sometimes only subtly, sometimes dramatically, to ensure that its assertion of authority would be convincing not only to others but, most importantly, to itself. A political class without the conviction of its right to govern has already lost half of the battle.

Chapter 1 demonstrates how in the 1820s and 1830s students sought to define an identity separate from the Portuguese. Ideologically, they were liberals, proponents not only of constitutional government and free markets but also of an antipatriarchal individualism that spoke to their own experience as young males. While successive generations never abandoned liberalism entirely, they found it inadequate for their purposes and often troublesome. This was particularly true in the 1830s when rebellions throughout the empire threatened to shatter the nation.[35] As students strove to master the discourse of liberalism, from the late 1830s to 1860 they also sought to redefine liberalism in terms they deemed appropriate for a slave society and less threatening to social stability.

By the 1840s, they also sought other means to assert the legitimacy of their authority, a topic I explore in chapter 2. They looked more to their literary and oratorical skills, abilities that separated them from the largely illiterate society over which they claimed the right to rule. (Even in the 1870s, only one in five free males was literate.) They played the role of the Romantic hero and considered the creation of a national literature to be a fundamental part of the larger goal of nation building.

Oratory and poetry remained key components of student culture for much of the imperial period, but more directly political concerns regained their cogency in the 1860s, as will be seen in chapter 5. Students were always

attuned to international trends and the impulses of the larger political national context in which they expected to soon play leading roles. They embraced a more combative liberalism, advocating abolition and, to a lesser degree, republicanism, which would not take hold fully until the late 1870s
and 1880s. Throughout the nineteenth century, young Brazilian males in
particular were alert to changing intellectual fashions and open to new
ideas. Students sought to portray themselves as idealistic youth, purer and
truer to the ideals of liberalism and not just its tarnished practice.

Chapter 6 examines the tensions within the imperial political system
from 1870 on, which threatened to end the long-standing political stability.
The pace of material progress accelerated, albeit largely in a geographically
limited area, primarily the province of São Paulo. The law students in this
period began to see the Brazilian monarchy as an impediment to the progressive needs of a society that was changing, but far too slowly for them.
At the same time, the dramatic explosion of student enrollment at the law
schools overloaded the patronage networks and inhibited the entrance of
many law students into the political class. In the waning years of the empire,
literary aspirations were being supplanted by a new orientation toward social science and a new claim that these young men could solve the problems
plaguing Brazilian society. Thus, these very state agents in training, who
had long been seen as the guarantor of political stability, now seemed to be
undermining it by embracing abolitionism and republicanism as never before. In doing so, they threatened the social and political pillars of society.

The students' redefinition of self within the peer culture created the possibility for a continued hegemonic role as the outmoded monarchical political system and slave-based social system were overturned. That could hardly
have been predicted on 11 August 1827 when the enabling legislation establishing the law schools was passed. The relationship between the identities
formed at the law schools and Brazil's changing society is a complicated
and dynamic one. To the opening phase in the creation of an indigenously
trained political class, I now turn my attention.

PORTUGUESE LEGACIES, LIBERAL ASPIRATIONS

The process of creating an indigenously trained political class was fraught with tensions. The political leaders of the new nation of Brazil were torn between the legacies of their Portuguese colonial past and their aspirations for a liberal American future. A desire for liberty and autonomy warred with a fear of instability and disorder, which was particularly acute in a slave society like the Brazil of the 1820s. In creating a new political order, Brazil's founders looked backward to Portugal and forward to England and France, their political and cultural models, while remaining committed to holding on to what they had. They questioned the traditions of centralized and authoritarian rule they had grown up with but feared breaking with tradition to an extent that might endanger their control over Brazilian society.

The law students, as well, were entangled in the attempt to define both a distinctively Brazilian identity and a form of liberalism that would not threaten their own future claims to power. More than any generation after them, the group of young men studying at the law schools in the late 1820s and early 1830s had to define themselves against their Portuguese cultural and political heritage. Their student culture and their understanding of themselves and of politics clearly reflected the deep ambivalence of the Brazilian ruling class about these Iberian legacies. To some degree, this generation had a chance to remake themselves. During the 1830s, however, as the unrest that followed the abdication of Brazil's first emperor continued, the students like their elders saw clear dangers in letting too many participate in defining a liberalism that was appropriate for Brazilian society.

The liberal founders of the law schools in Pernambuco and São Paulo were largely products of the University of Coimbra, as were some of the law students themselves. The institutions they created were significantly and necessarily based upon Portuguese traditions, even as they tried to improve upon that model and make it fit Brazilian society. In seeking to create institutions for a new nation, they worked within limitations imposed by three centuries of colonial rule. The newly independent Brazil of 1822 had little to build on in creating an appropriate educational system for a new nation. Inevitably, the early Brazilian legislators had to work from what they knew, and for the majority what they knew was the University of Coimbra.

COIMBRA AND THE FOUNDING OF THE BRAZILIAN LAW SCHOOLS

The men trained in canon and civil law at the University of Coimbra had seen their power increase since the 1400s as the Portuguese empire was created, the absolutist state solidified, and their job opportunities expanded. The law school graduates' power and interests were "intimately tied to those of the Crown," which "embodied legitimacy and authority." This link to the Crown had enhanced the Coimbra graduates' status in Portuguese society, placing them on a level of virtual equality with knights and *fidalgos*, in other words, minor nobility. Over time, they took on various characteristics of a caste, marrying into each others' families and virtually monopolizing judicial and other administrative positions in government.[1]

These *letrados* were royal officials, not civil servants. Imperial legislation attempted to prevent them from establishing ties with the local societies in which they served. The Portuguese Crown had long tried to maintain its own authority by preventing the establishment of rival, local authorities. In 1352, the Crown had established the *juiz de fora*, literally, the judge from outside, a royal appointee who was expected to be more loyal to the Crown's interests than municipal judges, who were elected by and beholden to local interests. The *juiz de fora* continued to serve as the representative of the Crown in remote areas of the Portuguese American colony.[2]

In the contradictory world of Brazil's constitutional monarchy the conflict between local power and imperial power carried over into the struggles over the location of power after independence in 1822. Loyalties to subnational regions remained strong, and those with ties to their local *pátria*, or region, resisted efforts to grant what they saw as too much power to the emperor himself and, by extension, to an imperial bureaucracy still tied to his interests.[3] Because the law schools were the institutions within which imperial agents were produced, their place in society, and therefore the relative importance of their graduates, would not be resolved until this crucial debate between centralized and regional power was settled. This would only occur after the years of instability that followed Dom Pedro I's abdication in 1831 and Dom Pedro II's premature accession to power in 1840.

A Coimbra education had primarily been, as Stuart Schwartz has argued, a socializing experience that "readied a man for the robe of office." Extracurricular activities, most particularly "drinking and brawling," created a certain esprít de corps and long-lasting personal ties among the young men. This camaraderie amounted to a virtual "class consciousness" that to some degree mitigated against a blind loyalty to the king.[4] The role of a law school education as a socialization experience would be just as strong in the Brazilian case, as I will show. Before I do, it is important to underscore at the outset that in both the Portuguese and Brazilian examples the expectations of professional independence of the Anglo-American world were distinctly different from the Iberian goal of molding state agents.

Coimbra students had been a privileged lot, enjoying until 1834 special *foros*, or exemptions from civil jurisdiction. Visually, students were distinguished from the townsmen of Coimbra by the cap and gown that between 1718 and 1834 they were required to wear both in and out of class. The cap and gown were intended to enhance the feeling of corporate solidarity, as it lessened distinctions between more and less wealthy students. Given their special legal status, the uniform may have shielded the students to some extent from punishment for their actions, although it also must have made them an easier target for spontaneous or planned acts of violence by those who resented their privileges. Indeed, hostility between town and gown often boiled over into physical conflict. (Students in Coimbra were an unruly lot; prohibitions against their carrying weapons were passed repeatedly beginning in the 1500s, but with little effect.) In Brazil, as we shall see, repeated proposals to establish a formal uniform came to naught. While formally, Brazilian students would lack any special legal protections, they frequently were protected by social custom and friends in high places from punishments for misbehavior.[5]

The ways in which the law school experience at the University of Coimbra created a political class conscious of its own place (to a large degree, apart from and over the rest of society) may not have weighed heavily on the minds of those who created the Brazilian law schools. What was clear to them, however, was that political independence created an urgent need for a magistracy trained in Brazilian, not in Portuguese, law.[6] The founding of the law schools was a highly conscious exercise in state building. Although critics later lamented the failure to establish a more broadly based system of education, the founders were probably correct when they maintained that the Brazil of the 1820s lacked the resources to staff a university.[7]

Early debates revolved around whether to have a law curriculum within a larger university (as was the case in Coimbra) or a law school independent of a university. The primary concern was more political than educational per se. The new state required men trained to fill its positions. The number of Brazilians educated at Coimbra was not sufficient for the demands of the new nation. In the early discussions over the founding of the law schools, it was envisioned that they would train "able men" who would one day be "wise magistrates." Furthermore, it was expected that some of the same men would eventually become members of the Chamber of Deputies and the Senate, the two houses of the newly established Congress. (Deputies were elected every four years; senators served for life.) Others would serve in the diplomatic corps. The graduates of the new schools would not just be bureaucrats, as they has been in the Portuguese empire but also professional politicians.[8]

The Constituent Assembly attempted to found a university as early as 1823, the year after independence from Portugal was declared on 7 September 1822. A university was necessary, one legislator argued, because of the mistreatment, even oppression, of Brazilian students attending the University of Coimbra. The larger struggle between the Congress and the emperor over the balance of power impeded the swift establishment of institutions of higher education, however. The initial proposals to create universities went nowhere because the emperor dissolved the Constituent Assembly on 12 November 1823.[9]

As legislators debated the fine points of establishing schools appropriate for an independent nation, they were concerned with avoiding what they saw as the mistakes of their alma mater. Although many of the statutes governing the University of Coimbra were provisionally adopted in 1823, they would have to be modified according to the "lights of the century."[10] Bernardo Pereira de Vasconcellos, a prominent figure in the postindependence period, always spoke disdainfully of the University of Coimbra. "I studied public law at the university, and I left it an ignoramus," he declared, claiming that he was "even forced to unlearn" what his teachers had taught him.[11] Other critics of Coimbra charged that the law school had produced "too many *bacharéis* who knew nothing [but] blind routines . . . lacking the principles and light of [juridical] science."[12] Furthermore, the Portuguese university had been a center of religious and intellectual intolerance, according to its not-so-loyal alumni in the Brazilian legislature. In Coimbra, Vasconcellos recalled, the Inquisition was "open continuously, ready to consign to the flames anyone who had the temerity to recognize any truth, whether in jurisprudence or in politics."[13]

As the legislators lambasted the weaknesses of their Coimbra education, they came to see as a key issue the place of Roman law in the curriculum. If training at the University of Coimbra produced a "sense of loyalty and obedience to the king," it was the Roman law tradition itself that had provided the ideological underpinning for the rise of the absolutist state in Portugal. The influence of the University of Bologna, which had led the revival of the study of Roman law in Europe, was particularly strong in Coimbra.[14] The inclusion of Roman law in the curriculum was hotly contested in succeeding versions of the law school's enabling legislation. It was banned in the 5 July 1826 proposal, for example, only to be put back in the 1 August 1826 proposal. Finally, it was excluded in the 11 August 1827 legislation that finally and definitively established the law schools.[15] Only in 1854 would Roman law be introduced in the Brazilian law school curriculum, when the need for centralized power had become part of the ideological consensus of the ruling circles of the empire.

The absolutist Portuguese model was to be replaced by a curriculum oriented around liberal understandings of the state and the economy. An early proponent of higher education in Brazil argued against the idea of having too many professors specializing in Roman law, a problem he believed Coimbra suffered from. As far as the deputy José Feliciano Fernandes Pinheiro was concerned, only two subjects were essential: constitutional law and political economy.[16] In designing the curriculum, lawmakers had a vision of a Brazil that had broken with the past and authoritarian traditions of

Roman law. They envisioned a nation moving toward a liberal vision of society, which placed constitutions above monarchs and extolled the virtues of a free-market economy over one based on mercantilist privileges.

When the law school's enabling legislation was passed in 1827, a yearlong course in constitutional law was required for first-year students, and political economy, a subject not taught at Coimbra, was one of the two main subjects offered in the culminating fifth year. Political economy became a key component of the law school curriculum. In São Paulo, this course was taught by major political figures, including a future member of the first three-man Regency in 1831. French and English liberal thinkers dominated the curriculum (and the extracurriculum) for the rest of the nineteenth century. For example, J. B. Say's *Catechism of Political Economy* was adopted as a textbook. The Frenchman's physiocratic emphasis on agriculture as the principal source of nations' wealth was agreeable for an elite whose own wealth came from export crops like sugar and, increasingly from the 1830s on, coffee. Pedro Autran, a dominant force at the Pernambuco school for generations, translated English liberal John Stuart Mill's *Political Economy* in the early 1830s.[17]

In addition to designing the curriculum, the legislators had to decide where the law schools should be established, and this too had broader implications for the location of power in Brazil. Olinda in the northeastern province of Pernambuco and São Paulo in the eponymous southern province were already the preferred sites for either a university or a law school as early as 1823. Difficulties of travel were certainly an important consideration. Olinda was expected to educate primarily young men from the north and São Paulo those from the south. Nevertheless, these two cities were hardly unanimous choices. Some feared that the intellectual stagnation they had witnessed in Coimbra would be reproduced in the new settings, which they argued were as isolated from the rest of the world as Coimbra had been. The allegedly "unpleasant pronunciation" of São Paulo natives was not the least of the defects suggested by that city's detractors, and certainly São Paulo was a far more rustic and less cultured setting than Rio de Janeiro in the nineteenth century.

Had the forces of centralization been ascendant, one would have expected Rio to be the ideal location. Certainly, Rio had much to offer as a setting for a university being Brazil's largest city as well as its political and cultural capital. If the founders of Brazil's law schools sought to create an elite for whom Rio de Janeiro would always be the central reference point, that city would seem to have been the logical choice for a law school. But since the law schools were established during a period of conflict between the centralizers, associated with Emperor Dom Pedro I, and federalists who were tied to local interests, the choice of Olinda and São Paulo seems to have been a triumph for the latter.[18]

Both cities had attractive liberal credentials. Olinda's connections to liberalism and education were established in 1800 when sugar-planter-turned-liberal-bishop Azeredo Coutinho revived an abandoned Jesuit high school and turned it into a seminary that shared some attributes of a modern secondary school. This advanced more than just the city's convents and churches, its traditional dominant institutions, however, since the graduates of the seminary also became associated with political causes. The school was seen as a "focus of liberalism," and as Gilberto Freyre somewhat breathlessly reminds us, "some even whispered of heresy." The bishop himself, according to José Murilo de Carvalho, was the first "to write on Brazilian economic problems from a liberal point of view." Many priests who studied at the Olinda seminary (and even some who taught there) were active in political revolts in 1817 and 1824, and some were involved in later revolts, such as the Liberal rebellion of 1842 in Minas Gerais and São Paulo.[19]

Although founded by Jesuits, São Paulo was never dominated by them, and the liberal spirit was strong there as well. São Paulo had been politically isolated until the eighteenth century. Perhaps because of the Paulistas' self-proclaimed personal independence, inhabitants of the city and surrounding province were actively involved in the drive for political independence. With independence, the town's political importance increased as it became the capital of the province. The first director of the São Paulo school was Lt. Gen. José Arouche do Toledo Rendon, who despite his military predilections had a doctorate in law from Coimbra. More importantly, he had been part of the core group of liberal São Paulo elites who had supported separation from Portugal. Rendon was a close ally of José Bonifácio, often called the father of Brazilian independence for his role in advising the young emperor to break from his native land.[20]

Other early law professors at the southern school also had liberal leanings. José Maria de Avellar Brotero, also a Coimbra graduate, was Portuguese and had only settled in Brazil after independence. An opponent of Dom Miguel, who had usurped the Portuguese throne, Brotero had been forced to flee Portugal. He taught in São Paulo from its opening in 1828 until 1871. He was known for his Broterados, which we would call malapropisms, and for a pretentiously annotated textbook with (critics charged) excessive citations in Latin and particularly French. Nevertheless, São Paulo law school chronicler Almeida Nogueira contended that Brotero's thinking was too advanced for his day and that this explains the rejection of his writings. (Brotero, for example, had suggested that the existence of God was a "doubtful point for many great spirits and philosophers.") This verdict is hard to square with the testimony of others that his lectures consisted of "undigested amalgamations of despotic doctrines, expounded eloquently if not methodically, and in sometimes incorrect Portuguese."[21]

Like many others in nineteenth-century Brazil, Brotero suggests the uneasy mix between liberal aspirations and the scholastic and authoritarian Portuguese heritage. The founders of the law schools wanted to move away from the Portuguese example of Coimbra, but their state-building project and Brazilian liberalism itself were ambivalent. One must look at the language of the enabling legislation itself, in which Dom Pedro I announced the creation of the law school for his "subjects." A liberal polity would consist of citizens; subjects suggested something less than liberal. As the leader of the new nation, Dom Pedro I himself was a profoundly ambiguous figure. Although championed as a leading proponent of liberalism both in Brazil and, after his abdication as Brazil's emperor, in Portugal, he acted frequently in an extremely autocratic and illiberal way. He had, after all, imposed the constitution that was to be the centerpiece of Brazilian legal study after he closed Congress.[22]

The legislators themselves, moreover, were not immune to the attractions of centralized control. Law school directors and professors were appointed by the imperial government; any changes in the curriculum or in the selection of textbooks had to be approved by Congress. This made the law schools relatively inflexible institutions and produced some of the very problems that the legislators had sought to avoid in moving away from the Iberian heritage.

To further complicate our understanding of the motives of the law schools' founders, we must look at the legislative act from the same year in which the law schools were created that called for the local election of justices of the peace. The position of justice of the peace was intended, in part, to alleviate the inadequate supply of trained personnel to fill positions in the justice system. More fundamentally, however, the justice of the peace (who would not necessarily have any legal training) was seen as a check on the power of the centrally appointed and Coimbra-trained magistrates, who were beholden and presumably sympathetic to Dom Pedro I and centralized power. As the most visible representatives of Portuguese power during the colonial period, magistrates had been hated and feared by many. The creation of the justice of the peace was a victory for those politicians who favored local over imperial power.[23]

It has been argued that the preexisting Coimbra-trained elite made a unified Brazil possible.[24] I concede that the Coimbra-trained magistrates played a key role in providing substantial continuity and stability in the early stages of state building. However, I would argue that the 1820s and 1830s were still a period of flux in which the centrality of the law school graduate was still an unresolved issue. The early legislators had profoundly mixed feelings about Portuguese colonial legacies. The law schools themselves reflected this combination of liberalism and authoritarianism, and the students would also reproduce these ambivalent traits in their own student culture and ideology.

STUDENT CULTURE IN A LIBERAL AGE

The first generation of Brazilian law students far surpassed its successors in rebelliousness and general unruliness. They sought to understand liberalism on their own terms in the changing conditions that political independence had created. The era of independence created new opportunities for self-definition. Student newspaper editors made clear their own sense that they lived in a new age by dating their newspapers with the phrase "tenth year of independence," for example, rather than 1831.[25] Students were coming of age in a highly politicized era when political ideologies were still in conflict and national and regional politicians had failed to achieve a consensus on the organization of the political system. As a result, they embraced a Brazilian liberalism that reflected a young man's distrust of authority as well as a desire for an identity that was, to a certain degree, democratic and egalitarian.

The students' deep engagement with politics was hardly surprising because much was at stake in this formative period. For them, one of the main unresolved issues was to what degree they would be running the show. In the politically charged times leading up to Dom Pedro I's abdication in 1831 and continuing with the widespread regional revolts throughout the 1830s, student newspapers gave scant attention to matters outside of the political realm. In an 1831 newspaper, for example, an Olinda student editor apologized for not discussing events at the law school itself, so pressing were the national events in that fateful year.[26]

Historians have frequently commented on the liberal bent of the Brazilian law student, not least of all during this period. "The São Paulo law school," as Pedro Brasil Bendecchi has written, "was marked from its birth by the sign of liberalism."[27] Some of the students who returned from Portugal after the law schools were opened had been involved in antiabsolutist political activities in Coimbra. They were returning to Brazil after Dom Miguel closed the university because of opposition political activities there.[28] As members of the anti-Miguelista Volunteers of Liberty, many early students had been forced to flee Portugal.[29]

Students in São Paulo followed closely the news from Rio de Janeiro, particularly "any new manifestation of '*exaltado*' liberalism."[30] They looked further afield for inspiration as well, namely, to events in France, the country that would be the primary model of a civilized nation for Brazilian elites in the nineteenth century. The revolt of the French people against King Charles X in November 1830 led to student demonstrations in the streets. Students saw hopeful signs in the successful removal of an autocratic ruler, which they hoped to see replicated in their country soon.[31]

During the first years of the law schools' operation, the gap widened between Dom Pedro I and the politically active members of society. Under pressure from England, though influenced as well by his own convictions, he had agreed in a treaty to end Brazil's participation in the transatlantic slave trade. Also, the emperor's costly attempts had failed to maintain control over some long-contested Spanish territory, resulting in Uruguay's independence as a nation in 1828. Brazilian liberals were increasingly vocal over Dom Pedro I's frequently autocratic ways. The emperor himself, for his part, was distracted by events in the native country, where Dom Miguel had seized power from the Brazilian ruler's underage daughter.

Some have characterized the late 1820s and early 1830s as a "revolutionary" period.[32] Certainly, to the extent that there were revolutionaries in Brazil during this period, the language they spoke was that of a decentralizing federalist liberalism opposed to the power of the emperor. To understand the political trajectory of many students during this time, the evolution of José Thomaz Nabuco de Araujo is instructive. Nabuco was born in Bahia, the great-nephew of a senator. His father had been a member of the Chamber of Deputies in Rio de Janeiro beginning when Nabuco was twelve and was the president of the northeastern province of Paraíba when Nabuco matriculated in 1831. Nabuco's father became a senator soon after the son's graduation from the Olinda school. Nabuco was himself destined to be a senator and leading "statesman of the empire" from the 1850s until his death in 1878. Like many of the more prominent law students, he came from a family in which visits from important regional politicians were a part of daily life during his teenage years in Rio. His experience in Rio at an impressionable age also gave him a certain cachet among his Olinda peers. From his first days at the Olinda law school in early 1831, he was politically active. Nabuco's own political bent was toward the *exaltados* who constituted the left wing of political discourse.[33] Like many of his generation, his heroes were primarily politicians and journalists. He aspired to emulate the aforementioned orator Vasconcellos and the writer Evaristo de Veiga, a prominent liberal newspaper editor in the imperial capital. (Like them, too, Nabuco would grow more conservative during the 1830s.)[34]

For those students in the São Paulo school, the influence of liberals closely associated with the call for independence was particularly strong. The opening of the law schools had created educational opportunities for young men of the middle sectors of society. José Antônio Pimenta Bueno, for example, was an older student (twenty-four when he matriculated) who was unlikely to have crossed the Atlantic to study in Coimbra. As a doctor's son in the port city of Santos, however, he was hardly the representative of the popular classes he is sometimes portrayed as being. Even before the founding of the law school, he had already been active in politics and had been an assistant to the secretary of the provincial government of São Paulo in 1824. He worked in the local press and became a close associate of some of the major political figures among the city's liberals, including some who would figure prominently during the period of the Regency. As an older student, his political leanings were less prone to the dramatic shifts we will observe during Nabuco's years in Olinda, although, as we shall see, local political conditions also helped to shape the law student body in São Paulo.[35]

Many students like Pimenta Bueno worked for local liberal periodicals, such as *O Farol Paulistano* (1827) and *O Observador Constitucional* (1829), the first newspapers established in São Paulo.[36] The student press was not as important as it would become in the 1840s. The influence of an Italian emigré, Libero Badaró, was particularly strong among the students.[37] When he died in 1830 at the hands of supporters of Dom Pedro I street demonstrations erupted in which many students joined members of the popular classes to demand the apprehension of his murderers. One of the local justices of the peace who pursued the case was himself a third-year law student. (Eventually, three German immigrants were imprisoned and charged with the crime.) A street near the law school was eventually renamed in honor of the martyred Italian, whose stirring last words were said to be, "A liberal dies, but not liberty."[38]

Other foreign-born residents of the southern city also had a strong impact on São Paulo students' political understanding. To promote liberal values among the students, the German emigré Júlio Frank, a teacher at the preparatory school next door to the law school, helped found a masonic student society, the Bucha. When he died, he was buried within the law school itself because as a non-Catholic he could not be buried in local cemeteries.[39] His tomb within the heart of the school symbolized São Paulo's distinctive liberal bent for decades to come. In a nation in which Catholicism remained the state religion, his tomb was a potent symbol of nonconformity and, to a certain extent, of anticlericalism.[40]

Badaró and Frank remained important figures for future generations of students at the southern school. Throughout the imperial period, law students wrote poems in their honor. No comparable role models existed in Olinda, particularly no powerful martyr figures like Badaró. This became an important element in the formation of the distinctive characters of the two schools.

The students did not see themselves as merely followers of older men, however admirable. They believed they had a special role to play in creating a liberal Brazil. For their part, the editors of São Paulo's first student newspaper, *O Amigo das Letras* (1830), promised to "profoundly implant the love of liberty" in the Brazilian people. They defined their project to be translating European thinkers of the eighteenth and nineteenth centuries. *Translation* is an appropriate word for the larger student project of adapting liberal ideas to Brazilian society. What was lost in the translation, some have suggested, was precisely the reality of the Brazilian situation.[41] What the students gained was a sense of themselves as distinct from their Portuguese forefathers.

The abdication of Dom Pedro I on 7 April 1831 — the event that banished other concerns from student newspapers — was a watershed event in the further definition of a Brazilian national project. Many of the more radical liberal students had supported his removal from office, and they celebrated his departure. For example, *A Voz Paulistano*, a newspaper edited by a sixteen-year-old student at the southern school, had found its reason for being in opposing the emperor and thus ceased publication after he left for Portugal.[42] The emperor, wrote an editor of another student newspaper, had tried to "make us slaves" and "suffocate the natural propensity of the Brazilian people for liberty, snuffing out the lights of the century." In the end, Dom Pedro had tried with a "coup d'etat to destroy liberty or lose the throne. He lost the throne." The confidence that history had but one direction, a liberal one, was manifest in almost every utterance of these first-generation students. "The human spirit is on the march," one student wrote, "despotism cannot make it retreat."[43]

Students' rejection of the authority of the monarchy justified, as well, a general suspiciousness of other forms of authority. While later generations of students were hardly compliant, the degree of conflict between the students of the 1820s and 1830s and their professors was particularly strong. Students were quick to challenge professors in the classroom. Outside of class, they often confronted their teachers on the streets or criticized them in print. The faculty lamented the seeming impunity with which they were attacked in the press. São Paulo director Rendon suggested that this was because these were no longer the times of "despotism," as had been the case in Coimbra.[44]

In another observer's eyes, these young men showed little respect for teachers because they had embraced "liberalism, badly understood."[45] This phrase is a key to understanding students' behavior during this era. Liberalism suggested to the students a new vocabulary of rights that allowed them to challenge their professors' authority. Brotero was hardly the only professor accused of engaging in "despotic and arbitrary acts."[46] Criticism of a teacher became linked in student phraseology to an understanding of the larger political context in which Brazilians were trying to break away from an authoritarian Portuguese past of despotism and arbitrary power.[47]

Professors appealed to the imperial government for help in gaining control of the students but received little support from the Congress in the early 1830s.[48] By the late 1830s, national legislators, concerned over larger questions of social order, grew more sympathetic to faculty concerns. Professors renewed their efforts to establish more control over students' behavior. The reforms passed in 1837 were directed only at "injuries, threats, or acts of violence of any sort," but students rejected the reforms as an unconstitutional infringement on their rights as citizens "not to be judged by special [courts or] judges."[49] After all, violent acts could be tried in an ordinary court of law, which could subject guilty parties to penalties far stiffer than mere expulsion from school. How much justice, students warned, could they expect from a system in which the ones making the accusations, the teachers themselves, would also be the judges and jury? This would relegate student rights to the "dominion of the arbitrary." The acts of youth, one student noted, are always presumed to result from a "lack of reflection, vehement passions, and the spirit of insubordination." If "our youth were not dominated by the noble spirit of independence and liberty," it would be much worse. "If there existed in our hearts the weakest germ of servility," he continued, the reforms would make it grow, and indignity and baseness would triumph. Students would lose their personal dignity and become "blind instruments" and "submissive slaves" of "arbitrary power."[50]

Ironically, even as it sought to define itself in antiauthoritarian terms, the student body reproduced Portuguese hierarchies in student life. The divisions between first-to-fifth-year classes had been strong in Portugal, and this carried over in the New World. First-year students bore the brunt of upperclass disdain and abuse. The hazing practices upperclassmen perpetrated on freshmen in these early years even led in some cases to murder. One young man lamented the "scandalous lack of hospitality" that had to be endured by a "young Brazilian, recently arrived after a young journey to which he was unaccustomed and full of longing for family and friends, whom he left for the love of study." By drawing attention to their shared identity as Brazilians, this student denied the value placed on the distinction between beginning and advanced students, especially when the latter acted as "persecutors" of the former. Moreover, these hazing practices were a part of the colonial legacy this student wanted his colleagues to reject. The fact that such behavior had the imprimatur of tradition meant nothing. Indeed, it "was a good reason not to" act in such a way in Brazil.

As the old saying went, "in Coimbra, a very small number of good things were practiced," according to Sérgio Teixeira de Macedo, who had attended the Portuguese university and evidently knew whereof he spoke. Brazil was "in the time of the reform of old errors and abuses."[51] This sense of the changed situation in the first decade after independence was highly charged. Social relations themselves were seen as mutable. The state of independence also suggested new possibilities, at least to some, for relations among themselves. The weight of tradition was strong, however, and the general societal belief in hierarchy even stronger. The ritual abuse of first-year students would continue until the 1880s.

The student culture in the first generation after the establishment of the law schools was an uneasy blend of the old and the new. As a language of rebellion, liberalism offered particular advantages for young men testing the boundaries of acceptable public and private behavior and belief. Students' fidelity to liberal values was soon tested by the political unrest that followed Dom Pedro's return to Portugal, and student liberalism, like Brazilian liberalism generally, would emerge transformed.

REGIONAL REVOLTS AND THE TRANSFORMATION OF LIBERALISM

The law students, politically engaged as they were, could hardly be exempt from the larger political transformations of the years following Dom Pedro

I's abdication. Their understanding of distinctively Brazilian liberalism was redefined until by the end of the 1830s many students turned away from the federalism of the early years and became supporters of a nation-state with power centrally located in Rio de Janeiro. The 1830s raised in a profound way the issue of the responsibility for maintaining "order" and locating power.[52]

Historians have long noted the contradictions inherent in nineteenth-century Brazilian liberalism, as did contemporary observers and in particular foreign travelers. It was a libertarian ideology for a hierarchical slave society and a parliamentary political system that was ultimately subject to the whims of a hereditary emperor who could dissolve Congress and call for new elections as he saw fit. The fight for independence had marked liberalism's "heroic age," according to Brazilian historian Emilia Viotti da Costa, when Brazilian landowners used these ideals to achieve independence to further their own economic ends. Landowners feared the attempt by the Portuguese to reimpose mercantilist policies on Brazilian goods that had found a better price in the free (largely British) market since 1808. That the Brazilian liberals did not live up to their ideals once they had achieved their immediate goals should not be too surprising. Liberalism, as da Costa suggests, was no more than "empty rhetoric" for many during this period.[53]

Liberalism in Brazil, as in Europe, however, was embedded in particular historical and social contexts, and these altered notably throughout the 1830s. The years 1827–37 marked "the heyday of Brazilian liberalism and the truly revolutionary phase of Brazilian independence," when the decentralizing impulse was at its height.[54] Devolution of power to the provinces accelerated after 1831. The combination of the loss of the traditional source of political authority and the internal struggles for power locally created opportunities for political unrest and insurgency on a scale never equaled, before or since, and in all regions of Brazil. The 1830s were a period in which the demands of the popular classes became most vocal if not most concrete or coherent. Many of these revolts drew on a vocabulary of anti-Portuguese nativism that created possibilities for coalitions that transcended racial and class lines.[55] Although students and recent law school graduates participated in some of these rebellions in the 1830s, the older generation of Coimbra graduates was largely absent. Other contenders for political and moral authority, such as radical priests and lower ranks of the military, were much more prominent in the revolts, however, and the ultimate failure of these rebellions marked a defeat for the military and the priesthood as major players in the political system for decades to come.[56]

Beginning with the abdication of Dom Pedro I, the discourse of liberalism in the student press began to emphasize the dangers of excessive liberty. For all of the students' unruliness or rebelliousness, they could be counted on to defend public order. Students in São Paulo offered to form an armed band to defend the newly formed Regency, although no actions seemed to have resulted from this proposal. In Pernambuco, where the resistance to the new political order was greater, students found common cause with officers and soldiers in May 1831 and supported the decrees of the regents against absolutist officials who sought to bar their execution. Students and military men called for the removal of the emperor's Portuguese allies serving in the provincial administration.[57] Although this protest led to the removal of some Portuguese officials, the alliance between soldiers and students in the northern city did not last. When the military took the lead later that year, the students did not follow them.

While revolts spread throughout the country, a rebellion in Pernambuco itself in September left strong impressions on the students at the northern school, particularly on their attitudes about popular insurrections and the military. In nearby Recife from 14 through 16 September 1831 (in what has become known as the *Setembrizada*), members of the military and the popular classes staged attacks on the local proabsolutist society, the Column of the Throne and the Altar, as well as on local Portuguese. Slaves seized the opportunity to join in the unrest in hopes they could gain their freedom. Prisoners were released from jail. Soldiers and what one student called "the horde of vile slaves" took over parts of Recife for three days. The revolt dissipated as many soldiers grew distracted by alcohol and pleasures of the flesh. Meanwhile, the Olinda law students played a key role in putting down the effectively leaderless rebellion. "Leaving behind the sanctuary of Minerva," as one admiring official wrote, "youths accustomed to study and well-versed in books . . . ran to the theater of war." Students took up arms to defend garrisons and other strategic areas around Recife, even disarming some of the soldiers. Officials praised their "acts of valor in defense of honor and public security." In the months after this revolt, students took turns standing guard at several fortresses around the city and helped suppress other minor uprisings.[58]

The *Setembrizada* and other revolts that threw the popular classes and disgruntled military men together deepened the students' distrust not only of the poor and slaves but also of a standing army, "with its tendency to insubordination and disorder."[59] The national government dramatically reduced the size of Brazil's army, cutting in half the number of "active duty forces from 30,000 to 14,342."[60] Students and the landowning class embraced the National Guard, formed through legislation passed on 18 August 1831, as the guarantor of their political liberties.[61] The military should only be used to guard the frontiers, one student argued; a militia composed of citizens was deemed sufficient to maintain order in the countryside.[62] (As an institution, the National Guard would soon be dominated by large landowners.)

By 1833, the formerly *exaltado* Olinda student José Thomaz Nabuco de Araújo was publishing a newspaper titled *The Old Man of 1817* that even an admiring biographer (namely, his son Joaquim) called "frankly reactionary." While the son attributed part of his father's political change of heart to "the intellectual versatility of adolescence," more fundamentally he credited the *Setembrizada* with giving his father a "lesson that he could not forget."[63]

If the times had been "revolutionary" before, the mood of students was soon marked by disillusionment.[64] Like their elders, students were disturbed by the revolts breaking out around the country. "There is no justification for insurrection against authority," one student complained, "unless that authority is failing to uphold the law." Since those conditions did not exist, how could these revolts be justified? Law students increasingly portrayed themselves as the voices of "moderation," of "union" and "order." Any "man of honor," a student wrote in 1831, "who is a friend of his country asks that its tranquility not be disturbed."[65] In defining the virtuous man, the student paper *Olindense* called for men who "love liberty" to also "love the law." Such a man "should respect and obey his legitimate superiors and dedicate himself to a job that is honest and useful to society." The students claimed to stand for a middle ground between despotism and anarchy. Students who supported the *exaltados* after 1831 were criticized for lacking experience and maturity; it was the time not for agitation but for calm reflection and a faith in the knowledge and patriotism of the nation's legislators.[66]

The ideals of order and nation over liberty and region were promoted in Olinda by an organization called the Patriotic Harmonizing Society, to which law students belonged (though they were hardly the most prominent members.)[67] Founded by Antônio Joaquim de Melo, the organization consisted of many of Pernambuco's wealthiest landowners. The organization intended to create a new political consensus, bridging the gap between *ex-altados* and the supporters of Dom Pedro I's restoration. If the two groups could accept his abdication as an accomplished fact, it was argued, they could also agree to move no further against those officials closely linked to him in the past.[68]

The very institutions that defined Brazil as a liberal society, a free press being among the most prominent, hindered the reassertion of the authority that students now saw as essential. "Among us journalism was born with the opposition [to Dom Pedro I] and therefore with a just hostility to government." The fight against Dom Pedro I had created a climate of liberty that was difficult to control. Given the stakes involved after 1831, students argued that newspaper editors had to recognize that a new government was in power and they should thus be responsible and refrain from excessive criticism.[69]

To delegitimize dissent, students sought to define their opponents as outside of the discourse of responsible liberalism, "equivalent," in fact, "to the Jacobins of 1792." Others were described as anarchists seeking to mislead the Brazilian people. They claimed that Brazilians were fundamentally passive when they were not being led astray by unwise agitators. "The Brazilian people love order and justice," one student argued. Although the people were often "deluded," one could always count on the "humane and peaceful character of our people."[70] Nevertheless, some students feared that "the people [were] better able to destroy than to create," as one student warned (quoting John Adams).[71] The difficulty of establishing order was "augmented by the difficulty of the trouble in which we are put by the slaves, that we unfortunately possess."[72]

To combat disorder, students embraced the status quo and championed the "need to conserve institutions."[73] "Only with the law religiously observed" could order be maintained.[74] This fear of instability led students to embrace the Brazilian constitution as a bulwark against disorder. This forced them into the awkward position of denying the role the deposed emperor had played in drafting the constitution.[75] From this period stems what Sérgio Adorno calls the *bacharéis'* "devotion to law and to order."[76] Their own future role as makers and interpreters of the laws guaranteed their status as the creators of the framework within which the rest of society would defer to their "superiors."

By the late 1830s, political unrest throughout the country had created an uncertain situation in the law schools themselves. Attendance was down. The São Paulo school in particular was in clear decline. Only six new students matriculated in 1836. Between 1836 and 1840 only sixty students attended the southern school.[77] Enrollment only increased in the mid-1840s when the political situation improved (and the advantages of attending law school for those seeking social and political prominence had become indisputable).

Despite its decline in enrollment, the São Paulo school maintained its distinctiveness as a more liberal and inviting place for student dissidents. Beginning in the late 1830s, the national consensus shifted rightward with the recentralization of power in Rio after the so-called Regresso or "Return." In this period, liberal students in Olinda found themselves more likely to be punished for their political views than their counterparts in São Paulo. This is demonstrated by what happened to editors of the Olinda student newspaper *Argos Olindense*.

As the Pernambuco school's historian Gláucio Veiga has (somewhat anachronistically) suggested, the *Argos Olindense* may have marked the "high point" of "left materialist republicanism" at the northern school. Its editors opposed state religion, for example, and local newspapers accused it of being a "subverter of order."[78] The editors did not, however, support the rebellion of the Farrapos in Rio Grande do Sul (from 1835 to 1845, the longest-sustained revolt of the nineteenth century). The young men who wrote and edited the *Argos Olindense* were, to a certain extent, sympathetic to the rebels. However, they still considered the leaders of the Farroupilha "deluded brothers" who had "rebelled against the communion of the Brazilian family" — hardly a wholehearted expression of support. Moreover, the students argued, the imperial government should offer the olive branch to the rebels, accompanied by a show of force. Nevertheless, these same writers left no doubts about their opinion of those they called "the apostles of tyranny" (generally, the Regressistas), and they rejected the path followed "instinctively" by the newspapermen of the late 1830s who "disgracefully" supported "anti-liberal views."[79] After receiving bad grades as punishment for their negative assessment of both Brazil's conservative trends and their professors' teaching abilities, the disgruntled students transferred to São Paulo.[80]

The Regressistas were the wave of the future, however. By 1840, the voices of dissidents like the editors of the *Argos Olindense* were muted. Despite one final major regional revolt toward the end of the decade in Pernambuco (called the *Praieira*), the *Regressista* modifications of the Brazilian political system would stand for the rest of the imperial period.[81] The disillusioned liberals of the late 1830s harnessed liberalism to the interests of the nation's new economic power, namely, coffee plantation owners in the Paraíba River valley near the imperial capital. In the process, they reduced liberalism to the special slang of a small group of powerful men.[82] "The liberalism of large landowners always was, in essence, one of privatism . . . a defense of their own privileges," as one Brazilian political scientist has written.[83] In this sense, Adorno's emphasis on "possessive individualism" as a cornerstone of Brazilian liberalism is well placed. The bourgeois values of "liberty, equality, property, and security" were dominant in the worldview of the Brazilian elite of the imperial period.[84] From this point of view, Brazilian liberals left behind a language that was, to a large degree, compromised. Some have argued that liberalism in the Brazilian context was an apologia for an authoritarian order and that the fundamental reality of private power, particularly in the countryside — over and above legally constituted public power — put the lie to liberal theory.[85]

It certainly is true that even the most radical of Brazilian liberals at the law schools during the First Empire and Regency never rejected the institution of slavery. Slavery had been a potent metaphor to use in the struggle against Dom Pedro I. The emperor had been accused of "trying to make slaves of" Brazilians whose "natural propensity" was for liberty.[86] The African or native-born Brazilian slaves themselves existed outside of the discourse of liberalism of this early period. So, for that matter, did the vast majority of the Brazilian population. The *pátria*, one student noted, was not the same thing as Brazil itself. Rather, it was limited to those "citizens that comprise political society.''[87] The law school graduates, as Adorno argues, were also able to "domesticate effective political opposition and expel democratic progressive forces." In Brazil, perhaps more than in any other country in Latin America, nineteenth-century liberalism became the privileged discourse of an extremely small group of men. As the language of the state its interpretation was up to the *bacharéis*, the state agents par excellence.[88]

Brazil's political elite never stopped seeing itself as fundamentally liberal, however. Perhaps this was because their ability to impose consensus enabled them to avoid confronting the dissonance between their ideals and their practices. Brazilian liberals, unlike their counterparts elsewhere in the Western Hemisphere, lacked strong organized enemies.[89] Liberalism in the Latin American context stood for the individual against traditional corporate privileges like those of the military and the Catholic Church.[90] In Brazil, however, such group prerogatives had always been weaker.

After the expulsion of the Jesuits, the Catholic Church was extremely weak institutionally (especially compared to a country like Mexico, where it was the major landowner.) In Brazil, there was never a sustained conflict with the Church over property and privileges through which anticlerical liberal and pro-Church conservative identities could be forged. Furthermore, in Brazil, unlike much of Spanish America, indigenous communities had not been protected under the colonial system; the debate over liberalism in Brazil did not therefore involve a conflict over communal land. The military was eliminated as a political force in the early 1830s. Lacking an abolitionist movement to contend with before the 1860s, moreover, the Brazilian coffee elite never had to develop a racial defense of slavery.

On the other hand, if Brazilian liberals feared the subordinate classes, and their response to the regional revolts showed that they did, this fact did not distinguish them from their counterparts in the North Atlantic world, let alone those in Spanish America. The attempt to yoke liberalism to conservative Brazilian social reality was challenging and continued to pose special problems for each generation of young men at the law schools. More than any other group, they continued to experience the cognitive dissonance between theories and practices. For young men seeking to master the discourse of liberalism during their student years, the meanings of liberalism continued to be, to some degree, in flux and open to reinterpretation.

By 1840, the triumph of the Regressistas had clearly contributed to a period of political quiescence on the law school campuses.[91] No student newspapers were published between the mid-1830s and the mid-1840s in São Paulo.[92] When the Liberals in rural São Paulo and Minas Gerais rose up in 1842, few from the southern school took notice. Young José Antônio Saraiva, eventually one of the dominant political figures in the late imperial period, was unmoved by the rebellion. His main concern was that the unrest might mean he would lose a year of school or be forced to transfer to Olinda. Some students did leave for Pernambuco, but order was soon restored after only minimal disruption of the law schools' operations.[93] When the Farrapo rebellion in Rio Grande Do Sul was finally put down in 1845, the long cycle of regional rebellions since 1831 ended. Students from every province celebrated. Rio Grandense students themselves held a dance to show that they too supported the imperial government in its victory over the insurgents. Saraiva, a native of Bahia province, expressed relief that Brazil's national unity had been affirmed and hoped that this would mean the end of disorder.[94]

WHAT HAPPENED TO THE CLASSES OF THE 1830S?

No one had spoken more bitterly of the authoritarian traditions of Coimbra than Bernardo Pereira do Vasconcellos. And yet this Coimbra graduate more than personified, he led the turn away from the decentralizing impulse in liberalism in the late 1830s. The regional revolts had turned him and the opinion of the entire Brazilian political class against the ideal of decentralized power. As a result, Dom Pedro II, grandson of the last Portuguese king of Brazil, would become a "man" before his time (when his majority was declared so that he could become emperor at fourteen). The centralized political system that marked his reign would be built around the magistracy.[95]

No single group in Brazilian society benefited more from the centralization of power that defined the Regresso than the law school graduates. The locally elected justices of the peace lost power to the imperially appointed municipal judges, district judges, and prosecutors, who were required by new legislation to be graduates of the schools in Pernambuco and São Paulo.[96] Local interests were served, however, as recent graduates found themselves forced to reach working arrangements with local landowners, who dominated the provincial towns where they usually began their careers.[97]

The founding of a secondary school named after the young future emperor Dom Pedro II in 1837 was intended to further the centralization of the empire. Graduates of the *Colégio* Dom Pedro II were automatically admitted into either the law schools or the medical schools without having to take entrance examinations. Not surprisingly, many of the Dom Pedro II students were sons of national politicians residing in the imperial capital.[98]

The first generation of Brazilian law students had not felt certain that they would be the future leaders of society or that their power would go unchallenged. The law school environment between 1828 and 1845 was an often fractious affair, with an extremely high level of conflict between students and faculty. Students in Olinda and São Paulo reflected the lack of national consensus. Some went on after graduation to participate in various regional rebellions, such as the *Sabinada* in Bahia and, especially, the Liberal Revolt of 1842. Most, however, experienced this period of instability as an object lesson in the need for centralized political control. (That such control improved their own career possibilities only reinforced the lesson.)

Whatever their earlier doubts, with the imposition of centralized power with the Regresso this group ultimately had the odds in their favor and the most to gain. The role of the magistrate as national, even imperial, unifier was reaffirmed. Because the number of young men with a law degree in the 1830s was relatively small, they were easily integrated into the political system by the Coimbra graduates, who largely controlled access to power.[99] Graduates of Olinda and São Paulo in the 1830s rose relatively quickly and easily to positions of authority, aided in particular by their legally sanctioned monopoly over access to positions as municipal judges and prosecutors. Of 108 members of the Chamber of Deputies in Rio in 1848, for example, 72 were *bacharéis*, while seven were doctors, six military men, and seven clergymen.[100] Between 1840 and 1853, the proportion of cabinet ministers with a degree from either of the two schools was 45 percent, increasing to 75 percent from 1853 to 1871.[101] By the 1850s, many law school graduates were serving as senators and ministers, at the pinnacle of the imperial power structure.

At the law schools themselves, a younger generation of students in the mid-1840s sought a new source of authority, not so much in the political as in the cultural realm, which is the subject of the following chapter.

2

LANGUAGE AND POWER

The debate over liberalism in the 1820s and 1830s marked an important initial stage in the development of a Brazilian political class at the law schools. The perceived threat to elite interests posed by the regional rebellions of the 1830s, however, led students to question the appropriateness of liberalism to Brazilian society. They began to seek ways to defuse liberalism's explosive potential in a hierarchical, slave society that they were committed to maintaining. By the 1840s liberalism alone could not sufficiently legitimize these young men's authority. Students were forced to redefine their identities and their roles in society. It was no longer enough simply to not be Portuguese. Liberalism could not be merely abandoned; it would continue to be redefined from the 1840s through the 1870s by each new generation of law students (as I discuss in chapters 5 and 6).

The students of the 1840s would redefine their identity so its primary emphasis lay in skill with the written and spoken word. The young men in Pernambuco and São Paulo found in literature, oratory, and journalism a renewed sense of a mission that could redeem and control society. The style they developed in the 1840s defined elite male identity for generations to come, and it marked, to some extent, a coming to terms with Portuguese legacies that the previous generation had rejected.[1]

One of the most enduring legacies of the Coimbra experience to Brazilian student culture was the *trote*, a form of public humiliation and verbal abuse imposed by upperclassmen on all first-year students or *caloiros*. *Caloiros*, easily identified by the rustic accents they often brought with them from their provincial homes, were surrounded by older students (particularly, although not exclusively, second-year students) and heckled mercilessly. The *caloiros* were expected to show that they could bear this form of hazing without complaint, with dignity, and, above all, silently. Moreover, *caloiros* were expected to listen and learn rather than speak at student association meetings and public gatherings. Without language, students were robbed of a crucial part of their understanding of themselves. This corresponds to what we know about rites of passage in tribal societies, where participants are "ground down to a uniform condition," as Victor Turner described it. The debased condition does not last, of course, for those "ground down" ultimately are invested "with additional powers to enable [those neophytes] to cope with their new station in life." Being silenced, therefore, prepared students for the time when they could demonstrate verbal skills befitting their status as members of the political class.

The link between language and power in Brazil had been strong for centuries. The Jesuits, who had a virtual monopoly over education before they were expelled in the late colonial period, were to a large extent responsible for the literary orientation of Brazilian education. Their pedagogy emphasized the fundamentals of a classical education: Latin, grammar, rhetoric, and philosophy. During the colonial period, moreover, literature had become a "defining leisure activity of the elite."[2] A Coimbra-trained magistrate for his part was expected to be adept at providing "learned citations and classical references."[3]

Many expected that the founding of the law schools would assure the hegemony of the literary elite. According to an early draft of the law school statutes, the ideal student would have a knowledge of languages and literature and would be eloquent, the better to perform well in a court of law or Congress.[4] Prospective students had to pass entrance examinations in French, Latin, grammar, rhetoric, philosophy, and, theoretically at least, geometry (although exemptions were often granted). In 1834, exams in English and history (including geography) were added.[5] The founders were also concerned about more mundane matters related to oral expression. They feared that the students in such provincial towns as São Paulo and Olinda would pick up the local accents. In the province of São Paulo, *lingua geral*, a standardized form of indigenous language that the Jesuits developed to promote the conversion of the native peoples, was used as commonly as Portuguese in daily life. And it was hardly unknown for sons of elite Pernambuco families to use "Africanisms" in their speech as well. The Brazilian elite hoped that its political class in formation would acquire a purified, polished speech like that increasingly promoted by the newspapers in the imperial capitol of Rio de Janeiro.[6]

Some of the professors tried to provide a model for appropriate elite male behavior and style that emphasized the cultivation of literature. São Paulo professor Brotero, although given to torturing the Portuguese language when he spoke, had a keen interest in literary matters and was the author of poetry and more than fifty published articles of literary criticism.[7] Lourenço Trigo de Loureiro, a teacher in Olinda, published adaptations of the French playwright Racine.[8] By and large, however, as one early director of the northern school complained, the faculty frequently lacked a "literary reputation" and were known as "zeros" in the "republic of letters."[9]

Although the idea of a literary-trained elite had its roots in Portuguese history, it did not take hold as a student ideal at the law schools in the 1820s and 1830s. For the first generation of law students, there were more pressing matters than literary production. Students were more often engaged in political activism, despite the clear interest of some of the founders and early directors in creating a more literary elite. The young men had focused on defining themselves against their Portuguese heritage and delineating a liberalism that matched their dreams and allayed their fears.

The students of the 1820s and 1830s were often unskilled in the use of language and ignorant about literature. The same administrator who criticized the professors for their lack of literary achievement had an even lower opinion of the students. Their inability to read Latin made it impossible for them to understand even the textbooks used in their courses. "Little or nothing distinguishes" law school graduates from any "idiot," he lamented. They "speak poorly," "lack the most basic ideas about literature," and in their writing employ "unpardonable solecisms, barbarisms, and neologisms."[10]

Student culture in the 1820s and 1830s was not yet devoted to acquiring and displaying verbal facility. It bears mentioning in this regard that when students of later generations looked back to the "noble traditions" of their predecessors at the law schools, they rarely, if ever, mentioned the young men of the 1820s or 1830s. This is largely due to the fact that the young men of these earlier times, such as José Thomaz Nabuco de Araújo, did not have — as Nabuco's son noted approvingly in his biography of his father—

the same "preoccupation" with "purely literary talent" that later generations came to have. Despite the hopes of the founders, students' interests
were more political than literary or even legal. Nabuco's heroes, as has been
noted, were politicians and polemicists.[11] The poetry that filled newspapers
from the 1840s through the 1880s was largely absent from the pages of the
Olinda and São Paulo newspapers of the 1820s and 1830s.[12] And some who
graduated in these early years continued throughout their political careers
to express disdain for the literary bent of the political class. Senator Zacarias
de Góis e Vasconcelos frequently rebuked his colleagues for their literary
pretensions. "I do not write novels or verses," he commented on the floor of
the Senate in 1875. On another occasion in 1870, when the minister of justice praised him by comparing him to a poet, he responded curtly, "I wasn't
speaking of poets or about sonnets."[13]

Even newspapers were not as prominent a part of student culture in
these years as they would be after 1845. When one newspaper ceased publication after only six issues in the mid-1830s, its editor complained about São
Paulo's lack of interest in belles lettres. He was particularly critical of the educated people who had failed to support his literary endeavors. The most
complete survey of student newspapers in that city does not list another student newspaper there again until 1846.[14]

The main cultural activity for students at both schools in the 1820s and
1830s was the student theater. Almeida Nogueira calls the passion for theater in São Paulo during the early years "the fever of the epoch." For the
northern school as well, the years in Olinda (1828–1854) marked the peak of
student interest in the stage.[15] The skills needed in theatrical productions
were not all that far removed from those required of a lawyer or politician.
When one of the early organizers of student theater in the southern school
later went on to great success as a trial lawyer, many a contemporary contended that his thespian background was the primary reason for his courtroom victories.[16]

Theater was particularly important because it gave future public men an
opportunity to present themselves to an audience primarily of their peers.
But it also provided opportunities for young males to play with gendered
identities; the students acted out the parts of both male and female characters on the stage. One student, who often played women's roles in theatrical

productions, was so successful at female impersonation that audience members frequently demanded to examine him more closely. It was a request he cheerfully complied with by offering them a glimpse at the apparatus that made his feminine appearance more convincing.[17]

Not surprisingly, some found the theater an unsuitable venue for a ruling class in training. Imperial authorities attempted to prohibit theatrical performances, particularly but not only during the school year. They argued that theater was "inappropriate for the character" of the students. Even the law school director himself was taken to task for attending a student play during Easter vacation. Rendon responded that the play had been attended by "constituted authorities and the good people of the city." Moreover, he insisted, the student productions represented "good order and seriousness." Despite repeated efforts to ban student theater, however, the young men persisted. The São Paulo students even took out a five-year lease on a theater in order to provide a better forum for the productions.[18]

THE RISE OF THE LITERARY ELITE

The theater notwithstanding, political aspirations were more important than literary ones for the first generation of law students. This would change dramatically by the mid-1840s, as the political climate changed and the centrality of the law school graduate in the imperial political system became firmly established. In the 1840s and 1850s, political stability was established throughout the empire, and enrollments at both schools rose. Accompanying these developments was the institution of the Romantic poet and the florid orator as the student ideal on both campuses.[19] As Brazilian politicians embraced the centralizing and more authoritarian Portuguese political traditions, the students rediscovered the value of an elite whose power was symbolized by its mastery over language.

Law student culture beginning in the 1840s was based largely on the display of verbal skills. In a slave society in which four out of five free men were illiterate, these students' facility with the written and spoken word set them apart. Their linguistic skill embodied status and power in a hierarchical society in which they would soon be the masters. From the 1840s through the 1880s, students used language competitively to celebrate their monopoly over what Pierre Bourdieu has called "linguistic capital."[20] Throughout the nineteenth century, students in other countries such as England and the United States turned away from an interest in literature and began to compete on playing fields.[21] In a society built on slave labor, such as Brazil, where physical labor was disparaged, athletic abilities were not yet prized. Students often referred disdainfully to what they considered the outmoded idea of competing in the manner of the ancient gladiators. "We don't need ... Roman exercises because nothing like this is conducive to our desideratum," one student wrote in 1860.[22]

They looked to the pen and the word for their arms. Gone were the days of warriors and conquistadors, one student wrote in 1849; in the "ruins" of the old world a "grand theater where intelligence predominated" had been erected.[23] Brazilian students now competed with each other, often in the privacy of the student residences known as repúblicas (an institution I will examine more fully in chapter 3), to see who had the best command of the written or spoken word.[24] This new style predominated at both schools for the rest of the imperial period, and to some degree beyond, and shaped elite male identity for generations. As one student wrote in 1860, these young men were ambitious in the areas "of letters, of power, and of brilliance."[25] Their command of language was a mark of their power, central to their "prestige and cultural leadership."[26] Like the priests of an earlier day, their privileged access to education in a largely illiterate society guaranteed their access to power.[27]

The students used language to shape their own corporate identity. In the revolutionary and early national periods of the United States, the link between law and literature had been largely broken, and the lawyer tried to present himself as a practical man of action. In Brazil, however, the link remained strong.[28] "What a sad degradation if the sons of this academy did not see anything beyond the horizons of jurisprudence," a São Paulo student wrote in 1859. "It is necessary for a jurist also to be, besides a philosopher, a writer, and a literary man."[29]

Demonstrating command of written and spoken Portuguese was a sign of manhood. If, as cultural anthropologist David Gilmore suggests, manhood is an achieved condition, much of these students' extracurricular lives was spent trying to show that they had arrived, that they were men and men of a particular social standing.[30] Their identities were shaped as members of a class and a gender that was expected to rule over society at large.

The new literary ideal, moreover, may have marked an attempt to establish a nonpartisan elite male identity that would unite the political class that had previously been divided and would justify in its own mind a faith in the right to rule over the rest of Brazilian society. The students' commitment to literature replaced earlier allegiances to particular political ideologies during the reign of Dom Pedro I and the Regency.

Emperor Dom Pedro II considered himself a cultured, educated man, and the *bacharéis* from the 1840s into the 1870s liked to see in him their ultimate patron, their mirror image. "I was born," the emperor claimed, "to occupy myself with letters and science." He translated such poets as Longfellow, Whittier, Byron, and Shakespeare, as well as texts from Italian and Hebrew.[31] When Dom Pedro II paid his first visit to São Paulo in 1846, the students recited their poetry for him.[32]

Student life gained a new vitality as the national temper cooled, particularly when members of both political parties, Liberal and Conservative, served together in the imperial cabinet during the Conciliation period. As a result, the law schools became the centers for the formation of nonpartisan and national identities. Literary matters seem to have served as a point around which all could agree. Student newspapers discussed the political matters of the 1840s and 1850s in only the most general terms. Politics itself was viewed as an inherently corrupt or immoral occupation.[33] Student writers bemoaned the seemingly irresistible attraction of political careers for even the most literary-minded graduates. "Today's politics ... [which] seduces and attracts ... is robbing the Empire of Letters of its best ornaments."[34] As late as 1867, a newspaper titled *Democracy* refused to accept political writings.[35]

If these literary men often rejected the demands of political activism, they embraced the need for nation building through literature. They defined literary activity as being in the "service of the holy cause of our country," to which they offered "great sacrifices."[36] These sacrifices were particularly admirable, one student wrote, in "youth in whose veins runs the blood of so few Januaries [at a stage] when the distractions of the physical world should

most exert their power."[37] For the students, the "cause" of letters was defined as "sacred." Religious metaphors linked nation and literature and suggested the purity of their project. The "written word," one student wrote in
1859, "is the most powerful element of social progress."[38]

Born after 1822, the generation that began arriving at law school in the
mid-1840s knew no other reality than that of an independent Brazilian nation. What they felt prevented Brazil from becoming a full-fledged member
of the civilized world was the cultural autonomy that a national literature
would symbolize. "Literature is gaining ground every day," one student
wrote in 1860, "thanks to the efforts of youth."[39] Among the students engaged in literary production in the São Paulo class that entered in the pivotal
year of 1845 were such future luminaries of Brazilian literature as José de
Alencar and Bernardo Guimarães. Alencar in particular typified the fusion
of the political and the cultural realms in the imperial period. He was the
prime exponent of nineteenth-century literary nationalism through such
Romantic novels as *Iracema*. A tale of a love affair between a Portuguese
man and an indigenous woman, the novel remains a pillar of the Brazilian
literary canon and is still taught in Brazilian schools today. Alencar became
not only a novelist but also a deputy, a senator, and minister of justice in the
imperial cabinet.[40]

In Brazil, as elsewhere in the nineteenth century, language and nationalism were intertwined. Brazilians referred to the language they spoke as the
"national language" as frequently as they called it Portuguese.[41] But this
national language had many regional variations, in part because of the lack
of urban development in nineteenth-century Brazil. The far-flung character
of the Brazilian empire naturally helped ensure regional differentiation in
speech patterns.[42] Linguistic diversity was viewed by some mid-nineteenth-
century Brazilian elites as just as much a threat to national unity as the re-
gionalist forces that played such a large role in the provincial rebellions of
the 1830s.[43]

The law students were, in many ways, learning a national language in
Pernambuco and São Paulo. As we have seen, one of the lessons students
learned in the early hazing process was that it was not good to have a distinctive accent. They sought to quickly lose the provincial manner of speaking
that marked them as *caloiros* and therefore objects of abuse. Ambitious stu-

dents sought to emulate the style of students from the imperial seat of Rio de Janeiro. By writing for the student newspapers and speaking in the student associations, they sought mastery over a national language that would serve them well in their future careers as agents of the imperial state.

Although the first poets of stature in independent Brazil tried to write classical Portuguese, over the course of the nineteenth century the literati began to embrace a more "Brazilian" language, and law students took the idea to heart. This was particularly marked in those who looked to indigenous themes for the inspiration to create a new Brazilian literature. "Indianismo" peaked as a literary trend between the 1840s and the 1860s.[44] Alencar himself promoted the learning of the indigenous Tupí language to help create a truly Brazilian literature.[45] A poem printed in an 1850 edition of the student newspaper *O Album dos Academicos Olindenses* exemplified this brand of literary nationalism; the poem made extensive use of indigenous words, all of which were helpfully defined by the author.[46] Another poem from the same period published in the student press employed the language of the Brazilian backlander, the *sertanejo*.[47] The need to explain the vocabulary of the indigenous population or *sertanejo* demonstrated the gap between the students' literary aspirations and the objects of their attention.

Like most examples of the "invention of tradition," Brazilian literary nationalism was, to a large degree, artificial.[48] Although Brazilian literary nationalism had its own culturally democratizing tendencies, bridging the linguistic gap between the illiterate and the hyperliterate, it also exemplified the cultural appropriation of the language of the popular classes and indigenous peoples. Moreover, the elite's real interest in the "people" was limited. The Indianismo movement was a diversion from Brazil's all-too-obvious African heritage and a sentimental celebration of those indigenous people who were safely dead or at least largely out of sight in the Brazilian context.

In any case, an interest in the African contribution to Brazilian culture developed more slowly. Indeed, in the rare moments during the 1840s and 1850s when student newspapers allowed their careful control of language to slip, one can glimpse some of the students' hidden prejudices. Students used the phrase "the language used by Africans in our kitchens," for example, to disparage the writings of rival students.[49] The place of the African in the Brazilian nation increasingly became a matter of concern among the law student body in the 1860s. For the young men of the 1840s and 1850s, however, the language they should employ had to keep its distance from the "kitchen."

In any case, there were inherent contradictions in the students' literary nationalism. Their models for creating a national literature as well as for the proper roles and sensibilities of poets were drawn from Europe, particularly from France and England.[50] France was revered as the country of light and civilization. Literary depictions of the young men suggest that they imagined themselves as being like Lord Byron or Alfred de Musset, favorites of students from the 1840s through the 1860s.[51] One graduate recalled of his classmates of the 1840s, "Every student with some imagination wanted to be Byron, and had as his inexorable destiny to copy or translate the English bard."[52] Independence, another student wrote, brought with it expanded possibilities for cultural relations with "civilized" Europe (Portugal not included). The result for Brazil was the "sphere of its knowledge being broadened after Portugal ceased to be the exclusive spring from which we could drink."[53]

Literary inspiration from these other countries created the possibility of a new national literature distinct from Portuguese traditions, even as political inspiration from these countries had helped to create a distinctly Brazilian political system. Unlike Spanish America, where the former mother country still played a major role as a linguistic model, Portugal lost virtually all of its cultural clout with its former colony when Brazil became independent. Favorite authors of the student body (besides Byron and Musset) included Victor Hugo, François Chateaubriand, and Walter Scott.[54] In one student's library of the 1860s, a little more than half of all the books were written originally in French. The rest were often French translations from German, Italian, and English literature. One modern literary historian has lamented the "virtual absence of Brazilian literature" in the same student's collection. Travelers to Brazil during this period suggested that, given the limited development of the Brazilian publishing industry, French books were more readily available than those locally produced.[55]

Faculty members sometimes expressed disdain for their students' interest in literature. One professor writing in 1861 suggested that this enthusiasm would not last; "when the students returned to their *fazendas* after graduation, the students' books would be burned and their brains become inert."[56] The purging suggested by this book-burning image hints at the irrelevance that literature would eventually have for many students. For in the years following graduation they would find their social authority amply displayed not in language but in the size of the family plantation.

During the student years, however, literary abilities were a defining aspect of these young men's identities. To demonstrate literary mastery was not only to take part in the construction of the larger nation but also and more immediately to gain the admiration of one's peers, whose opinion was central to a young man's opinion of himself. Moreover, it is crucial to keep in mind the extent to which these young men's understanding of themselves was imbued with the spirit of the Romantic era, in which the artist was seen as someone superior to the rest of society, a man with a mission to redeem the world. This was a central component of their identity during these years.[57] The Romantic style represented a "regeneration" in world literature, a type of "literary liberalism," as one student wrote in 1849.[58] Romanticism had become the predominant literary style in Brazil with the publication in France of Gonçalves de Magalhães's *Suspiros Poéticos e Saudades* (Poetic sighs and longings) in 1836. But Romanticism would take hold at the law schools themselves only in the mid-1840s.[59] From then on, the law schools were the "great focus of the Romantic infection," as one critic of the *bacharel* has written. It was an "infection" that "dominated the national spirit until the end of the 1870s."[60]

POETRY

Of all the forms of literary activity engaged in by the law students of the imperial period, writing poetry was the most important because it was the activity in which the influence of Romantic understandings of the self were most central. Poems were published in student newspapers and recited in club meetings in the privacy of student residences or in large auditoriums. Students not only read but also improvised poetry in public. The literary jousts between Antônio de Castro Alves and Tobias Barreto in the 1860s became legendary.[61]

The verse they presented in public was more than just the nationalistic boilerplate of a political elite. Writing love poetry, in particular, was an expression of their young manhood. It was a more demanding form of verbal expression whose content was more intimately connected with their masculinity. Love poetry was published in all the student newspapers from the 1840s on, even when the students' concerns grew political again after 1860.[62] "To write verses is today's mania; it is an epidemic," a student wrote in 1863, though the same had been true at the law schools since the mid-1840s.[63] Another noted, with some exaggeration, that there were no twenty-year-old men who were not poets.[64] Students without poetic gifts felt isolated, even when they demonstrated other skills with language.[65] Some law students wrote poems that rank among the major achievements of nineteenth-century Brazilian literature (one thinks particularly of Manuel Antônio Álvares de Azevedo in the 1840s and Antônio de Castro Alves in the 1860s). The majority of student poets were, as one would expect, of lesser rank, a good many merely poetasters whose poetic production was limited to their school days. Brazilian literary critic Antônio Cândido notes that "most significant poets *of the second rank* [italics mine] during the 1850s were students at the law schools in São Paulo and Recife."[66] Much of their poetry was formulaic.

Many students published a volume of poetry before graduation (their identity as law students was always announced on the title page), and most of them never published a poem again.[67] Law school graduates continued to give speeches and write editorials, but for the majority writing poetry was part of the process of becoming a man. Their love poems were, above all, public expressions of their maturing masculinity.

The ability to write poems was considered a defining characteristic of the student ideal. In one poem, for example, a São Paulo student portrays a young man flirting with a young woman selling flowers. She responds to his attentions by asserting that she trusts neither "doctors" nor "poets." A young law student would be recognized as both by his skill and by his presumption of a special attractiveness to women (about which more will be said in chapter 3).

By writing poetry one could make a name for oneself among one's peers far more readily than through the study of the law.[68] Castro Alves represents the best example of a student who seems to have rarely, if ever, attended classes but who was admired by his colleagues above all others. His public reading of his own poetry soon after his transfer from Recife to São Paulo in the late 1860s made him a hero to the student body of his time and for decades afterward. His poetry had a great emotional impact on his audiences. "I never saw an audience carried into ecstasy as it was in the São José Theater when Castro Alves recited his poems," one colleague recalled.[69]

Students often sat around their rooms while one of their number stood on a chair and improvised poetry. Romantic poetry was, above all, an oral art, meant not to be contemplated in private but experienced in public. As David Haberly notes, Romantic poems had all the earmarks of declamation: "the apostrophes that represent syllables artistically swallowed to save the meter; the forests of exclamation points and question marks that denote unheard verbal flourishes and unseen gestures; the dashes that once symbolized sudden and dramatic changes in pitch and volume; the reticences that are the last trace of dying voices."[70]

As Doris Sommer has suggested, the Latin American elite of the nineteenth century were "sentimentalized men," whose literary expression forged a link between literature, love, and nation building.[71] Her insights are particularly telling when one considers the fact that love poetry was considered appropriate fare for celebrations of the seventh of September, Brazil's independence day.[72] As Romantic poets, the law students' poetry was devoted to emotions, described as "perfumed songs," seeking inspiration in the "vehement pulsations of the heart [and] the melancholy palpitations of sentiment." Authentic poetry was recognized by its reflection of true feelings, particularly of young men awakening to life's pleasures, including the delights of the senses.[73] Student literati promised to "consecrate our dreams, our most intimate emotions."[74]

The students' love poetry reveals much about the attitudes and values of these men at a particular stage of their lives. Many of the poets addressed their poems to an idealized virgin, perfect in her purity and beauty and sometimes preserved in her perfection by death.[75] Women were idealized by Romantic poetry, according to some critics, partly because of the social segregation between men and women in a patriarchal society.[76] Women were presented in student poems "with the obsessive force that they have in adolescence."[77]

To cite one example of the way in which students explored their relationship to the idealized "other" they created, the poem "The Sleeping Virgin," represented one student's voyeuristic sexual fantasy. The author addresses another (fellow student?) who is evidently also watching the young woman sleep and urges him to be quiet. "This is the woman I have been imagining in my daydreams," he informs his companion, "the kind of woman I have been searching for at parties and dances." As she sleeps, her clothes fall open, revealing her breasts. The author continues to watch, admiring her physical beauty. The woman begins to stir, disturbed by the heat of his real or imagined kiss on her breasts. The young men flee, fearing her awakening.[78]

While this poem is almost certainly a product of the author's fantasy life, it does seem to reflect a man's sense of entitlement. Two men enter a woman's private space without her permission. They observe the woman in a semi-nude state, this in an age when São Paulo women still habitually wore the veil in public. And the author allows himself to kiss her quite intimately. Although a fantasy, the poem emphasizes the special liberties and privileges available to elite men in the author's society. Yet the final flight of the young men suggests, as well, an adolescent's ambivalent longing for and fear of sexuality.[79]

Not all of the love poetry was addressed to virgins. Certainly, there is an exuberant sensuality in much of the student poetry. In one poem, for example, Silva Nunes Junior writes of possessing his lover's body and imagines splitting his soul in two so he can be forever united with her. Vicente de Carvalho's series of poems dedicated to a woman named Dea are similarly passionate. A poem by Wenceslão de Queroz describes a woman's white and naked body.[80] The poetry of these young men placed an overarching value on the intensity of physical union as a secular form of transcendence, as other cultures' Romantic poets were often doing at this time as well.[81]

Moreover, through their poetry these young men were able to share their feelings with each other, whether they were celebrating physical intimacy or sharing the disappointments of love lost. They joined their lives together and staked their own special claim to passion as young men. They announced to the world that they were men. Moreover, they made their claim to a special access to young women through the use of language.

An important symbol of the student commitment to literature and poetry in particular was the premature death of a young talent just prior to graduation (usually of consumption, the poets' disease, although also of yellow fever, a recurring problem in Brazil in the nineteenth century). Perennially young and idealistic, eternally poetic and never distracted by political or bureaucratic concerns, the dead student poet was the student ideal par excellence, heir to the purity and martyrdom of Christ. Dead poets were more often invoked than living ones on public occasions, perhaps because they had not lived to graduate and thus had not been corrupted by the political system students professed to scorn but ultimately longed to join.[82]

A dead poet, such as the undoubtedly gifted Álvares de Azevedo who died during his fifth year at law school, became a symbol for generations at the southern law school. Álvares de Azevedo is said to have "so personified the spirit of youth . . . that no other name speaks more loudly to the heart of the Academy."[83] He was so closely linked imaginatively to the southern school that his mother was even said to have given birth to him in the law school library. Students continued to use selections from his poetry as epigrams introducing their own poetry long after his death.[84]

As student culture once again became more political in the 1860s, student poetry did also, much to the chagrin of more conservative professors and their student followers. Political poetry in the previous generation had been limited largely to celebrations of nationalist heroes. Castro Alves, in particular, almost single-handedly transformed the poetic ideal with the passion of his abolitionist poetry. (This, too, is reminiscent of popular understandings of Lord Byron, although it has been argued that the depth of Byron's political commitments has been exaggerated.[85]) As the literary ideal became more politicized, it could serve less effectively as a unifying factor. Thus, it actually helped bring about the fragmentation of student identities that first became evident in the 1860s and accelerated after the mid-1870s.[86]

In the golden age of the literary elite, their dedication to poetry helped define these young men as a breed apart. The Romantic exaltation of the artist, and particularly the poet, helped provide them with a particularly strong sense of themselves as people above and beyond the ordinary.[87] "The poets are the true apostles of God," one student wrote in 1856.[88] "The spirit of the true poet never loses faith in his principles, never denies his mission," echoed another.[89] The sense of the poet or artist as someone with a "mission" was the "typical contribution of Romanticism" to world literature and art, as Brazilian literary critic Antônio Cândido notes. As a literary style, moreover, Romanticism was particularly tied to a particular stage in personal development, indeed to adolescence itself.[90] In the context of the Brazilian law schools, Romanticism helped solidify the students' identity, both as men and as members of a particular class for whom literary expression was believed to be reserved but, above all, as people with a right to lead their society.

ORATORY

Far more than poetry, oratory linked the skills valued in extracurricular student life with the abilities necessary for public lives in provincial or national legislatures or, if all else failed, in the courtroom. Students' references to themselves as the modern-day equivalents of Demosthenes suggest the centrality of oratory in their self-image.[91] If the student press often gave pride of place to poetry, it also devoted extensive space to student speeches.

Some orators were particularly adept at speaking on solemn occasions. Others spoke wherever and whenever they could, "in academic gatherings, on the streets, at formal parties, in Masonic meetings, etc." Some students continued this pattern into adult life, offering their rhetorical services whenever a speaker failed to appear or when an improvised speech suddenly seemed necessary for a special occasion.[92] As in the classical tradition, leadership was linked to formal speech, which, according to historian Mark Szuchman, "provided the sensory medium of citizenship."[93] Students linked rhetorical mastery not only with citizenship but, even more crucially, with leadership. The ability to master formal speech, to know what and what not to say and the proper forms in which to say it, marked in this sense a fundamental "constraint on access" that helped separate the men from the boys, the elite from the popular, and the men from the women.[94] After all, not everyone could speak in a formal situation; access to the podium defined these young men. They helped select each other, and their superiors, particularly law school instructors and administrators, further weeded out those who could not speak.

Students practiced these more formal speaking skills in their student clubs. These met on a weekly basis, usually around noon or four in the afternoon in one of the student *repúblicas*, with around fifteen to twenty students in attendance. After one of the club orators delivered a speech, debate on a particular issue would be joined. Subjects for discussion included the death penalty, the influence of celibate priests on the Brazilian population, and whether wars had a negative impact on society. These could continue for weeks on end. The point, after all, was not to resolve an issue but to demonstrate one's ability to construct and sustain an argument, or at least to prove one had an inexhaustible capacity for wordplay.[95] The students' classical education prepared them to be articulate, if not always insightful. Toward the end of the school year, elections would be held for the club officials, which included primary and secondary orators.[96] Making a name for oneself in these clubs could have a major impact on a student's future, particularly when other club members were the sons of some of Brazil's most powerful politicians. "São Paulo is a small world," one student wrote to his father. "Any person can make a speech in a private gathering and soon he's known throughout the school."[97]

An orator was measured by several different criteria. Students orators, said their critics, were given to "hyperbolic phraseology" combined with a "rounded" and "impressive" style filled with colorful and elaborate metaphors.[98] Few used colloquial language in the student setting.[99] Finally, an orator also had to possess the physical equipment to produce sonorous tones.

In such an environment, young men who suffered from speech impediments tended to stand out. It may seem surprising that not all students so afflicted made a poor showing in the hyperverbal and competitive student culture. Almeida Nogueira notes that one stutterer "nevertheless was an orator, and curiously enough, a fluent orator." In orating or declaiming he lost the stutter that hindered his daily conversation, though "the slightest distraction" could cause a lapse back into stammering.[100]

At the celebrations of the law schools' founding on the eleventh of August oratory took center stage. Although these were largely all-male events, women were occasionally allowed to attend. Even then, their presence was primarily ornamental. As one student noted in the late 1860s, women were expected to provide the "flowers of beauty" to complement the men's intellect.[101] Certainly, no woman would have been expected to speak at such an event. The students may have felt reassured in their masculinity, as the women deprived of speech and active citizenship were expected to listen and admire the young men's facility with words.

NEWSPAPERS

Poems improvised and speeches delivered gained larger audiences and greater permanence through the student newspaper.[102] The student press, which had virtually died out by the late 1830s, was reborn in the mid-1840s. Students founded, edited, and published their own newspapers in the 1840s and 1850s with renewed enthusiasm and purpose and a renovated style. The student press during this period rejected partisanship. To be sure, the Liberal and Conservative parties, born in the late 1830s, had their ádherents among the student body. As a student corporate ideal, however, belonging to a particular party or faction was specifically rejected during those years. Newspapers defined their concerns as primarily literary. The look, as well as the content, changed in the 1840s. Newspapers were usually published on a monthly basis and, in this period, were primarily literary reviews. Each issue could run as long as fifty or sixty pages, and articles were frequently spread out over the length of a newspaper or carried serially through a number of issues. The contents of the student newspaper consisted largely of literary productions, short stories, poems, plays, and speeches. Student newspaper editors rejected the model of the regional political newspaper.[103] One student newspaper editor conjectured that people failed to support literary newspapers because they associated all papers with the "virulent language and odious recriminations" of the political press.[104]

The connection between the newspaper and the student body itself changed in the 1840s. While small clusters of dedicated young men, often roommates linked by political affinities, produced the newspapers of the 1830s, new student associations produced the papers of the 1840s and 1850s. After a time marked by what was repeatedly characterized as "indifference," student literary associations blossomed.[105]

In his important study of the *bacharel*, Sérgio Adorno emphasized the ways in which the newspapers promoted the formation of a political class. They provided a forum for debate on public issues and allowed students to stake a claim on the development of Brazilian society by giving them a direct tutorial role over the popular classes. While there is much in what he says, Adorno ignores the extent to which these newspapers were primarily written for an audience of other students or, somewhat more indirectly, an audience of other elite men with similar backgrounds and interests.[106] An occasional newspaper produced by students was directed to a particular audience outside the student body, and that target group was not the popular classes. Instead, when the students chose to educate a particular social group rather than express their sense of corporate identity through newspapers, the group they selected was defined by gender — the young women of Pernambuco and São Paulo, who were generally women of their own social class. *O Bello Sexo*, for example, published in 1850 in Pernambuco, was intended to remedy the lack of "intellectual education" provided for the sex that had been "created for the happiness and ornamentation of humanity."[107] These newspapers were particularly short lived. More than any other student newspapers, they demonstrated a faith in the students' ability to educate a particular portion of Brazilian society. They are not, however, representative of the student press as a whole.

Many student newspapers did attempt to link the student body to the nation's larger elite male community. Subscriptions to some of the Olinda newspapers were available in other important cities such as Rio de Janeiro and Salvador.[108] The students hoped to make a name for themselves and felt that their literary efforts deserved wider distribution, their formulaic disclaimers of their lack of merit notwithstanding.

Student editors had a grandiose vision of the role of the press and its place in Brazilian society. The editing of a newspaper was viewed as a "patriotic task."[109] Editors were the "apostles of a mission."[110] For them, the newspaper was linked to the key concepts of the spirit of the age. It was as much a symbol of progress as the railroad, the telegraph, and the steam engine. "Time and space," according to one enthusiast, "were annihilated" by the "powerful instrument" that was the newspaper.[111] The opening pages of a new student paper often included a lengthy discussion of the role of the printing press in furthering the development of humanity.[112] The newspaper had "an eminently civilizing mission."[113] The litany of "sacrifice" and "mission" was repeated endlessly in these newspapers.[114]

Many a newspaper failed, of course, but each new paper that took its place was launched with great enthusiasm. As many as thirteen student newspapers were being published in São Paulo in 1860.[115] The constant arrival of new students meant that their hopes could always triumph over their predecessors' experience.[116] The act of launching a newspaper was celebrated with great pomp and circumstance. Although the "grand mission" of founding a newspaper was "a difficult and burdensome business," it was also an "eminently patriotic task, a glorious sacrifice that those who aspire to work for the aggrandizement of their country cannot refuse."[117]

By the 1860s, student newspapers, which had previously been published by nonpartisan associations, began to develop explicit ties to parties: *O Constitucional* with the Conservative Party, *A Legenda*, among others, with the Liberal Party. This reflected the contemporaneous breakdown of Conciliation-era politics and the rebirth of the Liberal Party. The focus on literary values continued, especially in newspapers that sought to represent the entire student body rather than specific segments. However, the reintroduction of partisanship on the campuses led to a certain fragmentation, as well, of student identities.

As the student press became more partisan in the 1860s, politicians and commercial newspaper editors criticized student editors for addressing national issues when they were only eighteen, nineteen, or twenty years of age (if not younger). Clearly, writing editorials on imperial politics was an act of self-assertion, a way of staking a claim to status as an adult male. Acutely aware of being observed by the adult political world, students often justified their concern with national issues by making reference to their expectation that they would lead the nation in the not-too-distant future.[118]

While they sometimes responded to criticism from the adult male world, more often they directed their rhetorical skills against each other. An editorial in a student publication was read by the editors of other student papers; editors made sure that their papers were distributed within the community of newsprint whether political rivals or not. The Conservative Party paper quickly denounced what had been published in the previous week's Liberal Party paper, and the Liberal Party editor would respond in kind the following week. In a student body that numbered in the hundreds at any given time before the 1880s, an editorial writer would be known by all and a rival could confront him in front of a classroom he disliked what had been written. Anonymous attacks on fellow students were seen as a violation of the rules of the game, as poisoning the atmosphere, and were roundly condemned.[119] In such a small community, face-to-face relationships were central to the formation of identities. While the ease with which one's critics could retaliate does not seem to have lessened the harshness of the language students employed, it did enable them to discover whether they were ready for the rough-and-tumble world of politics.

At its worst, the criticism found in student newspapers could seem like pedantry to an outside observer because there was so much concentration on questions of style. But it was never merely that. The students argued over who belonged to the political class and who did not. Since command of language defined authority, when one student criticized another's use of adverbs in an article in 1850, for example, he was questioning the latter's right to membership in the literary elite. A person who could not use adverbs correctly clearly did not belong.[120]

The primary function of the student newspaper was more expressive than educational — it linked its authors to a community and a class. Student papers in this period enjoyed a prominence they never had before or since in Brazil (and, I would argue, an importance they rarely have had in any society or epoch). Through these publications the students made names for themselves among the elite male political community and became public figures imbued with a sense of mission that was linked to technological and political progress.

The literary bent of these newspapers was not without its critics, even among the students themselves. The student editor of *O Publicador Paulistano* (a semiofficial rather than student newspaper published in the late 1850s) argued that his fellow students misunderstood the function of the press. He noted that "A newspaper is not a poetic monologue in which the poet is free to choose the sounds, forms, and images that he desires . . . ; on the contrary it is a collective work in which the public's active participation is necessary."[121] The voice of the public, however, was absent from the student press.

THE STYLE OF THE LAW STUDENT, THE STYLE OF THE *BACHAREL*

An ideal student, then, would be a poet, an orator, a thespian, and a journalist. Within the student community, a particularly successful student would find others repeating his bon mots, imitating his style and even the sound of his voice.[122] A law student had the polish and ease associated with an aristocracy, although the *bacharéis* would be quick to argue that their special place in society was due more to their gifts than to their inherent social and cultural advantages. A *bacharel* was expected to have a style that would inspire respect and deference from the rest of society.

The students' verbal skills also defined, in large part, their relations with others. Students were known for their tendency to flatter and flirt with women.[123] One student was described as a "lover by profession and a skilled editor of love letters."[124] Facility with words gave students an advantage over many of the young women they encountered; even those of their own social class had an education limited largely to French, music, and drawing. Literary depictions of student encounters with young men (admittedly written by older men recalling and likely idealizing their youth) included conversations studded with literary references, many of which the young women cannot follow. For example, though the character of Adelaide in Bernardo Guimarães's *Rosaura, A Engeitada* is given to reading poetry and novels, she is not well read and has never even heard of Goethe. Women, Guimarães contended, were less intelligent than men and considered study only something to pass the time between "dolls and candies." Nor can Adelaide understand Latin, which the students employ to show off and to flatter. This leads her to request that they not recite verse in a language she does not understand. Students competed verbally with each other for Adelaide's attention, and the young provincial Belmiro, a portrayal of the author himself as a student, is said to be at a disadvantage in this regard because he is less adept with words than the others. Even so, he is clearly more verbally gifted than Adelaide.[125]

The literary leanings of the student defined an identity that was both class- and gender-based. Notable in this regard is one newspaper editor's pejorative use of the word *hermaphroditic* to describe the language used by a rival editor in 1850.[126] Language was defined as male, and students zealously guarded their rights to language and to their definition of what was male language.

After graduation, language continued to play a major role in the *bacharéis*' sense of themselves. Many continued to edit and publish newspapers. As provincial and national legislators, their ability to convince their political allies and opponents through oratory continued to be essential. Poetry, being associated with youth, grew less important.

For many, familiarity with a foreign language continued to be a marker of social and political status. For most, French was the preferred language, the language of civilization. Many chose to write and publish in a foreign language and to introduce into Portuguese what one Brazilian linguist has called "the avalanche of gallicisms in the eighteenth and nineteenth centuries in Brazil."[127] Perhaps the most extreme example of a *bacharel* enamored of a foreign language was Tobias Barreto, who rejected the Francophile tendencies of his peers. For him, the progressive language was German, which we taught himself after graduation in the 1870s, following the unification of Germany and that nation's increasing international prestige. Soon he was writing and publishing articles in German, first in the backwater of Escada and later in Recife after he returned to teach there. "Let it be for you as if I were in Berlin," he wrote a colleague.[128] The fact that almost no one besides Barreto himself could have read German in Pernambuco (that northeastern state not being a favorite destination for German immigrants) seems to have been inconsequential to him. Writing in German marked him as a civilized man, a man of the upper class. The status conferred by language was no doubt doubly precious because he could not claim it by birth.

As Angel Rama has argued, Latin America clung to "the tenacious myth, adopted from French thought of the independence period, nourished by nineteenth-century liberalism [and it literary correlate, Romanticism], and steadfastly maintained by each generation of *letrados* — that men of letters are best suited to conduct political affairs."[129] Their literary inclinations were, as I have suggested, a symbol of their status and power, a clear proof that they were gentlemen to whom deference was owed.[130] A knowledge of law, their ostensible object of study, was not sufficient to grant them this legitimacy in their own minds or in that of society at large. As Adorno has argued, building on the insights of Nelson Saldanha, the *bacharéis* defined "politics as an activity directed by intellectual criteria," which guaranteed their authority.[131] Power flowed not from the barrel of a gun, as it often did among Spanish American republics haunted by the omnipresent *caudillo*. The *bacharéis* of imperial Brazil basked in the certitude that as a civilized, progressive nation, Brazil was beyond that. Power flowed from the shaft of a pen.[132] The *bacharéis'* discourse may, as its critics charged, have marked an evasion of reality, filled as it was with "vague formulas, empty phrases, [and] the love of words for words' sake." Nevertheless, the literary elite's hegemony over society went largely unchallenged from the 1840s to the 1870s.[133]

3

PEERS, PATRONS, FAMILY, AND COMMUNITY

The political class that was formed at the law schools was not defined by words alone but through social relations as well. Historians have concluded that the students developed an identification with the nation over and above their ties to their families and their local power base. However, to the extent that these young men did develop such a national orientation while at school, I argue that the process was not as straightforward as the founders intended or historians have inferred it to be. In any case, they did so primarily within the student community itself and not in the classroom.[1]

I have already shown how from the 1840s through the 1870s students developed a sense of themselves as a group defined by mastery over language and that this characteristic set them apart from others in Brazilian society. The tension between commitments to the nation and ties to family and region, however, would not be so easily resolved in the short-term experience at school. The attempt to form a common identity at the law school was mediated through friendships; living arrangements; social, literary, and political organizations; factors of spatial and social mobility; symbolic attachments; relationships with women and older elite men as well as the larger communities of São Paulo and Olinda (Recife after 1854); and even through personal style. Identities were formed, as they always are, in relation to others. Nowhere is this clearer than in the attempt to create a community of law students, a national elite-in-training that saw itself as independent from the rest of society and united as a band of brothers but that was also bound up in the ties of patron-client relations that defined nineteenth-century Brazilian society.[2]

FAMILY, YOUTH, AND IDENTITY

To begin constructing a national consciousness, the founders of the law schools decided it was necessary to bring these young men from all over Brazil to two relatively accessible locations. By making the trip to Pernambuco or São Paulo, prospective students and their families made a statement about their place in society. Substantial family resources financed a son's trip, often from a plantation in the interior, to one of the law schools. Travel was difficult in nineteenth-century Brazil, and trips home would be rare. If the journey was itself an essential part of the construction of a national identity, it began by loosening ties to locality and family.[3]

Many of the tensions experienced by the law students of both Pernambuco and São Paulo reflected the changing role of the family in nineteenth-century Brazil. The family was the central political unit. Families constituted "electoral clans," even though they were never the "exclusive connecting bonds in politics," according to Linda Lewin.[4] At the same time, as some critics of traditional Brazilian society have argued, the "ethics of family was opposed to the impersonal norms of the state," which would soon employ the law school graduates.[5]

The family was also the central economic unit. Choices of marriage partners, for example, were crucial in guaranteeing a family's long-term financial stability. An important indicator of the degree to which these students developed a new orientation while in law school was whom they chose as a marriage partner after graduation. It is undoubtedly true that students often married the sisters of fellow law students from other provinces or that they married local women from Pernambuco or São Paulo. Both demonstrate the way the law school experience helped establish new networks of power and influence.[6] The tendency among elite Brazilians to marry cousins, so as to maintain family wealth and ensure racial "purity," also remained strong in the nineteenth century. The strength of family ties could not be wholly disrupted by the law school experience.[7]

The tension between the student as individual and member of a peer group on the one hand and as family member on the other reflected larger changes in Brazilian society as a whole. The rights of individuals had traditionally been subordinated to those of the family.[8] During the colonial period, families had been held responsible for crimes committed by family members.[9] A father had legal authority over his family and could even have sons who were still living at home imprisoned for misbehavior.[10]

The conflict between traditional understandings of familial relations and more individualistic, liberal notions of personal responsibility and identity continued throughout the imperial period. The law students embodied the contradictions of a patriarchal society in transition. Students sought to balance the interests of their families with those they faced as imperial subjects and public men. One student asserted in 1860 that while he had ambitions to acquire fame in letters and politics, he would "sacrifice with pleasure any of these ambitions for the happiness of my family."[11] His family's happiness, however, often could depend on the successful fulfillment of his ambitions.

Fathers in the imperial period would proudly say, "I graduated him," referring to their sons, because they believed they had made the critical choice in deciding to send a son to a professional school rather than forcing him to work in a commercial establishment.[12] Undoubtedly, they knew, as will be discussed in chapter 4, the extent to which a political favor or a letter to the proper authority might determine their sons' success in school. The assertion, however, that a father had "graduated" his son robbed the latter of any sense of accomplishment he might have gained from the experience. A father's financing of his son's education was no altruistic act, in any case; it was a good investment that often opened new political opportunities for the father as well.

A student's success or failure in law school was clearly not just an individual matter; it also represented familial success or failure. For example, an uncle of Rui Barbosa (a prominent student orator in the Recife and São Paulo law schools and later a key political figure) referred not to Rui's own goals but to "our hopes" for his reaching "our target." Rui was not to be allowed to let even the tragedy of his mother's death in his early student years distract him from the completion of what were largely familial responsibilities.[13] "You are the future of our family and the hope of our family," Olinda graduate José Thomaz Nabuco de Araujo wrote to his son Joaquim.[14] The pressures were at times unwelcome, and the conflict between familial expectations and the law student's growing sense of independence could be painful. A young man could see himself as an individual and a member of a student community, as I will show, but to his relatives he was still a family member, no matter how far from home.

Even before he began his legal studies, however, the law student had begun to leave his family behind. From the 1820s until the late 1870s, students had to travel to the cities where the law schools were located to take the entrance examinations. They generally spent a year or so in the cities preparing to take these tests. Accompanied perhaps by a family slave and a friend from home, they began their first steps toward autonomy and adulthood.

Even then, however, students did not leap into the new world of the student community completely alone. That the reality of familial ties preceded the dream of independence is illustrated by Barbosa's experience after transferring to the southern school. Before finding housing to share with other students, he stayed in the home of the provincial president, who was a friend of his father.[15] Moreover, students usually were taken under the wing of a "correspondent," that is, an older man directly related to his family or linked by financial or political ties. Designated by the student's father to look after his son while he was away at school, the family friend's primary responsibility was to dole out the student's allowance. This financial hold over the younger man gave the correspondent a degree of insight into the student's personal habits that he could then share with the distant father. Generally, the correspondent was expected to keep an eye on his father's son and report any indiscretions.[16]

The ties to patrons and family back home were often frayed by physical distance, however. One way that family members sought not only to maintain these ties but to exert some measure of control, besides engaging a "correspondent," was by writing letters. Letters served to reassure parents of their distant son's well-being, of course, but they were also part of the larger framework of personal obligations, which were defined by emotional ties to be sure but also by a sense of benefits previously received. Letters could help maintain influence over a distant son no longer under a patriarchal father's control. Bonds between fathers and sons were loosening and parental power weakening during the young male's transition to manhood. A son's response might be the rough equivalent of the Hispanic formula, "I obey, but I do not comply." And a father's attempt to place emotional pressure on a wayward son was not always enough to reestablish control. Familial expectations and individual desires were not always compatible.

REPÚBLICAS: AUTONOMY AND BROTHERHOOD

Despite ongoing efforts to restrain young men, to a large extent Brazilian society allowed these young males to define their own rite of passage into manhood. The students' autonomy contrasts strikingly with what we know, for
example, of other contemporaneous models of elite male socialization. Consider the English model. While Brazilian students lived on their own in
the group living arrangements known as *repúblicas*, English students lived
either on campus or in licensed boarding or lodging houses. In the *repúblicas* (which grew in importance in students' self-depictions after the 1840s),
one writer has suggested, "everything was permitted, except study."[17] Walls,
gates, and ditches surrounded English colleges to restrict the students' mobility, while nothing impeded the Brazilian elite male's access to public
space. Young Brazilian males of their class could go wherever they wished.
In England, curfews were strictly kept; bills from local wine merchants were
sent to the student's tutors. For a young Brazilian elite male, everything was
permitted. For an English student, the emphasis was on self-control; for his
Brazilian counterpart, on control over others.[18]

If the English comparison seems a bit distant, consider Brazil's neighbor
Argentina for a markedly different approach to elite male socialization. Concerns about the breakdown of social norms in postindependence Argentina
led Argentine legislators to pass laws that required "the police to place in
debtors' prison any student found in 'the streets . . . cafés, or other public
places during school hours.'" University officials were required by law to report student absences from their classes to the police.[19] Brazilian society was
not averse to some types of regulation of student behavior. Grades and the
names of absent law students, for example, were printed in the local newspaper, but the Brazilian method suggests a greater reliance upon shame as
a motivating factor in controlling student behavior. As it was, however,
shame does not seem to have been particularly effective. Public space belonged to these young men, and they were able to define their own private
space as well.

One of the central institutions of law student culture, and a key component in these young men's socialization into the peer group, was the *república*.[20] A private space in which students practiced being public men, the *república* constituted what anthropologist Anthony Leeds has described in the

context of twentieth-century Brazilian society as the *panelinha*, in his words, "a relatively closed, completely informal primary group, held together by ties of friendship or other personal contact acting for common ends."[21] The affective ties forged in the *república* may have been an unintended consequence of the Brazilian law student experience. However, *repúblicas* were no less effective in forging a cohesive elite for being relatively spontaneous and unplanned, in contrast to the more controlled environment of the college dormitory in the United States. Moreover, in a society in which, even to this day, face-to-face relationships are more important than impersonal bureaucratic ties, the *república* was a crucial institution for forging identities and creating alliances.

The financial difficulties of student life forced many to live together. The first thirty-three students at the São Paulo law school, for example, boarded together in groups of three or four. Even if they did not live in the same house, many lived on the same block, often close to the law school itself.[22] Although housing was frequently a problem, solutions tended to be improvised rather than resolved by creating student residential housing. This failure to develop student housing is curious, given the constant complaints that the schools lacked control over their students. However, this ad hoc approach to housing has continued largely unchanged to this day in most Brazilian universities. The failure to provide housing threw students back on their own, largely familial resources while encouraging them to make their own associations, which would, in many cases, last a lifetime.

The autonomy structurally embodied in the *república* was quite different from the patriarchal Big House celebrated in Gilberto Freyre's *The Mansions and the Shanties* (1936). The students' sense of being in control was reinforced by their distance from their fathers. In this patriarchal society, students relished escaping the shadow of their fathers' house to set up their own living arrangements and make their own friends. For Joaquim Nabuco in the 1860s, the São Paulo law school provided a liberating environment, a time of "rebellion and independence." He tried to contrast his way of thinking with that of his prominent politician father — himself a graduate, as we have seen, of the Olinda school. In his first year at school, Joaquim founded a newspaper to attack the Zacarias ministry that his father supported. (The older man suggested that he stick to studying and leave journalism and poli-

tics alone.)[23] This sense of independence also expressed itself in more pro-
saic ways. "During my very first days at law school," he later remembered
warmly, "being absolutely my own master, with no inhibitions arising from
paternal supervision, I began to buy the furniture, the china, and the other
things for the quarters I shared with three of my colleagues."[24]

The students spoke of the *república* as constituting a new "family," but
it was a family without mothers or fathers.[25] The differences between the
república, a community of peers, and the nineteenth-century Brazilian patriarchal family, a hierarchical institution, are more striking than the similari-
ties. Lacking a strong central authority figure, these campus families consisted only of brothers, as the students frequently called each other, both
inside and outside of the *república*.[26] Former roommates described themselves as being "brothers in affection."[27] This was a fraternity on a more intimate scale than the North American variety. (The sense of brotherhood
was reinforced by the fact that many students who attended the schools did,
in fact, have brothers in other class years.[28])

The students' belief in equality within their own ranks is reflected in the
pride they took in the lack of "chiefs" in the *repúblicas*.[29] Internally, student
residences were supposed to be run democratically (although, in keeping
with the hierarchical realities of student culture, first-year students might
have special tasks[30]). Members, for example, had responsibility for paying
expenses on particular days of the month.[31]

The *república* was an essential building block for the community of students and provided them with an opportunity to develop a closeness they
claimed they could not otherwise find in Brazilian society. The friendships
created there were seen as unlike any experienced outside of student life, as
one recent graduate longingly described them in 1870: "frank, loyal, capable
of self-abnegation." Life in the *república* was a life "of the heart."[32] These
friendships, moreover, often lasted throughout men's political careers.[33]

The friendships that were formed in the student residences often built
on provincial ties as often as they created new national linkages. *Repúblicas*
were frequently shared by students from the same province.[34] As one visitor
to the São Paulo school observed in the 1860s, "They conserve in this
way, in the midst of the promiscuity of their general relations, a provincial spirit." Students from Rio Grande do Sul often lived together; students

from Rio de Janeiro did the same. Young males from the province of Minas Gerais were said to be especially prone to choose fellow Mineiros as room-mates.[35] Many *repúblicas* consisted of students who had first met each other in the secondary schools located in the capitals of their home province, as can be seen in literary depictions of student life.[36] Furthermore, provincial loyalties helped bridge the hierarchical divisions within and beyond the student body by including both "animals" (students preparing to take their entrance exams) and students already enrolled.[37] Regional loyalties often played a major role in student elections (for the choice of class orator, for example), with votes split along regional lines.[38] Provincialism in student housing and in the law school generally was important, and it needs to be seen as mitigating against any simplistic indoctrination into national values. However, the *repúblicas* also clearly provided a place in which students could feel at home in the company of their fellow provincials while establishing broader ties that would serve them well in the classroom and in the more nationally oriented student literary and debating societies.

Associations in the *repúblicas* also sometimes drew together men from different provinces. In choosing whom to live with, some students, often the most prominent and most well-connected politically, could draw upon previous ties at the Colégio Dom Pedro II in Rio de Janeiro. This institution was, not surprisingly, a particular favorite for national politicians based in the capital to send their sons. Boys whose fathers served in the Senate or Chamber of Deputies usually grew up in Rio, no matter what their families' provincial origins. Those with Rio ties always had a special place in the student body and could count on being the ones other students wanted to meet.[39]

Although *repúblicas* were seen as the archetypal student dwelling, not all students lived in them. An interesting aspect of student life was that some student "bohemians" lacked a permanent place they could call home. Instead, *repúblicas* vied for the honor of putting them up for a time. Students granted these bohemians special status largely because they exhibited the student ideal of independence in its purest form, and yet, paradoxically, they were also the most dependent on the student community as a whole.[40] There were others who could not even afford to live in the student *repúblicas*, where the sharing of poverty was proverbial (if somewhat exaggerated — few students lived without slaves or servants). Some of the less privileged lived as pensioners in local convents and monasteries.[41]

For most, however, the *república* played an important role in the formation of students' self-understanding. They saw themselves as brothers linked in solidarity and as independent, set apart from the rest of society.

The conflict between students' loyalty to their families and to their peer group is humorously described by Almeida Nogueira in a story from 1860s São Paulo. A student who still lived with his father (an unusual situation) was friends with the members of a nearby *república* composed of students from Rio de Janeiro. The "republicans" had long admired the older man's turkeys, chickens, and ducks. They soon tested their friend by proposing to enlist his aid in the time-honored student practice of larceny most fowl. In this case, the birds to be robbed belonged to the student's family. To whom would the young man be loyal: his family or his peers? One night after letting the family dog out for an evening run, the young man let his fellow students into the family household. Entering cautiously, the "republicans" suddenly were surprised to find the door to the next room opening, revealing a brightly lit interior. "Grab the thieves," they heard the owner of the house say. The students started to run, only to discover that the outside door had been locked behind them. Realizing that they had been betrayed, they expected the worst. Instead, the father of the house invited them into the dining room where they found a lavish meal already prepared for them. Their host welcomed them, saying, "You have only accelerated the date of a party that I have planned for a long time, to celebrate your friendship with my son." In this ingenious manner, Almeida Nogueira concluded, the young man had been "freed from committing a betrayal of either his colleagues or his family, and to conciliate his collegial duties with his loyalty to his family."[42]

Family and regional loyalties were subsumed, however, in the short term at least, by national ties formed in the student literary and debating societies that became so prominent a part of student life in the 1840s.

ASSOCIATIONS

The *república* as an institution predated the rise of the literary ideal in the 1840s. The development of autonomous student associations as a major focus of student energies, however, dates precisely from the mid-1840s. The occasional student organization had existed before, such as the federalist Philomatic Society. However, most of the local voluntary societies students joined in the early years were already-existing organizations formed by older men outside of the student community.[43] Moreover, these early organizations were largely devoted to political and not literary activities.

Beginning in the mid-1840s, however, student associations proliferated, reaching their peak in the late 1850s and early 1860s, when roughly ten to fifteen existed at either school.[44] Some associations were patterned after similar organizations in Rio de Janeiro, borrowing their names and pursuing similar purposes.[45] A few of them were semiofficial organizations. Particularly important associations celebrated the anniversaries of their founding within the confines of the law schools themselves, although weekly meetings were held in student homes.[46] Moreover, students took the initiative for maintaining these organizations and for creating new ones. Like common living arrangements, the associations were central to the construction of student community and identity.

One of the first student associations, the Epicurean Society, founded in 1845, was devoted to what its members considered Byronic excesses, particularly drinking, frequenting brothels, and general bohemianism.[47] On one occasion, the society's members "stayed together for fifteen days on end in an enclosed room lit only by candlelight."[48] By experimenting with sensory deprivation and depriving themselves of all other human companionship, they joined their lives together (and undoubtedly did nothing to improve their performance in their classes). The Epicurean Society's excesses even led to the early death of some of its members. The survivors, through the shared testing of physical experience and endurance, became closely tied together.

Students also formed secret societies, such as the Burschenschaft (students' association) in São Paulo. Although little, unsurprisingly, has survived regarding the activities of these organizations, it is known that many of the most prominent politicians of the imperial and republican eras belonged to the Burschenschaft as students. In keeping with the hierarchies within the law student body, the head of the Burschenschaft was always a fifth-year student. New Burschenschaft members were chosen by existing members, thereby creating a certain continuity in the personal qualities most admired by these particular members. For law students, membership in such a clandestine organization demonstrated that one had reached the apex of the student community social structure. That the Burschenschaft, to some extent, represented a meritocracy is suggested by the fact that it also paid for all or part of the tuition of some of the poorer members. The details of their nocturnal rituals have not been preserved. New leaders of the organization, however, received a special key that was passed down for generations. This key, one might surmise, symbolized their right of access to social and political power. Future presidents of Brazil during the republican period had held prominent positions in the Burschenschaft during the imperial period. Afonso Pena, for example, was the "chief of general communion," and Rodrigues Alves, the "chief of the Council of the Apostles," the two highest positions in the organization.[49]

The roles of the Epicurean Society and the Burschenschaft, while important, have been overemphasized by scholars. This is perhaps because in the case of the former they are more colorful than the average student society or in the case of the latter because they seem to offer answers to some secrets of the working of Brazilian politics during and after the imperial period. But it was the closed but still "public" institutions like the *Atheneu Pernambucano* or the *Atheneu Paulistano* that brought in a larger number of students and, therefore, played a greater role in defining student identity. The *Atheneu Pernambucano*, for example, had roughly seventy students in the 1860s in a student body of around five hundred; the *Instituto Científico* had eighty.[50] And these were but two of many societies during these glory days of association building. Student societies drew young men from various provinces together and provided opportunities for the gifted, the ambitious, or the lucky to establish national ties and reputations. To cite but two examples, northerners such as the poet Castro Alves and the orator Rui Barbosa, both from the province of Bahia, became dominant figures in the Atheneu Paulistano in São Paulo.[51]

For the students, the attempt to create a cohesive student body through association building was an active process. Particularly threatening to student unity was what students referred to as the "spirit of indifference" demonstrated by some of their fellows. This spirit hindered all efforts to form effective associations and to publish newspapers that could last more than a few months.[52] Student editors and orators were particularly disdainful of those they called *zoilos* — bitter, envious critics who knew how to tear down but not how to build (the name, appropriately enough, derives from a critic of the Greek epic poet Homer). Within the student body, the *zoilos* were the ones who worked against the unity the associations sought to foster.[53] When in 1850 a small group of Olinda students proudly embraced the label and published a newspaper criticizing the literary pretensions of their fellow students, one student indignantly replied, "How dare a half-dozen boys attempt to criticize an entire corporation?"[54] The editors of newspapers and the founders of associations claimed to speak for the student body as a whole and to represent its true spirit. By 1860, one newspaper proudly proclaimed, *zoilos* were almost extinct as a species. The literary ideal had triumphed, and the goal of association building had been embraced as a primary student responsibility.[55]

Within these organizations, young men sought to foster individual goals as much as the broader ones of community formation. Making a name for oneself entailed creating an identity within a group, first within the student community.[56] In pursuit of this goal, it was often necessary for an ambitious student to found a new association and create a new newspaper in which one's name could become known.[57]

Being accepted into an already existing association meant a great deal to these young men, for acceptance by one's peers was paramount.[58] Moreover, the *repúblicas* and the associations provided the perfect setting for the gradual accumulation of public influence discussed by Anthony Leeds and, more recently, by Glen Dealy. "The public man seeks to become the 'surrounded' man," Dealy has argued. Reserve and a disinclination to make friends were not qualities admired by Brazilian law students. Dealy's much-criticized model accurately describes important characteristics of male identity in the law student community of nineteenth-century Brazil. The law student experience did help students "prepare a following." These associations even more than their classes helped socialize these young men into the norms of elite political society. This seems to have been even truer for those rare law students who did not by birth belong to the upper class, but through ambition and an ability to make the right connections at school could aspire to leadership roles in Brazilian society.[59]

Dealy and others go wrong, however, in depicting this type of activity as merely a Machiavellian means to an end. Friendships were not only instrumental but central to the process of identity formation and gaining a sense of belonging. The law student associations were celebrated as being a "meeting of intimate friends," where one's most private thoughts, "one's most modest ideas find an echo, a sympathetic ear, a constant loyalty."[60]

The student societies could contribute to a sense of common identity in most ways. However, some feared that the increasing number of groups, while a sign of the vitality of student life, could also fragment the student community into factions, where "egotism" predominated.[61] Like the *repúblicas*, although to a much lesser extent, associations sometimes built upon preexisting provincial ties. The organization Culto á Sciencia (Devotion to Science), for example, was formed by graduates of a high school with the same name.[62] There were a variety of mutual aid organizations for students from the same province, such as the Benevolent Societies of Minas Gerais and Rio Grande do Sul. Since these organizations did not produce newspapers, however, they had much less of a role in defining student identity.[63] The rivalry between particular student associations was frequently criticized in the student newspapers for its harmful effects on the student body as a whole.[64]

One organization of particular importance in Pernambuco was the Monte Pio Acadêmico, which was intended to provide needy students with financial aid. Even the existence of such an organization is significant, given the frequent (and justified) complaints about the elitist nature of higher education during the imperial period. Monte Pio did help poor but talented students attend the Recife law school, although how many they helped cannot be determined. In 1858, students complained that not enough of their colleagues were willing to provide the necessary financial resources to sustain other students. Although in previous years, one student predicted the association had been able to provide support for five students, Monte Pio would soon not be able to help anyone at all. Indeed, the organization had all but disappeared by the following year. When the organization was revived in the mid-1860s, one professor opposed it on the grounds that making financial aid available to students would mean the school would produce too many law graduates (a problem that did occur in the 1880s, as we shall see).[65]

Although the various student organizations absorbed much student energy, not all students were active in extracurricular student life, and not just because they were apathetic *zoilos*. Older students in particular were less likely to participate in either the bohemian or the literary activities of student life. Married students, however old they were, rarely belonged to student associations; they were seen as occupying a different category. Marriage separated the men from the boys, so to speak, and kept married men from being prominent figures in the student community.[66]

In a social universe configured partly by rituals, the student community achieved its apotheosis on the anniversary of the founding of the law schools, the eleventh of August, an event that grew in importance for the students after the 1840s. All associations were represented by at least one orator on this annual celebration. The mistreatment of first-year students was deferred for the evening (after they had completed their assigned task of making the building presentable). Theoretically, the *trote* was suspended for the remainder of the year.[67] The façade of the law school building was brightly illuminated for the evening, and bands played martial music and overtures. After the student orations and other entertainments, the student body paraded through the streets of their city.[68]

The anniversaries of the founding of associations were themselves important events, not least because they demonstrated success in creating binding ties. Reports on these events in the student newspapers always emphasized the "order" and "harmony" that was sustained during the course of the evening. Rivalries between the various societies and between particular people were always set aside, at least in the imaginative reconstructions of these events that appeared in the papers. Whenever students gathered together, their unity was supposed to be on display. One student described the assembled students as "forming one individual."[69] After the regional rebellions between 1824 and 1842, the political class had at last achieved a national consensus. In their celebrations of student community, the future leaders of Brazilian society were demonstrating that they were not ultimately divided by their internal diversity.[70]

Another important day for the student community, as for the nation as a whole, was, of course, Independence Day, the seventh of September. It is highly suggestive that the inaugurations of many of the student societies were set for this day in celebrations that were marked by the singing of the national anthem and shouts of "Long live the independence of Brazil." By doing so, student linked the fate of their associations with that of the nation. They staked their claim to membership in what Roderick Barman has called the "official nation," in which they were united "as much by a shared outlook and culture as by the possession of any common racial, social, or economic standing."[71] The creation of associations, like the writing of literature, was seen as a patriotic and progressive act, designed to further the intellectual and political development of Brazil. The time spent establishing associations was seen as part of the sacrifice the students made for the nation.[72] Furthermore, this symbolic linkage heightened the sense of personal and political independence that was so central to the ideal of Brazilian youth, while deepening the conviction that one belonged to a group with a special vanguard role to play in society.[73] Associations were linked, metaphorically, to the founding of Christianity; as Jesus's apostles had spread the gospel, so the students' societies would enable them to spread the new gospel of nation, progress, and civilization.[74]

Through their associational life the students were therefore doing more than just making valuable contacts (although certainly they were doing that). They were creating the institutional framework and personal ties necessary for student community and, beyond, for a cohesive elite. To belong to a student organization was a crucial part of becoming an elite male. As one professor lamented, the "most talented and most admired students are those who most take advantage of these associations and least apply themselves to the law."[75]

HIERARCHIES

To understand the type of community the law students envisioned, one can also look to fictional depictions of the law school experience, particularly because so many such novelistic re-creations of student life were by former law students. Consider, for example, Bernardo Guimarães's *Rosaura, A Engeitada*, which was a representation of student life in the 1840s when the author was, as we have seen, a literary-minded student in São Paulo. In describing the student world, Guimarães made clear that, whatever the students' other faults, they did view themselves as belonging to a community unblemished by the racist attitudes of the larger society.

Guimarães presented as one of his major characters Major Damásio Augusto Bueno Aguiar de Andrade, a muleteer of mixed-race ancestry who had successfully risen through São Paulo society. In attempting to solidify his social status, Andrade sought among the law students an appropriate suitor for his daughter. After a *mestiço* student accompanied the young men on a visit to the older man's house, the major asked a student to leave this person of mixed race home the next time they wanted to pay a call. The law students considered this insult to their friend an affront to themselves as a corporate body, in which the ideal of equality and fraternity reigned. They resolved to exact revenge. After several modest efforts toward this end, one anonymous student wrote a satirical love poem in which the daughter's own multiracial ancestry was revealed to her for the first time. Not surprisingly, both she and her father considered this a vile insult. By writing the poem, the law student (whose anonymity signaled that he represented Every Law Student) mocked the social pretensions of the nouveau riche from the position of one secure in his social position. He did so in defense of his law school peers, to whom he owed ultimate loyalty and for whom all other social distinctions of race and class were secondary.

In their student culture, racial origins were deemed to be, according to Guimarães, irrelevant to the assessment of a student's qualities.[76] Within the student community, the more democratic values of merit and the communal values of solidarity were assumed to prevail, enabling the students to be the rightful aristocracy in society at large. However truthfully Guimarães's novel reflects daily social relations, his otherwise critical and unsentimental portrait of student life does suggest how strongly graduates continued to believe in the law student community even decades after leaving it.

The students developed a corporate ideal that professed fraternity and solidarity, but it was not without internal divisions. It certainly had its own hierarchies. All students were brothers, but not all brothers were equal. Particular associations, even particular *repúblicas*, had more status than others. A young male's status within the community was confirmed by having key leadership roles, such as president, club orator, or newspaper editor, within one of the best organizations.[77] In a society such as Brazil's that placed such a high value on hierarchy, this is hardly surprising.

The distinction between upper and lower classes among the students was understood as a natural one. In a rigid five-year curriculum like the law schools', where specific classes were taken each year, the student body could easily fragment, and the differences between classes were always pronounced. This occasionally frayed the communal bonds so essential to creating a cohesive elite.

The insulting labels and demeaning treatment first-year students received kept them aware of their status outside of the accepted law student body.[78] Hazing of *caloiros* sometimes amounted to little more than verbal abuse, shouting, and whistling. First-year students also had responsibilities that were considered demeaning, such as, as we have seen, cleaning and preparing the law school building for the celebrations of the eleventh of August. And they were denied certain privileges, such as the right to vote for editors of student newspapers and to speak on public occasions (see chapter 2).[79] Second-year students did not rate much higher on the social scale than *caloiros*. They were known as "rubbish." Third-year students had their "foot on the bench." Fourth-year students had almost arrived. A fifth-year student, perhaps reflecting that year's lax academic standards and the presumed ease with which it could be survived, was known simply as a *bacharel*.[80]

The hierarchical relationship between the classes is best illustrated by most of the following phrase: "the fifth-year students asked the fourth-year students to say to the third-year students that they should order the second-year students to" — followed by the surprising twist that this last group should — "indulge the first-year students."[81] (Only rarely did upperclassmen impinge on the prerogatives of second-year students regarding their social inferiors.) These categories were an inescapable result of the fact that the five-year program was divided into distinct courses of instruction. But they were also a reflection of a larger world in which, as Richard Graham has insightfully argued, no one was equal.[82] Social hierarchy at the law school cemented students' awareness and ultimate acceptance of gradations of power and authority in which they anticipated playing a commanding role.[83]

Over the years, the *trote* experienced by generations of entering classes varied in intensity and severity, but the potential always existed that incidents could escalate to more dangerous levels. On 29 March 1831 in Olinda, for example, a *caloiro* named Francisco da Cunha e Meneses, son of the Viscount of Rio Vermelho, was standing at the entrance to a billiard hall when a fourth-year student named Joaquim Serapião de Carvalho started insulting him. Generally, hazing involved a group of older students heckling an individual adolescent in his mid-teens; in such cases, the outnumbered boy had no recourse than to suffer his indignity silently. In Francisco's case, however, his assailant was alone, and he chose to answer this insult with vigor. The two young men began to strike each other, first with fists and then with canes. Carvalho then struck Cunha e Meneses in the side with a knife; the *caloiro* died later that same day.[84] After his death, the editor of a student newspaper lamented the "barbarous custom" of hazing *caloiros*. This "reprehensible form of distraction" was "shameful . . . immoral, undignified, and the enemy of good order."[85] Despite the concerns expressed by students and faculty, however, the ritual abuse of first-year students remained standard practice at the law schools throughout the imperial period.

For that reason, when entering students were not mistreated the upperclassmen's restraint seemed noteworthy. The amount of heckling endured by the entering São Paulo class of 1861 was so tremendous that many expected the following year's class to suffer in kind. Indeed, it was generally the second-year students, dismissed by upperclassmen as "dressed-up *caloiros*," who were loudest in their abuse of the first-years. Instead of giving as good as they had gotten, however, the second-year students in 1862 decided to welcome the incoming students with a band playing "festive music and other demonstrations of fellowship."[86]

Besides the hierarchies based on the accident of entrance year, there were those based on student definitions of merit (as we have seen, particularly in oratory and writing poetry). However, status could also derive from the political and social prominence of one's father. Everyone knew who the other students' fathers were because their names were printed periodically in daily newspapers. This practice could be embarrassing for some, particularly in the early years when the student body was a more diverse lot, and some students of more modest background suffered the indignity of being listed as "being of unknown parentage."[87] Class differences within the student body were a subject seldom broached and usually denied, given the felt need to emphasize unity over division.[88]

Student hierarchies also reinforced "national" or at least Rio-centered longings. As the center of political and cultural life, Rio de Janeiro set the tone for elite Brazilian society. Students from the capital city had a special familiarity with power and displayed a certain style that students from "the provinces" tried to emulate. *Repúblicas* composed of Fluminenses (people from the state of Rio de Janeiro), particularly those from "the Court" itself, had an especially prominent place in the student community. The style of Fluminense *repúblicas* was said to be more aristocratic than that of the "modest, economical" dwellings of students from Minas Gerais, for example. Perhaps the best example of the Rio native as student was the future Baron of Rio Branco, the man who would define Brazilian diplomatic style and substance for more than a generation. In his youth, he was already known for his lavish spending, for his ease around women and in the presence of the powerful, and for his stylish dress.[89] Although one hardly need accept his own urban prejudices, Adorno is clearly right when he describes the law school as a "school of customs," where the "brute-like student from the countryside was humanized."[90]

Despite these evident hierarchies, students' desire to advance their community and make themselves into a band of brothers more remarkable for their unity than their divisions was also expressed in the longing for a uniform. Periodically, students and faculty expressed regret that there were no required cap and gown for law students in Pernambuco and São Paulo. "The military academies have their distinctive outfits," one student complained in 1856. Even the Colégio Dom Pedro II, "which already enjoys so many privileges" (and from which so many students had graduated), had one. A uniform, this student argued, would "make us physically recognized, as part of national sovereignty." Moreover, another student continued, a cap and gown would be conducive to greater economy for the student by providing poor students with a "refuge from their poverty, freeing them from the shame of appearing badly dressed among so many of their friends, whom fortune favored" with greater familial wealth. The universities in the civilized countries of Europe had their own uniforms, it was argued. And the

University of Coimbra, which "has served, more or less, as the model for our school," had one as well.[91] (That Coimbra should be cited approvingly suggests one way in which this later generation of students differed from those of the 1820s and 1830s, who had defined themselves in opposition to Coimbran traditions.)

Even if they had no official uniform, students at both schools adopted an informal one of their own, one that was centuries removed, however, from the medieval cap and gown of traditional Portugal. Instead of wearing academic robes, they chose the wool suits favored by the business classes of France and England, outfits ill suited to the Brazilian climate. The student type, par excellence, was a bit of a dandy, and new students had to learn to look the part. Students also often wore glasses when they did not need them in order to appear more serious.[92] Where a required uniform would have reduced hierarchies based on familial provenance, the attire they chose accentuated them. Furthermore, students resented attempts by outsiders, such as clerks, to dress in the same kind of suits. They considered the exclusive right to wear a frock coat one of the prerogatives that accompanied their status.[93]

"OTHERS"

The hierarchical reality of student society did little to diminish a fundamental sense of brotherhood. An important aspect of the law school experience was to differentiate the students from the rest of Brazilian society. In this sense, the five years in Pernambuco or São Paulo were as much a "rite of institution" as a rite of passage, to cite Bourdieu's useful distinction.[94] While internal divisions were important for defining status within the student body, others in Brazilian society already referred to (and deferred to) the young law students as "doctors."[95] As one poet suggested in the 1860s,

> Perhaps he never opened a book,
> and didn't devote himself to knowledge,
> but his name was on the list of São Paulo law students,
> and that was all that really mattered.[96]

At the same time, all outside of the law school were derided as *futricas*, which is defined as "ordinary, egotistical" men "of low sentiments."[97] In chapter 2, I discussed the ways in which an ability to manipulate language allowed students, in their own minds at least, to stake a claim for authority over society at large. Equally central to creating a sense of identity was a recognition of "others" in relation to themselves.[98]

The law students, that is, made a clear distinction between themselves and the rest of the community. *Futrica* continued from the 1840s to the 1880s to be the dismissive designation for those outside of the community.[99] Students in São Paulo corresponded with those in the Pernambuco school and exchanged copies of their publications, hoping to enlarge the "imagined community" of students beyond the confines of their own locale. Law students clearly saw themselves as having more in common with each other than those who were not similarly schooled.[100] While the townspeople were expected to defer to the students, the students in turn often condescended to the townspeople. One student disparaged the *caipiras*, or country people from the surrounding province of São Paulo, "who seemed not to be of the human race."[101] Extracurricular student life often revolved around pranks; a favorite target, other than *caloiros*, was, by definition, any *futrica*.[102]

Among those "others" who lacked such access to higher education were, of course, women, whose contrasting condition helped define the students' identity as young men. The law students' freedom at school, particularly their access to public space, was not shared by the upper-class and middle-class Brazilian women of their day. Elite women in the nineteenth century were expected to remain at home unless they were accompanied by (the presumably male) head of the household; only slave women, mulattas, and prostitutes walked the streets alone. Ladies in nineteenth-century Recife were transported in enclosed sedan chairs carried by slaves.[103] The students' primary opportunity to meet women of their own class, therefore, was at the highly formal ballroom settings in which the students themselves were the honored guests. (Student poetry was filled with descriptions of these dances.)

Marriage to a woman of "good family" could wait until after graduation, however, as far as some of the young men were concerned. For the moment at least much of their attention was often lavished on local actresses, whose very occupation was linked in popular perceptions — and in reality — with an older profession. Castro Alves, whose long-standing relationship with the Portuguese actress Eugênia Câmara titillated and scandalized Brazilian society in the 1860s, was himself referred to as a "satellite," a common euphemism for pimp, as David Haberly informs us.[104] Poems were written in honor of favorite actresses; students divided into camps in support of one or another of the leading ladies. Actresses, however, were not considered marriage material. Instead, access to these women's sexual favors was considered one of the perquisites of elite male status.[105] And prostitutes without any known theatrical gifts were also central to the students' sexual life, to such an extent that some of them are even celebrated in the semiofficial histories of the schools.[106]

The consequences of an active sexual life could leave some students constitutionally unable to attend to their studies. One student in his fifth year in 1863 had to miss more than a week of class because of the "French disease." Despite various treatments, Prudente de Morais (eventually the first civilian president under the republic) continued to suffer horrible pains and to seek alternate medications. His doctor recommended marriage as the most effective remedy for what ailed him, although (based on what his older brother told him about matrimony) he seem disinclined to follow this advice.[107] That his case was hardly unique is suggested by the comments of a traveler who, returning to São Paulo years after graduation, noted the existence of a pharmacy that had been much trusted by the "better part of the young men of our time" for its help in curing "certain illnesses" in the 1850s.[108]

The law students prized what they considered their special appeal in the eyes of the women of São Paulo and Pernambuco (not unconnected, of course, with their own social background and future expectations of power and wealth). Not surprisingly, this led to conflict with other young males. One student complained that certain young men of São Paulo, whom he referred to disparagingly as "Zé Povinho" types (common men of the people), were introducing themselves at parties and elsewhere as fifth-year law students.[109] The student was outraged by this usurpation of his and his fellow students' identity and prerogatives. On another occasion, some young males unconnected to the law school attempted to form an organization in São Paulo that would allow no more than three or four law students as members.

The students gleefully noted the failure of this organization to attract young women to their social events, proving once again the students' greater attractiveness to women.[110]

Their disdain for contemporaries of lesser social status is demonstrated by the particular enmity that existed between students and men employed in commercial establishments. Usually from poor families, these latter young men had their own form of group living arrangements, known as "castles," which were usually located above the warehouses or stores where they worked. Gilberto Freyre noted the medieval symbolism of the castle, which expressed the workers' more conservative tendencies, in contrast to the presumed "progressive" stances of the law students.[111] Students zealously guarded the reputation of the student body from attacks by other young men. Any affront to corporate solidarity could lead to a fight, and some students considered their bruises from brawls with outsiders as badges of honor.[112]

In turn, law students treated other social groups' sense of identity cavalierly, for example, parodying publicly the practices of military men. In 1854, this led to a near state of war between members of a local military battalion and the law students in São Paulo. What became known as the "incident of the cadets" started when a young soldier stood in line for a theatrical performance wearing his military cap. (The theater, as we have seen, was a public space that the students felt they owned, as sometime actors and playwrights and as full-time patrons.) A fifth-year law student named Francisco Gonçalves Meirelles began making loud noises to draw attention to the cadet and what he considered his inappropriate attire and location. Other students joined in by yelling and shouting, as well as by stamping their feet and beating their walking sticks on the ground. Meirelles then stood on a bench and started giving mock orders as if he were a military officer. "Turn to the right! Present arms! Aim! Fire!" The sound of whistles and the pounding of canes built to a deafening roar. Finally, the cadet could not stand the public humiliation anymore and ran away, much to the students' delight, for they continued to hoot at the fleeing man mercilessly. Other soldiers, who happened to be nearby, and failed to appreciate Meirelles's impersonation of an officer, tried to seize him, but his fellow students interceded.

In the days and nights that followed, repeated conflicts between law students and military men broke out around the city. As a result of one incident, a young cadet who had been thrown into a ravine by some students was gravely, perhaps even fatally, injured. His comrades responded by threatening that if he died they would take their revenge on the students, leaving none alive. The students, in turn, marched two by two to the provincial president's palace and demanded to know "if the government could and wanted to guarantee their safety." "If not," they declared, "the students themselves would be ready to defend themselves." The president cautioned the students to take no untoward steps and sent the whole battalion to the port city of Santos to cool off. Of the fate of the injured cadet, history remains silent.[113] The incident confirms the relative immunity of the students and their privileged and protected status within the community, despite their frequent protestations of mistreatment.

An editorial in an 1863 issue of the newspaper *A Actualidade* noted that students felt they could do whatever they wished without fear of reprisal because they were the sons of "counts, viscounts, marquises, and successful capitalists." A student would receive only a slap on the wrist for any wrongdoing. The school's director might call a misbehaving student in for a conference and, in the course of the discussion, reveal that he and the student's father were friends. Despite the director's disciplinary intent, this knowledge would confirm the student's feeling that he could get away with anything.[114]

Students' sense of community was enhanced by incidents in which they were mistreated by outsiders. In 1867, after a law student from Ceará publicly criticized a minor public official in Recife, the latter hired a couple of thugs to beat up the young man. When the local police were slow to act, fellow students held demonstrations in the streets and gained the support of the community of Recife in demanding punishment for the perpetrators. Castro Alves, soon to depart for the southern school, led the demonstrations and displayed a new political style that would soon grow in prominence, particularly in the abolitionist movement: a politician making direct appeals for support from the popular classes. Order was restored, however, when the student decided to take advantage of the legal means available to him and bring his persecutors to trial. As young law students, he and his fellows knew the limits to which they could question authority because a direct attack on it could backfire and, ultimately, put their own future claims to authority into question.[115]

The students' sense of community and identity was defined partly in relation to the larger communities in which they resided: Olinda (Recife after 1854) and São Paulo. It has been suggested that the students and residents in the latter city "formed two different entities that were in a certain sense, even separate."[116] But the students' relationship to these larger communities in the northern and southern cities was not always the same. The differences between the two cities were particularly evident to those students who had transferred from one school to the other. This was a fairly common practice and one that deepened the ties between the two schools' student bodies by enhancing the sense of a national student community.

Both São Paulo and Recife were the capitals of their provinces. This gave them more political prominence than they would otherwise have had; the increased political activity in the schools created many opportunities for the young men. But there were critical differences between the two cities. Recife, which local promoters still call the "Venice of Brazil" because it is divided by two rivers and linked by numerous bridges, would seem to have been less provincial than São Paulo until late in the imperial period. However, it was also less open to the energizing impulses provided by the students themselves.[117]

In São Paulo, in particular, the students were on center stage (often quite literally), and they knew it. São Paulo was a small town even in the 1860s, numbering hardly more than twenty thousand people. It had changed little since independence. Oxcarts were still a primary means of transport.[118] The town was "provincial, conventional, and bourgeois," while the students did their best to be worldly and bohemian.[119] The students were always a highly visible presence in São Paulo; when they were on vacation, their absence was palpable. The city without the students was a proverbially dull place; they provided a "fictitious life that was but an interruption from its habitual somnolence," as one traveler put it in the early 1860s.[120] São Paulo was truly a college town until almost the end of the imperial period.

Students, often readily identifiable by their frock coats, were hardly universally admired by the residents of São Paulo. For one thing, their predilection for stealing pigs and chickens from neighbors' yards or nearby monasteries hardly endeared them to the surrounding community.[121] Students also occasionally abandoned their formal attire to parade around the city in a state of near total nudity, a clear indication of their privileged access to public space.[122] They made themselves noticed at theatrical performances, as well, in ways that were often considered offensive by local people. The *Aurora Paulista* in 1852 complained, for example, of students lighting their cigars and blowing smoke in the faces of nearby audience members as well as uttering obscenities in loud voices.[123] Students were also known to disrupt theatrical performances by shouting out comments in the middle of a scene.[124] In the small town of São Paulo, for example, while the rest of the population was usually fast asleep by 9:00 P.M., the students were awake and unconcerned with the nuisance their noise may have caused neighbors.[125]

Thus, in one literary depiction drawn from life in Recife in the late imperial period, townspeople considered the student *repúblicas* to be the "headquarters of revelry" or even the nearest thing to an insane asylum. When some students' neighbors asked the local police officer to arrest the revelers for immoral behavior, the students joined together to defend "the honor of their class," characterizing the neighbors' actions as a threat to the "liberty we have always known as students." The special status reserved for students was a result of their being "youth from good families, who were educated and who knew how to give respect when necessary." They clearly did not find it necessary with this particular official, since they displayed themselves naked before the hapless individual and pretended to stab him with a banana.[126] Although a certain degree of tension is perhaps inevitable in any college town, what is clear in the Brazilian case is the extent to which these young males were granted freedom to live life as they wished. Public acting up, though criticized, was nevertheless expected as part of the normal behavior of elite young men.

Although the experiences in the northern and southern cities were similar in many ways, there were also striking differences. Students were able to define their own terms, both politically and socially, to a much larger degree in the college town of nineteenth-century São Paulo than they were in Recife. Castro Alves, who had attended both schools, stated the difference succinctly: "As for liberty, I prefer São Paulo."[127]

The differences between the northern and southern locales deepened after 1854. In that year, after years of complaints from students and faculty alike, the law school in Pernambuco was transferred from the quiet college and religious town of Olinda to nearby Recife, a bustling, commercial city with a population of more than sixty thousand.[128] Directors had complained for years that Olinda was too isolated, too provincial. Professors had often been reluctant to make the relatively short trip to Olinda from their homes in Recife because the latter offered more opportunities to earn extra pay through legal work and to make valuable political connections. Moreover, the Olinda monastery that had housed the law school had been falling apart since the early 1840s. In 1852, some classes had to be transferred to the former governor's palace. Other classes continued to be held in the crumbling monastery, however, until one day students were forced to make a spectacular escape from the imminently collapsing walls and ceilings by jumping out of the building.[129]

The need for a new location was clear, but not long after the move to Recife complaints were already being heard about the inadequacy of the new building.[130] The relocation, moreover, had a negative impact upon the northern school's student community. Unlike in São Paulo or Olinda, the students could not set the tone in the much larger city of Recife, where sugar plantation owners dominated urban life. It may seem surprising, but if anything the transfer made the intellectual atmosphere in the northern school more, and not less, provincial since the students felt more restrained and less a central focus of the city's dynamics.[131]

Whether in Pernambuco or São Paulo, the students valued their temporary distance from Rio de Janeiro (while it nevertheless remained the location of their ultimate aspirations). Repeated suggestions were made in the national congress to close the schools and consolidate them into one school in the imperial capital of Rio. Students rejected these proposals as politically inspired, however, and a threat to their much-prized autonomy. Apparently, they feared that a move to Rio would allow authorities to monitor their activities more effectively.[132]

THE CHARACTERISTICS OF "YOUTH"

Living on their own together, making their own rules, having such a prominent role in their communities, celebrated or resented by their fellow citizens, these students came to identify more with each other as independent youth who had a special mission for Brazil's future. Their belief in their own independence, in their own minds at least, set them apart in a society built on obligations of dependence. Living in the *repúblicas* enhanced the sense of distance they already felt between themselves and the rest of society. Living on their own as men, defining their own private as well as public space, separated them from elite women as well and also from their fathers. They were "free" youth, above whom they recognized only God and the law. Such freedom and liberty were key defining characteristics of youth.[133]

To be independent in nineteenth-century Brazil was to be eligible to participate in political life. According to the law of the land, people who did not make above a certain minimum salary were considered as lacking "independence of character" and were therefore ineligible to vote. Such people were presumed to be dependent on a large landowner or other patron. Those under the age of twenty-five were also considered to be dependent unless they were (1) married men, (2) military officers, or (3) graduates of law or medical schools. Law school graduates were, by definition, independent, and law students sought to demonstrate by their daily actions that they already were so.[134]

Moreover, as young men training to be the rulers of society, the students had a special claim to the future. They defined themselves as the "Brazilians of the future," restricting their definition of the nation to themselves and imagining the time in which they would dominate Brazilian society.[135] In their rhetorical visions, the students were the "star that was beginning to shine brightly on the country's horizon." This star was the "free youth that was being born." Others were trying to hide their "brilliance" because they feared the future in which they would be judged.[136] The narrative that the students constructed in their August eleventh and September seventh orations defined the future as uniquely theirs. "Destiny belongs to youth," one student proclaimed in 1847.[137]

Though the young are usually considered the hope of the future, the law students were talking not about youth in general but themselves in particular when they referred to the *mocidade* (the term, meaning "youth," that they most commonly used to refer to themselves). The Brazilian "youth" were not yet men, but they were no longer children; they were "missionaries of progress and liberty."[138] The mission of youth, as they saw it, was to "regenerate" society from the larger spirit of "pernicious indifference" that plagued the current generation and Brazilian society.[139] "My heart is elevated like a mountain top," one student wrote in 1860, "and when I feel great and noble passions, I feel immense pleasure in comparing my heart to those of the paltry souls I see around me."[140]

The peer group that played so decisive a role in developing such an exalted sense of these young men's identities could not, however, separate them from the larger web of relations in which they were enmeshed. And to put this law school-engendered sense of independence in perspective we need to look at the role of patronage in their daily lives, even as we shall see, in their student culture.

THE REALITY OF PATRONAGE

Patronage, as Richard Graham has so masterfully shown, was the glue that held Brazil's vast empire together. Within the patronage networks, the law students played a crucial role as both the sons of powerful men, whether plantation owners or professional politicians, and as future agents of the state. But it is not enough to merely say that these young men benefited from, and were partially defined by, patron-client relations. During his law school career, a student evolved from being the client of a powerful patron, often a family member, then frequently through a transitional stage as a rebel against these very patronage networks, and then, as the peer group demanded, to potential client of others—with the ultimate goal being to become a dispenser of patronage himself. An examination of this process will reveal the heightened tensions that existed during a period in young males' lives when they sought to achieve a degree of autonomy and self-definition. They were not simply going through the motions of a rather mechanical, contractual process. Some actively sought new patrons, often with the aid of their families. Frequently, they came into conflict with their fathers and other older men upon whom they were dependent precisely because they were trying, at the age of eighteen or so, to become independent and define themselves.

A peer group that prized independence, as we shall see in chapter 5, put pressure on the law students to create identities independent of and to embrace political positions antithetical to those of their families. Clearly, even if their sense of themselves as independent political actors was highly compromised by their own links to, and dependence on, the patronage networks that held Brazil's hierarchical society together, the process by which they absorbed the reality of dependence was a complex and difficult one.[141] In becoming men, they first tested the boundaries of their social and political order and, ultimately, came to terms with it. Freyre and others have understood this conflict as representing the conflicting values of city and countryside. The students, living apart from their landowning fathers, represented the progressive city, while their fathers and patrons represented the countryside.[142] Graham has convincingly argued that this conflict between urban and rural interests was more apparent than real and that the interests of rural and urban Brazil were, in most cases, congruent. Yet it is important to see that the law students experienced real conflicts finding their place in patronage structures and sought to project an identity that was outside of them.

The very friendships that served as the emotional undergirding of their sense of community were bound up with the need to find allies and build a political career. It could be argued that the primary function of the law schools was to provide a setting in which the sons of the national elite could forge the ties that made political stability possible. Although they were distant, fathers were happy to provide advice on how to succeed. They instructed their sons in the ways of patronage, as illustrated by a letter from the Baron of Paty Alferes to his law student son in 1854: "I am glad to learn that you are becoming a friend of the son of Eusebio [de Queiroz Coutinho Mattoso da Câmara, himself an early Olinda law school graduate], whose friendship can always be an advantage. But you must also set him a good example, as studious, prudent, and well behaved, for he is an awesome eyewitness to your future. His father will always be one of our best men of state and can help you a lot later, but you must not let on that this is your motive because then people will say that you favored him out of some ulterior motive, and all that you will do for him will lose its merit."[143] It would be wrong, as I have argued, to think of student friendships as merely instrumental, even exploitative. Parental understandings of the role of friendships were not necessarily shared by sons. The strength of affective ties is proof of that. Nevertheless, the law school experience clearly enhanced opportunities for the fortunate few.

Rui Barbosa's father, although no baron and only a moderately successful politician himself, also was concerned with teaching his son behavior that could aid him in his political career. He urged him regularly to write letters to political leaders, particularly Conselheiro José Antônio Saraiva (an 1845 graduate of the São Paulo school, discussed briefly in chapter 1, and by the late 1860s the leader of the Liberal Party in Bahia, Rui's home province). His father offered advice on subjects to discuss and even words to use in his letters to Saraiva. Despite the young man's professed disdain for mainstream politics during his student days, Rui evidently complied with his father's request in this regard.[144]

Older men of means in nineteenth-century Brazil cultivated relationships with the younger law students, and novelistic depictions suggest how complicated these relationships could be. It should not be assumed that the older men always had the advantage. Both older men and younger had something to gain from such connections. The young men might have had something their elders coveted. This may have been particularly true when the older men were members of the nouveau riche and the students were from established families. Such students often had a self-assurance and a polish that the newly arrived lacked. (For that matter, these older men often sought through association the youth they had lost and could not regain.)

Older men, for their part, could offer a free meal, companionship, and often an attractive daughter as the prize for the young men's social status. For fathers like the newly risen Major Damásio in the Guimarães novel *Rosaura, A Engeitada* having a *bacharel* for a son-in-law could guarantee a higher social standing for himself and certainly for his grandchildren. The older men had to court the younger men, which gave the latter a certain edge. Major Damásio deferred to the students by calling them "Doctor." Nevertheless, the major faced risks in courting the students. Not all of the students were from rich families, and these young men of more humble origin might have been even more anxious to marry into money than the men from wealthy families. Though Guimarães's character tried to attract the sons of prominent men from Rio, he could not always be so discriminating because the students, as we have seen, tended to stick together.

Even when some students repaid his hospitality by mocking his social pretensions and revealing his daughter's mixed-race ancestry, other students took their place. His social pretensions got the better of him. Among these new students, the major found a suitable husband for his daughter Adelaide in a twenty-three-year-old from a prominent family in the province of São Paulo. All of the leading members of provincial society attended the wedding, including the provincial president, law students and faculty members, and the major's patron, Rafael Tobias de Aguiar (a leader of the Liberal revolt in 1842). The risks all this entailed for the major soon became apparent. After the wedding, the son-in-law, never more than a mediocre student who had used all of his social connections to make it as far as he had, dropped out of school. Ultimately, he was a failure in almost any business he took up and spent much of the novel chasing after the family's mulatta slave.[145]

For students from less privileged backgrounds, the ability to find patrons was crucial, for without it they sometimes were unable to undertake the financial sacrifice required to finance five years of education. Balthazar de Silva Campos, a popular figure in the São Paulo student body of the 1860s, was not the only one able to continue his studies because of the financial aid provided by relatives of his fellow students.[146]

Patronage sat uneasily with imported North American notion of the "self-made man," a phrase that entered the Brazilian vocabulary *in English* during this period. It is fitting that when Almeida Nogueira praised a student for belonging to this category, he also revealed that this Horatio Alger character had a patron from his home province.[147] Patronage did make a degree of social mobility possible, but only for those who were willing to play by the upper class's rules. In any case, as Graham argues, those with fathers at the highest levels of national politics were "at least twice as likely to make it into the same circle as a classmate who did not."[148]

Even in creating their student culture, these young men also had to rely upon the kindness of strangers. The act of publishing a newspaper of necessity involved students directly, perhaps for the first time on their own initiative, in the world of patronage. Without financial support from "illustrious men" or "protectors," a student newspaper could neither move from the planning stages to the printed page nor continue for years once it had been established (though students helped support the papers by paying association dues and providing the necessary creative energies).[149] The choice of a print-setter was important in this regard. *Ensaios Litterários*, for example, was printed by the provincial government in the capital itself. In the inaugural issue of a newspaper, students often expressed their anticipation of support from cultured men.[150] Students prided themselves on being able to survive on their own; ultimately, however, they had to seek aid from patrons if their newspapers were to survive.[151] Alumni were a critical source of financial support. Recent graduates, naturally enough, seem to have had a particular interest in guaranteeing the stability and continuity of the student associations they formerly belonged to.[152] Furthermore, students basked in the reflected glory of their "prestigious patrons."[153] Visiting journalists and politicians were also invited to be honorary members of the student associations. One organization, which had sixty-eight student members in 1859, had twenty honorary members in May and thirty-four by August.[154]

Students even sought to become each other's patrons. They knew the social rules and, at times, could play with them. Desiring entrance to a particular dance to which neither had been invited, two law students showed up elegantly dressed. As law students, they knew the society to which they belonged required that you know somebody to be acceptable. They therefore proceeded to introduce each other to the host and give testaments to the other's character. They were certain enough of their own social status to be able to present themselves as people competent to present each other to polite society. Their ploy worked; the host of the dance enjoyed their skillful playing with conventions, and they were allowed to enter the dance.[155]

Students also knew the rules of the game well enough to make promises of future patronage to each other. For example, one told another that his true vocation was to be a law professor. His interlocutor responded that his chances of ever attaining such a goal were small because he "lacked a protector." "That doesn't mean anything," the first student responded. "If one day I am in the Cabinet, your nomination is guaranteed." And this, indeed, was what happened many years later.[156]

If students understood the reality of patronage in their lives, and often chafed under its restrictions, they had reasons not to discuss it openly. To understand these reasons, one must look at the language students used when writing to their patrons privately. To the man who raised Rui's father, Rui Barbosa closed his letters by referring to himself as the man's "friend and servant" or his "very attentive and obligated friend and servant." In another letter, he described himself as being "at the disposal of [one] to whom my father, my family, and I owe so much."[157] The dependence inherent in the patron-client relationship contrasts strongly with the student ideal of independence. Students did not speak of themselves in their public discourse as being servants but as future leaders of society. Yet these larger networks of friendship and patronage made it possible for students such as Rui Barbosa to stay in school when their own family fortunes took a turn for the worse. When the Liberals were turned out of power and Rui's father lost his seat in the Chamber of Deputies in 1868, the older man was unable to maintain his son in school. An old family friend had to pay Rui's tuition and other expenses. In gratitude, Rui asked the older man to become his "confirmation godfather" to "consecrate" and thereby make this bond "indestructible."[158] In this way, ties that were both personal and political took on a larger spiritual connotation and a deeper emotional texture. Without patronage networks these students could not hope to lead, but the justification for their future authority could not be based upon their having been, at any time, just clients.

Youth's frequent failure to respect authority often tested the limits of socially sanctioned discourse and behavior. New friendships could lead to different understandings of politics that conflicted with former loyalties. For all the promise of independence inherent in student life, however, practical concerns forced students privately to recognize the centrality and inevitability of patronage in their lives. Their independence was, to a large extent, an illusion.

THE COMMUNITY OF FORMER STUDENTS

Despite the frequent factionalism among the students as well as the personal animosities, jealousy, and envy they sometimes felt toward each other, and apart from the patron-client system, students at the law schools imagined a community that was clearly distinct from the rest of Brazilian society. The unity between students could often seem a sham in the early years after graduation, when career opportunities depended more on one's familial background than on one's accomplishments in school. "For men in my circumstances," Sancho de Barros Pimental complained to his close friend Joaquim Nabuco, "the time of crisis is that which follows the departure from law school." A couple of years after graduation, Sancho de Barros Pimental was working in the backwater of Aracaju in Sergipe. The well-connected Nabuco, for his part, was living in Rio de Janeiro.[159]

Upon graduation, a *bacharel* would often return to his hometown. There he would be greeted with appropriate pomp and circumstance, and the family would gather to celebrate the return of their transformed son.[160] The years after graduation would determine the extent to which the new ties forged at law school would take priority over the traditional linkages to family and patrons. In the first years after graduation, most *bacharéis* would be isolated in a provincial community, working as magistrates as part of the imperial bureaucracy. In such a community, where they were addressed as "doctor" by the usually illiterate townspeople, they felt their own distinctiveness even more strongly and often longed for the stimulating law school environment and the friendships they had left behind.[161] They felt connected less to the provincial town and more to the national community of Brazilian men with the same law school training. *Bacharéis* founded newspapers in their small towns in which they addressed not the needs of the local community but the national issues that interested them and the literary and political issues that defined their social status.

Nevertheless, the realities of life after graduation posed the necessity of creating new identities. The bohemian life of their student days, for example, was frequently abandoned after graduation, not least because such eligible young men quickly married and acquired a gravitas heretofore lacking.[162] By marrying soon after graduation, they, to some extent, put their past behind them and entered a new phase of life, demarcating the student experience even more as a distinct phase. "Youth," in this sense, was finished.

Men like Barros Pimental would look to men like Nabuco and others with the same training to help them escape from their unsatisfying positions in the hinterlands. They hoped that by properly using their connections with family and friends from law school, they would find themselves at the center of political life in Rio de Janeiro.[163] New patrons would not necessarily supplant old ones but would instead allow the *bacharel* to be more flexible and upwardly mobile. Political necessity, as much as nostalgia, would link them to the community they had imagined while in school. In a politically prominent position made possible by his law school ties, the *bacharel* would then in turn be in a position to find employment for less influential members of his family.

4

TEACHERS AND STUDENTS

The peer group played a decisive role in the development of the young law students' identities, but a study of the student community would be incomplete, at best, if it did not also take into account their relationship with the law school professors. The students' transition to manhood and to political power was mediated in part through relations with teachers.[1] As this chapter will demonstrate, the teacher-student relationship itself took on the appearance, as well as many of the stresses and strains, of a patron-client relationship. Moreover, only by examining the ways in which professors and their presumed disciples interacted, can one can evaluate the degree to which the law schools served as conscious centers of indoctrination.[2] I argue in fact that they never succeeding in filling this role, at least not in any simplistic and straightforward way (not even in the way the founders intended them to). This was due to the disarray among the faculty, the schools' failure to maintain consistent academic standards, students' resistance to discipline and academic demands, and the ways in which the law schools as institutions and the faculty and students themselves were caught up in the patronage networks that bound Brazilian society together. The law school experience served more as a rubber stamp, conferring status on a select group of largely elite males.[3] Without an examination of the pedagogical practices at the schools and the interpersonal dynamics, even the power struggles, between teachers and their pupils, one would have an incomplete understanding of the law school experience and its role in the formation of an elite male identity and a political class.

DISARRAY

If the law schools never served as model indoctrination centers for apprentice mandarins, it was not least of all because they were so disorganized.

Central control from Rio de Janeiro never overcame certain fundamental problems (although critics charged that central control was a major contributor to the schools' problems). The imperial government often had trouble finding directors to run the law schools and professors to teach the courses. These problems continued throughout the imperial period, making it extremely difficult for the schools to fulfill their educational mission. Directors themselves did not always take their responsibilities seriously. This pattern established itself early in Olinda when the first man appointed director of the law school, Pedro de Araujo Lima, a leading figure in postindependence politics, was too busy looking after matters in Rio to serve. He even failed to attend the school's inauguration ceremony.[4] Another early director of the Pernambuco school neglected his duties because, he reportedly said, he was "born to live for love affairs and not to direct students."[5] The director in São Paulo from 1837 to 1842 was Nicolau Pereira de Campos Vergueiro, one of the first members of the three-man Regency following Dom Pedro I's abdication. He was more interested in politics and agriculture than the school itself and did not pay much attention to school matters. In any case, he lost his job after taking part in the Liberal rebellion of 1842.[6]

Faculty members also often found other activities more attractive than teaching. Olinda professors in the early years often considered opportunities to earn money practicing law in the nearby capital city of Recife more enticing that the prospect of teaching young men. Teachers even occasionally refused to leave their homes in Recife to go over to Olinda to teach classes. One twenty-five-year-old professor in the 1830s showed up for no more than twelve to fourteen classes a year. Despite attempts by the imperial government to require professors to live in Olinda itself, absenteeism remained a serious problem.[7] Of the required fourteen positions in the early 1830s, for example, only ten were officially filled in Olinda; of these ten, only four professors were actively engaged in teaching, the remainder having been granted leaves of absence. Examinations had to be administered late, if ever. (It is nowhere made clear how students were supposed to pass examinations for classes they had not been able to attend.) Conditions were not much better at the southern school.[8]

At both schools, particularly in the 1830s and 1840s, the professors often lacked experience in teaching or in practicing law because they were often themselves recent graduates. Moreover, these young professors were expected to grade other young men with whom they had formerly spent much of their leisure time (not to mention the fact that they lacked the deep knowledge of the subject they would have gained from extended years of study or legal practice).[9]

Conditions at the law schools continued to hamper the smooth functioning of these institutions, even during what I have argued was a peak period at the schools after the mid-1840s.[10] The São Paulo school, for example, did not have a full-time director from 1842 to 1857.[11] The comings and goings of the faculty continued to harm the quality of instruction in São Paulo and Pernambuco. Remaining faculty often had increased responsibilities. In speeches on the floor of the Chamber of Deputies in Rio, politicians accused the law school professors of letting their substitutes teach so they could rest. Substitutes did indeed teach a large number of classes, often on subjects in which they had little expertise.[12] Teachers, as much as their pupils, were remembered as being more talented than hard working, which demonstrated their lack of affection for the art of pedagogy itself.[13] And professors continued to miss classes. In 1868, for example, four professors missed more than twenty classes at the São Paulo school.[14]

Professorships were nevertheless eagerly sought-after positions, despite the fact that the reputation of law school professors among the general public was not particularly good.[15] To land such a job, political connections were important. The Olinda director himself complained that many professors had been awarded their positions through "scandalous acts of patronage."[16] A position at the law school was often seen as a springboard for political office. As one historian has suggested, the professors were "masters, not of law, but of politics."[17] Indeed, faculty members often clearly saw their positions as no more than a way station or stepping stone to political offices. They left the school at the earliest opportunity for positions in the magistracy or in provincial or national politics, while attempting to hold on to their position at the law school in the event of a change in political fortunes. Professors often asked for leaves of absences and then repeatedly requested extensions for years on end. This made it difficult for the schools to attract effective short-term replacements since they could not offer the prospect of long-term employment. Directors, teachers, and students complained bit-terly about the impact of these practices on the quality of teaching. (Given what was generally agreed to be the low pay of the professors, it was hardly surprising that many left, but the primary reason for the departures seems to have been political rather than financial.)[18]

The faculty were no model of unity or collegiality. In 1830, Pedro Autran publicly criticized his colleague João José de Moura Magalhães for being "incapable of exercising the noble functions of a magistrate." Autran fur-ther charged that Moura Magalhães "wanted to abuse" his office to "satisfy his own abominable vices" (which though unnamed presumably involved sodomy). Autran even encouraged a student to bring the wayward professor up on charges. Fortunately or unfortunately, the "embarrassing facts" Au-tran claimed to have to back up his accusations were not brought to light.[19] Other professors, as well, aired their disagreements in the Recife press. Another teacher accused Autran, his "worst enemy," of waging "cruel war" against him. (He further suggested that Autran's translation of John Stuart Mill's *Political Economy* was inadequate.)[20] The interpersonal con-flicts among the professors often made it difficult for them to maintain a united front in disciplining the students.

This fractiousness led the first active director of the northern school to leave his job early, exhausted by the internal faculty conflicts and those be-tween faculty and students. Conflict between professors was no less a prob-lem in São Paulo. The divisions among the professors and the frequent turn-over of the faculty and directors made it difficult for them to effectively indoctrinate their students. Given that students' ultimate goals were to work as magistrates or politicians, it hardly hurt their career chances to have professors who were well-connected politically. Awarding positions on the basis of patronage, however, sent a clear message about the real priorities of the imperial government in Rio. Instruction, even effective indoctrination, was less important than the obligations and favors exchanged by the power-ful to maintain their own social and political position. The mixed messages sent by the imperial government and mediated through the law school fac-ulty were not lost on the students themselves because they were reflected quite clearly in the quality of the teaching at the law schools.

PEDAGOGY

To understand more clearly how even the goal of indoctrination was compromised by the way the schools were run, we must look carefully at the way faculty taught classes and awarded grades. Only minimally did professors play the role of gatekeepers before the entrance into the political elite.[21]

Pedagogical practices at the law schools and the power dynamics implicit in them certainly give the impression of having been adopted with indoctrination in mind. On any given day, a professor would explicate a particular point of law, drawing usually upon the textbook or *compendio*, adopted for the course. (Students and faculty alike in nineteenth-century Brazil criticized the imperial government's requirement that a professor adopt an approved *compendio* or synthetic textbook expounding the fundamentals of an important aspect of the law. In the eighteenth century, the adoption of such a textbook was part of reformist efforts to improve the quality of instruction at the University of Coimbra. The *compendio*, it had been hoped, would solve the problems of professors getting lost in obscurantist detail and failing to teach the fundamentals of the subject slated for class discussion.[22])

On the day following the explication of a particular subject, one or more students were required to "repeat" the lesson "the way parrots would," as one critic of the system put it. The advantage of this teaching method, it was argued, was that students ended up hearing the lesson twice, and the professor was able to correct any misapprehensions before too much time had elapsed. For the student, the putative advantage was that he gained experience speaking before a public "that could evaluate his discourse." (This was, of course, in keeping with the style of the rhetorically inclined, verbally gifted student ideal I have already discussed.) The student would be "obliged to study for fear of being ashamed" in front of his peers. Peer pressure, therefore, was expected to reinforce the authority of the professor in the classroom. Furthermore, the frequency with which students were forced to perform publicly could make professors' evaluations more just since the final grades would not simply be based on the final exam.

Nevertheless, the disadvantages of this pedagogical style were obvious to the students. Those who tried to go beyond merely repeating what they had heard in class were told to "shut up," according to one disgruntled student.[23] Moreover, teachers, critics charged, often lectured at and rarely discussed with their students the fine points of law.[24] Professors often were windy and unorganized, relying heavily upon a showy use of citations.[25] Even a good teacher was known as much for his oratorical skills as his learning. It was a rare professor who was known for concise speech.[26] The lack of outside observers at professors' lectures in Olinda had a harmful effect on the quality of instruction, according to an early director. A professor, "certain that he is only heard by his students, pays little or no attention to his lessons, limiting himself, many times to the aridity of perorations."[27] As a system of indoctrination that had its roots in the teaching practices of the University of Coimbra, the emphasis on rote memorization may have been considered effective. For our purposes, it is less important to dismiss this style as pedagogically ineffective than to note that the students themselves by and large rejected it.

The first generation of professors in Brazil, in any case, lacked a systematic body of knowledge from which to draw in designing their courses. No tradition of legal scholarship by professors or independent scholars had yet been established, which reinforced a pedagogy that emphasized learning merely practical information and close attention to the ordinances and rules of the empire.[28] Students with excellent memories were highly prized, and the ability to reproduce the exact words of a legal text or commentary represented the ultimate goal. One Olinda professor was said to require his students to cite ordinances exactly or be forced to repeat the entire year, an approach better suited for training lawyers than magistrates.[29]

Despite the requirement that students demonstrate some measure of active, in-class participation, their grades were largely determined by tests at the end of the year. These examinations were public events, attended by local political authorities and people of high social standing. Not surprisingly, final exams were necessarily the tensest period for the young men. First- and second-year students were tested in groups of four; the remaining students were tested individually, in most cases by three professors (except for fifth-year students, who were tested by four). Examiners used either a black ball or a white ball to register their grade. A student who received only white balls would receive the grade of *aprovado*, or approved. Any student who received one black ball was given the "S" grade. (While this was considered a "satisfactory" grade as far as the professors were concerned, it did not satisfy the students who received it.) Two black balls equaled an "R" for *reproval*, or failure.[30]

Outside observers, however, complained that the examination methods themselves were defective. For example, the particular legal issue to be examined was announced only twenty-four hours before the final exam. Thus, students who had only attended class irregularly, at best, could cram and study a fairly minor point of law and do quite well, especially if he was particularly eloquent.[31]

The lack of "rigor" in these exams was frequently lamented, not least by the director of the law schools, but even by the emperor Dom Pedro II himself.[32] Citizens of São Paulo wondered how the students they saw wandering the streets of the city day and night could end up passing their exams. Students, for their part, complained that the ignorant public who attended the exams was awed by the "vain loquaciousness" of the students' answers to exam questions. The tendency to pass students contributed to the prevalent notion among students that a diploma was conferred on them as much for their social standing as for any individual accomplishments. Professors' resolutions one year not to advance "lazy students that kept themselves busy in creating pranks and disorder" were seemingly forgotten in the next.[33] By the 1870s, one professor complained that the exams were "almost turning into vain formalities," though many critics charged that they had always been just that.[34]

In fact, lax grading practices at the law schools were a constant source of concern for directors, professors, imperial officials, and outside observers. Of 251 students in Olinda in 1836, for example, 208 received the highest grades, and only three received R's. These undemanding grading practices continued to be the norm throughout the imperial period. All 106 second-through fifth-year students in Olinda received the highest grades in 1844. Of 160 second- to fifth-year São Paulo students in 1853, only ten students received less than the highest grade. None of the fourth- and fifth-year students in 1859 at the northern school received an R. Finally, of the graduating São Paulo classes of 1855 and 1870, all received the highest grade possible. In the latter year especially, the first-year students must have been exceptional because 40 out of 42 did the same.[35]

Professors often complained that the entrance examinations were not administered with the appropriate severity and that "noticeably incapable" students were let in.[36] This put pressure on teachers of first-year students to weed out the least prepared. Professors in the upper classes argued that it was the responsibility of those teaching first- and second-year students to give failing grades.[37] The first year clearly was the most difficult both in terms of academic and emotional demands. Professors handling the first-year classes seem to have taken their gatekeeper role more seriously. (As did the second-year students who subjected the *caloiros* to the rigors of the *trote*.) Students were given a bit of a respite in the second year, because they rarely received the dreaded S grade, much less the far more serious R.[38] The third year was also thought to be quite demanding, but after that it was smooth sailing for the fourth- and fifth-year students. By then, their identity was assured. Grades of R were rare by this point.[39]

With the R grade a rare exception, students were disgruntled when they received anything less than the highest grade. They resented the S grade, even though it had no impact on their chances of advancing to the next year or of graduating. In the 1850s, the S grade was rather common, although the ten given to the graduating class of 1857 was considered a bit excessive. Almeida Nogueira argued that these grades were often clearly unjust and "motivated by the bad temper of some professors."[40] One São Paulo newspaper lamented the large number of S grades given in 1857: "These do no good to anyone and only serve to disgust the families and sadden the young men" on the day that should be the happiest of their young lives.[41] Students, as we shall see, knew how to respond to these slights.

By the 1860s, there was already talk of an overabundance of law graduates; the system would be overwhelmed in the 1880s. Both students and faculty complained about the increasing popularity of the law degree. Everyone wanted to be a "doctor," one student complained in 1860.[42] By 1863, the entering class in São Paulo was the largest ever, with 157 first-year students matriculating. Although there is no paper trail to suggest a deliberate policy to fail more students, nevertheless, the attrition rate that year was particularly high.[43] Of the 91 students who graduated in the São Paulo class of 1868 — the most ever up to that point at the southern institution — 11 received the humiliating S grade that year, also an all-time high. From this distance, the number looks like a final gesture of authority, a fit of institutional pique.[44]

Students, for their part, thought grades were assigned arbitrarily out of personal animosity or affection. They complained that professors would attack a "student's self-respect" and embarrass him in front of peers merely because the teacher took a disliking to him.[45] The law school career of Teixeira de Freitas might serve as a good example in this regard. The future codifier of Brazilian civil law consistently received poor grades, yet a sympathetic professor described him as one of the best students and suggested that his poor showing was the result of the "caprice" of other faculty members.[46] That grades were often arbitrarily awarded is illustrated by the success of the student hero and poet Castro Alves. Although a prominent member of the student community first in Recife and later in São Paulo, he was never attentive to his studies. In the final examinations one year, he launched into a beautiful, but uninformed, discourse on a particular point of law. After he concluded, the examining professor remarked, "Mr. Castro Alves, I appreciate your poems very much; but about law, you know nothing." Nevertheless, the professor gave him a passing grade.[47]

On a more serious level, charges and countercharges of grades traded for patronage poisoned the academic atmosphere. As we have seen, access to higher education itself would have been impossible for many without the aid of patrons. But even success or failure on entrance examinations could depend upon a father's pull with the examining committee.[48] Students frequently joked about someone being examined "without letters of recommendation," and professors in turn complained about requests received from students' patrons or fathers to go easy on them.[49] Professors allegedly whispered answers to favored students.[50] They also were accused of punishing the student sons of political rivals.[51] In the 1860s, a student charged that a law professor had invited students to his house to solicit the support of the young men's prominent families in his bid to represent their home province of Paraiba in the Chamber of Deputies. "The professor refuses to grant favors *to* students, but expects favors *from* them," the student complained. Woe to the "unprotected" student, many young men complained.[52]

The professors were as prone as anyone else to need favors from patrons, even when they had done work that merited reward. In 1861, Pedro Autran, who had already been teaching in Pernambuco for thirty years, had to appeal for financial compensation for the book he had written, which had been adopted as the school's political economy textbook. He turned for protection to José Antônio Saraiva, a leading figure in Bahian and national politics, asking for recognition for his years of service and for help in maintaining his large family, but to little avail.[53]

Patronage could even enable a student to make up for a year of absences due to sickness. Joaquim Nabuco, for example, became ill during his fourth year and missed more than the minimum number of classes required to take the final exams. He petitioned the Chamber of Deputies for a waiver of this requirement. Whether his father's status as a prominent senator and frequent member of the imperial cabinet had an impact on the decision is unknown. In any case, the younger Nabuco was able to take his exams on time. That a student could pass the final exam after missing most of the year's classes speaks volumes about the quality of instruction at the law schools.[54]

STUDENT RESISTANCE

In a world defined by patronage, students sought to enforce their own understanding of the law school experience by resisting the demands placed upon them by their teachers. Professors complained bitterly about students' lack of discipline, the failure to establish a code of regulations regarding student behavior, the professors' lack of authority over their students, and, not least of all, the students' lack of interest in their studies.[55] Students, for their part, complained about having to attend two classes a day, but however poor the quality of instruction often was the amount of time they spent in class was hardly excessive.[56]

In 1844, the Olinda director complained about a state of "sheer confusion, anarchy" at the school. Students' distance from their families, many believed, was the main reason for their unruliness.[57] If, as one professor noted, quoting Savigny, the legal profession was one in which "the respect for legitimate authority is the primary duty," Brazilian law students were noteworthy in their frequent failure to concede legitimacy to teachers' authority.[58] Students denied that teachers had a right to reprimand them and sometimes resorted to threats of violence when they anticipated receiving bad grades.[59] In one instance in 1873, a student followed his examiners after they left the building, hurling insults and then threatening violence. Ultimately, the local police had to intervene. The student eventually was prohibited from taking classes for two years.[60]

Students also committed what might be called "daily acts of resistance." Rare was the student who entered the classroom sooner than fifteen minutes after the class hour had begun. Professors frequently adapted to this student practice, although some stubbornly lectured to empty classrooms. With classes beginning chronically fifteen minutes late, and with five minutes required to take attendance, only forty minutes were left for the day's lesson.[61] To protest against unpopular teachers, students would simply walk out of class or fill the hour voicing challenges to the doctrines espoused by the professor.[62] Their resistance, not surprisingly, often demonstrated their linguistic abilities. One young man, stumped by a professor's question on an obscure point of law, was able to use up the remaining class time with formal expressions until he was, quite literally, saved by the bell.[63] Many challenged the professors' authority directly and criticized what they perceived as poor teaching. A member of the fourth-year class in São Paulo in 1866 left a note on the teacher's desk that read: "I want to learn law and not bullshit. You should study so that you can teach us, and not come here to fill our ears with nonsense." Upon reading the note, the professor slammed his desk, left the room in disgust, and never taught that class again.[64]

Student absences, moreover, tended to increase as they advanced one year to the next. Fifth-year students were particularly prone to miss classes.[65] Despite the attempt to shame students by publishing attendance records in local newspapers, there is no evidence that this did anything to improve attendance.[66] The professors lamented the lack of clear guidelines regarding comportment and discipline as well as their own lack of internal unity, which prevented them from taking effective action against students who misbehaved. Professors sought the right to "paternal jurisdiction" over their students, though this remedy was unlikely given the lack of student housing owned and operated by the school.[67]

Students regularly turned to local (and not only student) newspapers to air their grievances over the way they were being taught. They knew what the schools' governing statutes contained and they criticized those who

"scandalously" violated these precepts by, as one student claimed, "ostenta-
tiously, and vainly parading" their alleged knowledge. According to the
schools' regulations, professors were expected to be "brief and clear in their
expositions," to avoid excessive demonstrations of "erudition motivated by
vanity," and to stick to "useful lessons."[68] One student complained that a
professor cited thirty-two authors in one lesson, some whom the teacher
himself had not read and others he had not understood. A good professor
seeks the betterment of his students, the student argued, not "a vain reputation of belonging to the literati."[69] By and large, the students were able to
criticize the faculty with virtual impunity, particularly in São Paulo. They
manipulated their status as public figures (of a sort) to make their case in
the press — the forum for the public, more than the common, man in Brazil. Clearly, the professors were touchy about the way they were treated in
the student press. After a discussion of teaching styles appeared in *O Olindense* in 1831, one professor wrote to say that *he* was not guilty of the abuses
mentioned in the article. The *Olindense* editor assured the anxious teacher
that they had not been referring to him.[70]

The student body's sense of itself as a community (formed in part in opposition to its instructors) is reflected in students' marked preference for
choosing an orator who had suffered the indignity of an S grade to represent
them at the graduation ceremonies.[71] Faculty members accused students of
electing those classmates most likely to criticize the professors during com-
mencement. The faculty often prohibited such speeches from being delivered; the students, in turn, might have the banned text published at their
own expense by a local typesetter.[72]

The problem of how to control students is suggested by the following
story from the law schools' early years. Despite a broad consensus that a particular student deserved to be corrected after arguing loudly with a professor, the faculty backed down and gave the student the highest grade possible. The aggrieved professor took this opportunity to resign his teaching
position.[73]

In another incident from 1833, discontent led to the demotion of a faculty
member who was particularly disliked by the students. Similarly, one student complained of his professor's "dictatorial manners" at a *sabbatina*, the
Saturday meetings in which the students were expected to lead discussions

of a legal issue. Professor Loureiro, who was evidently prone to shouting and gesticulating wildly and was known by his students for his "arrogance and impudence," complained of being "insulted atrociously." In the following weeks, Loureiro got into further shouting matches with students, and the faculty convened to discuss what to do. They demoted Loureiro from teaching the fifth-year class to a less prestigious second-year course. Undoubtedly, the internal conflicts among the faculty made it easier for the students to win cases like this.[74]

It was the fifth-year students who were most likely to miss class or challenge their professors when they bothered to attend class. For example, the fifth-year students in 1865 in São Paulo were clearly feeling their oats with their political economy professor, constantly bringing up "objections, requesting explanations, and making observations" and impertinently embarrassing the professor, whom they considered hopelessly out of date. The professor responded by giving a record number of R's, sixteen, in fact, but this did not prevent any of the young men from graduating. (No fifth-year student had received an R since 1851, and then only one.)[75] To speak at graduation the fifth-year students chose not the student recognized as the class's best orator but one prepared to criticize these grading practices. The faculty then refused to let the young man speak. When the student tried to give his graduation speech anyway, the law school director quickly declared the ceremony over, which led to noisy protests by the students. Although the orator had his degree suspended for one year and the rest of the students had theirs suspended for thirty days, these penalties ultimately were reduced on appeal to six months and fifteen days, respectively.[76]

Most problematic of all for the faculty was the students' perceived "right to a diploma."[77] Although students demonstrated "little fervor for their studies," they expected to get good grades. Faculty members considered the young men to be arrogant. Students, it seemed, had nothing to learn from their teachers; the teachers instead should learn from them.[78] "Not even the director, let alone the teachers, can make the students apply themselves more," one early director of the São Paulo school lamented. Autran complained that when the students did not receive the highest grades, "they became indignant."[79]

Professors were not totally without resources when they wanted to discipline their students, however. In the late 1830s, the editors of *Argos Olin-dense*, a student newspaper discussed in chapter 1, criticized a number of professors and suggested that if the students were bad, they merely reflected the vices of their instructors. One professor reportedly told students that the editors would receive R's in retaliation for the views they expressed in their publication.[80] The director complained to the imperial government that the *Argos Olindense* was founded with the "manifest intent" to undermine the "current administration" of the empire and to cause bad feelings against the law professors by labeling them ignorant. The director hoped to enlist the aid of Bernardo Pereira de Vasconcellos, the proponent of centralization and order, since the "government is ignorant of nothing regarding the law schools."[81] In the fifth-year exams professors retaliated by giving the students involved in the paper's operations a grade of S, which, as we have seen, was always seen as a slight. In response, a number of recent graduates and current students invaded the law school building and proceeded to surround some professors and shower them with epithets. The provincial president called in the local police force to remove them from the building. The ultimate limits of the professors' power over their students, however, is suggested by the fact that two students involved in the incident were able to transfer to the São Paulo law school and graduate.[82] (Although students wishing to transfer from one school to another were required to get a "letter of good conduct" prior to the transfer, this clearly was not an insurmountable obstacle, as examples from successive generations of student could attest.[83])

Professors could suspend students. They also could imprison a student for libeling a professor. One student was imprisoned for three, another for four months.[84] The faculty did not have many ways to chastise students for conduct they considered inappropriate, however. The grade itself was the primary weapon, and students, as students will, complained bitterly about grades they thought were assigned unfairly (although, as we have seen, few suffered greatly from the law schools' grading practices). Nevertheless, there were times when a young man went too far. A student who threatened his teacher with violence was prohibited from attending school for twelve years.[85]

Whatever the level of student resistance, many believed that discipline improved in the 1840s because the students were less involved in political activities. Nevertheless, the directors and faculty members continued to complain about their lack of authority over their students' conduct. The overseers of activities at the law school appointed a bishop, a traditional source of authority, as director at the Pernambuco school.[86] Still there continued to be problems making punishments stick. In 1851, the faculty forbade three students who disrupted the fifth-year examinations from enrolling for six years, but the imperial government reduced the penalty to one year.[87]

Students themselves argued that there was a "new spirit of order and morality" among them after the school's move to Recife in 1854. After all, they no longer insulted and attacked professors in broad daylight, as they had done in Olinda. This change in student behavior resulted "not only from the respect that His Excellency the director and the professors inspire but also and principally from an awareness among the students of their own dignity."[88] It was the students' own sense of themselves that determined their behavior.

Although discipline at the northern school was said to have improved after the move to Recife, the faculty continued to express regret at not having more control over the students' extracurricular life.[89] "Students in Belgium cannot be out of their house after ten at night, nor can they form associations, make collective demonstrations, or go to the theater or to houses of ill repute," one teacher complained in 1864. The faculty should consider measures to "ensure the morality and application of our students," such as making the students wear uniforms. Nothing came of this suggestion, as we have seen.[90]

There were repeated attempts to establish more discipline in the schools, particularly in the 1850s. Students could be expelled from class or put in a special prison for one to eight days. Only in the case of a physical assault on a faculty member was a student likely to receive any significant and lasting punishment. However, the stipulation that students complained about most bitterly was that they could fail a year if they missed forty classes. The young men ridiculed the choice of forty as an arbitrary number (as any number inevitably would be), but the students tended to dance around this number, moving perilously close to the edge. More than one took pride in getting away with thirty-nine absences.[91]

By the 1870s, the need for reform at the law schools was palpable. To improve the examination procedures, it was decided in October of 1871 that students would no longer be informed what the examination topic would be twenty-four hours in advance. On 28 October in São Paulo, students responded by invading the exam rooms and destroying the furniture, shouting out *vivas* for the teachers who had voted against the new practices and "down with the subservient teachers" who had supported them. Exams were postponed until the following February. In the weeks after, police banned student meetings, and leaders of the demonstrations were banned from taking classes for two years.[92] More serious reforms would be attempted at the end of the 1870s, as we will be see in chapter 6, but the fundamental problems remained the same.

TEACHER-STUDENT RELATIONS

The complications of the teacher-student relationship are suggested by the graduation ceremony itself. These ceremonies, attended by local and national authorities as well as family members and local residents, required each student to thank his professors publicly for the grades he had received. This practice suggested the way in which education was embedded in Brazil's patronage networks. Students did not view a grade as something earned through individual achievement but was conferred on them by their teachers as a favor. At times, students refused to play along. Francisco Joaquim da Costa Pinto, for example, did not thank his teachers at his graduation ceremony. It is hardly surprising that he did not seem particularly grateful because he had received the dreaded R. (The grade did not prevent him from graduating, but he must have seen it as a final example of arbitrary authority.) In retaliation for this public insult, the faculty attempted to withhold Costa Pinto's diploma. Ultimately, however, the imperial government refused to back the professors, and Costa Pinto received his diploma.[93]

In another instance in 1860 at the São Paulo school, the future abolitionist Antônio Bento was more selective in his criticism of his professors and only partially grateful for his degree. He thanked two of his former professors but went on to say that he did not thank "Mr. Furtado, who besides being an immoral man and an undignified teacher who knows nothing of justice." Fortunately for Furtado, Bento was stopped before he finished his statement. Bento had his degree suspended for two years (which kept him from practicing law).[94] Another similarly ungrateful student in 1852 was less explicit in his remarks and relied on a heavy use of irony, it was said, to make his point. He had his degree suspended for one year.[95]

The conflict between students and teachers suggests the complexity of the issues at work here. Professors caught up in their own patronage networks sent mixed messages about the value of education itself. If a grade or a degree was perceived as being bestowed as a favor, so was a teaching job. An ethos of merit conflicted with students' expectations that they had already been assured a place in the larger society. Students who were already referred to as "Doctor" by people they met on a daily basis did not expect "reproval." The young men anticipated being passed from year to year because they expected to be recognized for what they already were. Professors used a language of merit and achievement yet succumbed to the temptation of treating these future Brazilian leaders as if they had already arrived, as well, particularly after the first year. The function of the law school remained to reaffirm a social identity already inherent in the vastly unequal access to education, which prevented the vast majority of Brazilians from even dreaming of attending an institution of higher education.

It would be wrong, however, to suggest that the students developed their sense of themselves only in opposition to their teachers or that the teacher-student relationship was only a negative one. Students often saw their teachers as role models and perhaps more frequently as potential patrons whose influence could be crucial in attaining the students' goals of becoming future political leaders. Students sometimes referred to their teachers as "friends and masters."[96] For their part, faculty members sought to protect students from the outside world. When local residents complained about student antics, professors reminded the police that they were strictly prohibited from entering the school building (which, in this way, could serve as a kind of sanctuary) unless specifically requested to do so by school authorities. The director wrote to a local official, "Inside the building, I will maintain order by the use of school employees. Outside of the law school building, you can take the actions you deem necessary."[97] Even there, however, the faculty could protect their charges. The Professor Furtado whom Antônio Bento disdained also served for many years as a local police official, which often enabled him to prevent students from being punished for their misbehavior.[98]

Professors were frequently compared and contrasted with fathers, even as the relative independence of law student life was defined by the lack of paternal authority. When the first director of the Olinda law school retired, he was celebrated as having treated his students with the "care" typical of an "excellent father of a family."[99] Like the father, the professor was expected to exert authority over the student, but it was an authority based on love and sweetened by tenderness. "I always considered teaching as a type of fatherhood: the master and the disciple are in the moral order in the same relation that the father and the son are in the physical order," one professor remarked.[100]

Faculty members served as honorary presidents of the student associations. Although their role was largely symbolic, a sign of respect, it also served as a form of protection. Professors provided a certain respectability to the student associations as well as, potentially anyway, a curb on their activities. Honorary presidents also provided a degree of continuity, for their tenure in office was usually longer than that of the student officers themselves. One student in 1860 complained that student association officers had to be reelected every three months, while faculty members continued to serve long after their enthusiasm for the office had waned.[101] Moreover, the search for patrons to nominate honorary members often got out of hand. At one point, the number of "honorary members" had grown so large that the Atheneu Pernambucano, for example, had to suspend the nomination of any more.[102]

An occasional student association would function without a faculty member as a sponsor. One student noted that the Club Acadêmico did not have one and did not want one.[103] But though some chafed under the restrictions they feared the faculty presence entailed, most understood the honorary president's function as an inevitable reflection of the reality of patronage in their daily lives.[104] One student described a teacher as "our protector, a man truly dedicated to the cause of letters and a friend of youth, because he does not limit his sacrifices to help them in their work" (by which the student clearly meant their extracurricular rather than their academic work).[105] Nevertheless, it should be noted that faculty members did not attend the weekly association meetings held in student *repúblicas*.

The question of student associations was particularly sticky for the professors, and faculty opinion regarding them was far from monolithic. Some faculty members considered the student societies to be positive institutions that helped train the young men for their future careers in law and politics.[106]

Yet in Pernambuco, in particular, student associations were often seen as, at best, distracting; in any case, unimportant; and, at worst, dangerous. One professor suggested that only religious associations, which were not harmful, should be allowed.[107] While it was good to study history, poetry, and religion, one instructor said in 1858 that he would not "tolerate those who make these studies a necessity of the first order in a school destined to create men who work in a particular profession."[108] Some professors scorned the students' attempts to direct public opinion by creating their own newspapers "when they were not yet old enough to exercise civil or political rights." The students were writing about subjects before they were old enough to understand them, and that would be damaging to them, one professor opined.[109]

Those professors who wanted to see only religious associations thrive in the law schools were most evident in Pernambuco. If the northern school had more of a Catholic atmosphere, it was in part due to the influence of one man who taught there for more than forty years. Pedro Autran, a follower of Adam Smith on economic questions and of the Catholic Church otherwise, dominated the school like no other from 1830 until his retirement in 1871, despite the distraction presumably provided by his fourteen children.[110] He was known for his participation as a lay leader in the celebration of the mass and always dressed in a suit and wore the image of the patron of the Brotherhood of Our Lady of Good Counsel. Autran's religiosity did not lead him to challenge the importance of secular authority. His liberal economic views melded with a style that was essentially scholastic in nature. Student folklore maintained that he was enshrined in a London gallery of paintings of outstanding economists, among whom he was placed in fifth place. (Foreign recognition figured prominently in student appreciations of faculty merit; another professor was said to have had his book translated into German for use as a textbook at the University of Heidelberg.)[111] As a man who devoted his life to teaching, however, Autran's prestige among the student body was, ultimately, limited.

The Pernambuco professors, following Autran's lead, played a more active role in promoting religion and in exercising tighter control over their students' literary production in Recife. The *Faculdade do Recife* was published under the direction of Autran himself, who had a distinctive notion of what a newspaper's proper function should be. Like the students, he saw the press as a "progressive" force; unlike them, he saw its progressive nature as determined by its sense of morality. Students in Recife for their part were also said to "possess the most profound respect for their teachers." In Recife, teachers saw the need for cooperation between teachers and students. Professors were often profiled in student publications there, and their writings were often published in student newspapers.[112]

Other professors in Pernambuco were noted opponents of the institution of civil marriage. They also generally supported the ultramontane trends in the Catholic Church, which stood in opposition to the mildly anticlerical spirit of the age.[113] The conservative tendencies of the faculty at the northern school did not always please the students. Soon after graduation, one young man mused that "with some most honorable exceptions, youth belongs to the party of freedom, they [the professors] to that of power; youth thirsts for knowledge and eloquence, but they are wells of stagnant water from the Middle Ages, and like wells, they have an echo but no voice."[114]

Religious brotherhoods were particular favorites of the professors. By participating in them themselves, students hoped to counter the popular opinion that equated student with heretic, but it was always the professors who provided most of the support for these organizations. Professors who led these organizations were treated with respect, but evidently the *irmandades* suffered from the disease they sought to cure because they failed to attract the financial resources necessary for their long-term success. The brotherhoods so close to the hearts of men like Autran did not provide a setting that the majority of students found conducive to the formation of their identity. Student energies were largely directed elsewhere.[115]

In contrast to Autran in Pernambuco, the major figure at the southern school for decades was a dramatically different type, José Bonifácio, "*O Moço.*" Known for his political and literary interests more than for his teaching abilities, José Bonifácio was a grown-up example of the student ideal. A poet in his law school days in the 1840s, he was a mainstay of the Liberal Party in São Paulo and a hero to many law students, who saw in him a valuable patron in their efforts to gain a prominent place in the party ranks.[116] In a speech to the law students in the 1860s, Bonifácio addressed the assembled students, saying, "The present and the past belong to today's combatants; the future belongs to youth. Youth is the sun that is rising, the butterflies seeking the light." One member of the crowd responded, "You are the light."[117] Some claimed that he was more of an orator than a teacher, but his students did not seem to mind. His predilection for oratory over legal niceties matched their own inclinations. "*O Moço*" invited local attorneys, politicians, and intellectuals to his classes. His own "almost permanent individualism" and loyalty to ideals and ideas made him a special favorite of his students. (His legendary impracticality also made him the object of some playful teasing by his charges.)[118] Even Bonifácio's very nickname, which was used to distinguish him from the so-called father of Brazilian independence, suggested his identification with the students: it meant "the younger" or, literally, "the youth."

The example of José Bonifácio brings us full circle. Student identity was formed partly in resistance to the ideological indoctrination represented by the teaching styles at the law schools. The professors themselves were valued more for their ability to help students find their way in Brazil's networks of patronage than as teachers, a role that, in any case, was compromised by its connection to those very same patron-client relations. The students, for their part, sought recognition of their identity. It was a recognition they believed they had already achieved and deserved as befitting their status as law students, and they admired those professors who were most like themselves.

5

STATUS QUO LIBERALISM
AND ITS DISCONTENTS

After the regional revolts of the Regency period and the early years of Dom Pedro II's reign, Brazil achieved a level of political stability unmatched in the rest of Latin America, with the possible exception of Chile. As Dom Pedro II matured, he came to dominate the political system in his own measured, moderate way. He used his power to dissolve parliament, form cabinets, and selectively call for new elections, according to his own understanding of the national mood and interests. This guaranteed that each of Brazil's two major political parties would have their opportunity to share in making national policy. He saw himself as above party and only interested in helping Brazil progress. Despite his interests in seeing his country evolve along European lines, he was not impulsive like his father and rarely pushed for reforms in such a way that conflict might result. While Dom Pedro II's method of governing kept the nation orderly, it could not help it transform itself beyond the traditional, agricultural, oligarchical, and patriarchal society it would remain well into the twentieth century.[1]

As Dom Pedro II developed his own style of governing, the _bacharéis_ came into their own as the primary agents of state power. Student life became less overtly politicized, as literature took a leading role in the formation of student identity. Students never completely abandoned politics, despite the tremendous importance of literature in student life and in students' understanding of themselves and despite a rhetoric that students had adopted to distance themselves from Brazilian political practices in the 1840s and 1850s. Poetry had its place and time in the lives of young men, but politics remained the ultimate aspiration of ambitious youth.

The politics of the young men of the 1840s and 1850s was more clearly conformist than that of the generations of students who preceded them and those who followed them. If the law schools ever served as effective centers of ideological indoctrination, it would seem to have been during this period. As I have shown in previous chapters, however, it was never the curriculum per se that created such well-indoctrinated agents of state power. The same curriculum was in place when students in the 1860s embraced republicanism and abolitionism. Students took their cues from their reading of national and international political events, and they learned much about politics in the informal world of the extracurriculum that occupied the bulk of their time and energies. Many of them, as the sons of politicians, had grown up being exposed to regular political meetings in their own homes.[2] The peer group built upon these prior experiences and had more importance than the faculty in determining the contours of student politics.

In this chapter, I will explore the young men's understanding of the political system and their own role within it because their interpretations of the political world was never far removed from the way they viewed themselves. I will discuss how they participated in the national consensus of the 1840s and 1850s and how they took part, as well, in the breakdown of that consensus. That process began with the rebirth of partisanship in the early 1860s and accelerated with the War of the Triple Alliance, in which Brazil joined with Argentina and Uruguay to subdue the tiny nation of Paraguay. After exploring the imperial political system as it looked from the door of the law schools (or, perhaps more precisely, from the window of the student *república*), I will examine how liberalism came to be reworked during the 1840s and 1850s. Classical liberalism never ceased being the dominant discourse of the imperial period, whether a student was a member of the Liberal or the Conservative Party.[3] If liberalism had been translated and manipulated by the plantation owners whose interests the imperial political system served, it never stopped being a rather troublesome language for the young men seeking to master it.

After 1860, the memories of the regional revolts began to dim, particularly for students born after the rebellions had been successfully put down, and at the same time competition between the two national political parties became more heated. In the wake of these two developments, students began to reclaim liberalism as a contested language. This was nowhere clearer than in the rebirth of abolitionism among law students in the 1860s. Party identity, which had always meant more to the young men than to many of their elders, helped mediate a response to changing times. It allowed particularly Liberal students in São Paulo a chance to rebel in the 1860s as they had in the 1830s. By embracing a liberalism that rejected slavery and the status quo, students renewed their claim to lead Brazilian society. While only a minority actually became abolitionists, abolitionism became a key component of the student ideal from 1860 on. From that point on, the student ideal required a young man to reject a central institution of his society. The image of the law student, son of a slave owner, rejecting the basis of his family wealth has been passed on in the historiography and mythology of Brazil's law schools during the imperial period. The model served, in part, to question the role of patronage in the formation of identity and to demonstrate the students' independence. If sons and clients of slave owners could join in the call to abolish the institution responsible for their families' economic well-being — challenging that which made it possible for them to study at law school — then patronage and family were not all. A student was not just his father's son or his patron's client. He was, as liberalism would have it, an independent individual actor.

It is important to understand that this model of Brazilian manhood served as a continuing justification for the authority of the *bacharéis* over society at large. Each new generation after 1860 wished to be seen as true to the ideals of liberalism that were so badly tarnished in the rest of society. Thus could their continuing claim to authority be maintained in changing times.

THE IMPERIAL POLITICAL SYSTEM

How was the Brazilian political system understood? Nineteenth-century political theorists saw in it a search for perfect order, a definition that the young men at the law schools also sought to refine in the 1840s and 1850s. The institutions of the monarchy, the bicameral parliament, and the centralization of authority in Rio de Janeiro were understood as the bulwarks of social and political order. The division of powers among the various branches of government, for example, was seen as "calculated in the perfect interests of order and public prosperity." Brazilian elites (and visiting Europeans as well) viewed the parliament and the existence of an electoral system in which two parties alternated in power as evidence of a political order as advanced as any of their European models.

José Antônio Pimenta Bueno, São Paulo class of 1832, was the author of the first general study of Brazilian public law, published in 1858. For him, the parliament was a guarantor of stability and unity. He saw the Senate, made up of men over forty who had been appointed for life, as a necessary check on the possible excesses of the Chamber of Deputies, whose members were up for election every four years. Senators were representatives of "conservative ideas" and "general interests." For Pimenta Bueno, had members of both houses been subject to election, the legislature would have been open to the irresponsible passions and errors of the general public.[4]

As the two houses balanced each other, so too were national and local interests supposed to be balanced. We have already seen how the law school experience itself was expected to help these young men achieve this balance in their own lives. On a national level, the senators were supposed to be above purely regional interests. Deputies were thought to have at least some greater responsibility to their particular constituencies, although even their ultimate allegiance was to be to the "public good, the good of the Empire as a whole."[5]

The legal discourse of Pimenta Bueno and the law students themselves linked the creation of a national identity to the maintenance of order. Pimenta Bueno saw a need for a closely supervised national educational system that would guarantee that the provinces would not develop different regional customs, characteristics, and languages. Such diversity would reinforce the tendencies of people in Minas Gerais province, for example, to see those in Bahia as "jealous rivals" instead of fellow members of "one Brazilian people." The provinces themselves were only an "administrative necessity," for the nation is one, Pimenta Bueno maintained.[6] For their part, students in the 1840s and 1850s feared the fragmentation of Brazil's vast empire into tiny republics like many of their Spanish American neighbors, which were destined, as they saw it, for no important role in world affairs. A decentralized federal state would break up into "incoherence, rivalries, and an internal antagonism that would destroy the sentiment of nationality which consists in the perfect fusion and brotherhood of the same people." Nationality was "above provincialisms." A student in 1849 argued that the increasing conflict in the United States between the northern and the southern states was proof of the dangers of decentralization.[7]

Students in the 1840s and 1850s largely accepted these and other components of the conventional political wisdom. A central element in the national political consensus was a belief in the traditional legitimate authority of the monarchy. One professor wrote, with an almost audible sigh of relief, that students had an appreciation for the emperor's moderating power, "despite the interest in new ideas circulating in the area."[8] According to theorists like Pimenta Bueno, the imperial family was the fundamental guarantor of Brazilian political stability. "Brazilian reason" had dictated the choice of a monarchial form of government. The emperor and the monarchical government "symbolized unity" and also continuity: "The monarch does not die." While a particular emperor might die, the dynasty itself guaranteed perpetual stability. "A dynasty is a series, succession, order in one family."[9] For the good of all Brazilians, providence would ensure that the dynasty would never be extinguished.

The Brazilian political system was the form of government most appropriate for Brazil, according to its material conditions and economic and cultural development.[10] Brazil was not a barbaric nation, one student wrote in 1859; therefore, an absolutist government was not appropriate. A hereditary constitutional government was right for a "civilized nation" like Brazil where "sovereign power was delegated within the circumscribed limits of a particular family." A polity in which ultimate political authority was open to competition could lead to a "bloody fight to the death, disrespect for property, [and] disrespect for other sacred rights, such as the honor of the family. . . . In short, horror, confusion, the moral and physical ruin of the state." Because the monarch knew his power is eternal, he was "not merely taking care of personal interests but the interests of the state and nation." Change in such a system would take place only over centuries and through the founding of a new dynasty, not through periodic elections. A constitutional monarchy provided the "truest and most truly understood form of liberty."[11]

The students' understanding of the imperial political system was influenced by their reading of European writers. Joaquim Nabuco's own account of his ideological development during his school years is instructive in this regard. Nabuco had read widely in French and English political theory of the time. The son of a prominent politician (a graduate of the Olinda law school, as we have seen), the younger Nabuco considered himself a liberal when he arrived at school, and the events of the late 1860s for a time seemed to radicalize his thinking. By the end of his law school career, as he reconstructed it decades later in his memoirs, his extracurricular reading had led him to a new appreciation of the Brazilian imperial system. In reading the work of the British political theorist, Walter Bagehot, Nabuco came to the conclusion that democracy as practiced in the United States was too unpredictable and not in keeping with the spirit of the Brazilian people. Brazil needed a political system that was slow to change. Above all, Brazil needed a constitutional monarchy under Dom Pedro II.[12]

Historians have often suggested that there existed a strong sense of identity between the young emperor of the 1840s and 1850s and the *bacharéis*. A self-styled intellectual, Dom Pedro II was not only the national symbol par excellence but also the ultimate patron in the Second Empire.[13] In his role as "teacher of the Brazilian nation," he participated in the "direct, personal encouragement of large numbers of talented, young men."[14] Many law students were graduates of the *colégio* that bore his name, where the emperor occasionally sat in on classes and tested the students. He saw his goals as meritocratic and sought out the better students and not merely the sons of more prominent fathers.[15] As part of its graduation ceremony, students at Colégio Dom Pedro II were required to kiss the emperor's hand in the traditional expression of respect and deference that had been reestablished in 1838.[16] The young law students were happy to see in him a reflection of themselves. "The destinies of this vast empire were entrusted to a young Brazilian," one student wrote, "and on him were deposited the hopes of the country."[17]

Dom Pedro II was described as the nation's ultimate magistrate, and the students themselves were largely training to become magistrates and representatives of imperial authority in the hinterlands.[18] The students' identification with the royal family is also evident in the rather sycophantic poem Tobias Barreto wrote during the visit the Princess Isabel and her husband, the French Count d'Eu, paid to Recife during the future law professor's student days. Isabel's greatness did not derive from the fact that she was a princess but from the fact that she was the "hope of the future" who "opens the pathway to the future." (As we shall see, the students' own sense of themselves as the proprietors of the future is echoed here.) For the *bacharéis* to maintain their unquestioned loyalty to the imperial political system, this identification with the emperor and his family would have to continue. When it broke down, so would the *bacharéis'* sense of national purpose.[19]

The new Brazilian national identity that was an important part of this political consensus was a strange blend of traditional dynastic identifications and modern nationalism. As heirs to the Braganza dynasty, the Emperor Dom Pedro II appealed to more traditional notions of authority than did the Spanish American republics, where constitutions had replaced monarchs as the ultimate legal authority. As a constitutional monarchy, Brazil tried to have it both ways. The traditional Portuguese understanding that "where the king is, there is the fatherland" continued to obtain.[20]

But the definition of Brazil, nation and state, was also more specifically restricted to the *bacharéis* as a group. This comes through in random phrases scattered throughout the texts of student newspapers. One student in 1860 wrote that "Brazil is in its adolescence."[21] An almost identical phrase refers to the "Empire of Brazil still adolescent."[22] As they identified themselves with the nation, so they identified with the state. They strove "to make the State the image of man; like him, the state should be free, and like him, the state should be intelligent."[23] The qualities they presumed to possess uniquely as a class, intelligence and independence, were also the values of the state. "From our ranks come the profound legislators," one student wrote, "the defenders of our principles in the parliament." Even the law schools themselves were seen as the "two forces that maintain us [meaning the Brazilian empire] in equilibrium."[24]

We should hardly be surprised by the emphasis on balance and order or by the students' characterization of the state and nation in highly personal terms. As a result of the reforms of the Regresso period, the *bacharéis* were, in effect, destined to embody the state quite literally. But by restricting the nation — and to a large extent, citizenship — to themselves they also disclosed, as Adorno has so astutely noted, the limitations and restrictions they placed on liberalism.

A BRAZILIAN LIBERALISM

Liberty and order are the two principles that dominate us. **José Antônio Pimenta Bueno**

Victorious over the regional revolts that had shattered the optimism of the early liberals, politicians such as Pimenta Bueno looked forward to a period of political stability. That the national political temper had cooled is illustrated by the inclusion of both Liberal and Conservative Party members in the imperial cabinet during the Conciliation period of the 1850s. Brazilian politicians believed they had found the perfect balance between liberty and order that had eluded their Spanish American neighbors.[25] That they had achieved this balance on the backs of African slaves did not trouble them during the 1840s and 1850s.

Despite the negative conclusions political leaders reached regarding the appropriateness of liberalism for Brazil society, the majority of Brazil's politicians continued to define themselves as liberals throughout the nineteenth century. Their continued use of the language of liberalism warrants some explication because the actual content of the liberalism of the 1850s and 1860s, in particular, has only been superficially examined. As I argued in the previous chapter, law students lived out the contradictions of the slave society. Nowhere was this truer than in the conflicting demands made on them by liberalism and patronage, by a peer group sense of independence and by future aspirations to power and prestige.

Some have contended that the "elite's commitment to liberal notions was . . . a mere gesture of cultural mimicry, an expression of a colonial and peripheral culture subordinated to European ideas and . . . to the European market." One can imagine these young men acting out the gestures accompanying liberal discourse to achieve mastery and then getting so caught up in the pantomime that they took the play more seriously, at times, than their elders. As Emilia Viotti da Costa has argued, liberalism may have "continued until the end of the Empire to be a utopia, a promise to be fulfilled," but this was especially true for young men who defined themselves as independent and idealistic. No more than the rest of society did they question liberal theory's premises. If liberal slogans were more than "badges they used to mark their 'civilized' status," it was because students were in a crucial period of identity formation in which language was of vital importance. The tension between discourse and practice was often unbearable for them.[26] Moreover, this unease interacted with the ambivalence they felt toward the often uneducated patrons on whom their future political success depended.[27]

An important function of the *bacharéis* was, in Adorno's words, to take "care of the form in which liberal ideas could and should be expressed."[28] As their elders did, students in the 1840s and 1850s were particularly interested in reining in the previously explosive potential of liberalism. "The most important service one can provide to nations and to legislators is to eliminate disturbances by way of a definition at once clear and precise of the word liberty," one student wrote in 1856. "How many instances of disorder . . . have resulted from words?"[29]

The political ideology of the 1840s and 1850s represented the complete triumph of Regresso values. Dom Pedro I, pilloried as a despot in the student press of the 1820s and 1830s, was now celebrated as the founder of the law schools and the "magnanimous heart that came to give us a nation."[30] The Regency period, on the other hand, was viewed as a time of disorder in which "the popular element through a violent reaction . . . attempted to dominate everything."[31] The Praieira revolt of the late 1840s, the last of the regional rebellions, represented the dangers of politics carried to its ultimate consequences: "a bloody revolution . . . born in the heart of the nation, [which] drank insatiably the blood of brothers." (This rhetoric must have been particularly powerful for a group that defined itself as a community of brothers.)[32]

Students concentrated their intellectual, as opposed to their creative, energies on defining the limits of liberalism. Restricting individual liberties was necessary for public order, one student wrote, for a man living in society could not have the liberties of a man living in a state of nature.[33] Furthermore, a constitutional monarchy provided proper constraints on the "tyranny of the people's sovereignty."[34] "Order is the consecration of liberty," another student wrote in 1860.[35] The fear of chaos and disorder was prominent in student discourse. To prevent disorder, their own duty was to "harmonize social forces."[36] São Paulo students valued prudence and political moderation and saw themselves, as well as the schools they attended, as "points of equilibrium."[37] This was true as well for their northern counterparts (although, I am arguing, it was particularly true in the 1840s and 1850s). The Liberal revolt of 1842, according to Liberal Party students in 1861, resulted from the breakdown of the "union between the aristocratic and the democratic element, whose harmony constitutes the beauty of constitutional governments" (particularly monarchical ones).[38]

Brazilian elites by the 1840s had rejected the possibility of further negotiation over the meaning of liberalism. Even more so than in many other Latin American countries, liberalism became, in effect, the privilege of one group.[39] Brazil, no less than the nineteenth-century Peru described by Florencia Mallon, "repeatedly repressed and marginalized popular political culture," and yet Brazilian elites achieved a degree of stability and hegemony unimaginable in most of Latin America.[40] Liberalism in Brazil was the language of the state; its interpretation was up to the *bacharéis*, the primary state agents. The *bacharéis* were able to "domesticate effective political opposition and expel democratic and progressive forces," according to Adorno.[41] Students of the 1840s and 1850s rejected the "absurd and liberty-destroying idea of the sovereignty of the people," arguing that the "will of the majority of the people was nothing more than the echo of demagogues." The people, they argued, can be equally tyrannical.[42]

Liberalism, as an ideology, was seen as a defining component of law student identity. "The majority, if not the totality of our body, has fought for, fights for, and will fight for the true ideas, the ideas of disinterest and liberalism."[43] "The law school is one of those places where the liberal spirit, inherent in every Brazilian, is most developed."[44] Students praised the "good done for people by liberal beliefs," while the "people condemn [conservative principles] as prejudicial and fatal to their existence."[45]

Although students frequently attempted to place limits on the discourse of liberalism, particularly during the 1840s and 1850s, they also saw themselves as representing true liberalism. Writing in 1869, Joaquim Nabuco defined the "sacred words of the Masonry of youth" to be "God, Country, and Liberty, the traditional legend of Brazilian students, the banner of the New Crusades in search of the ideal Jerusalem that is glimpsed among the mists of the future."[46] Each generation made its claim to liberal beliefs, a claim that justified their right to the reins of power after graduation. The mission of the students was renewed periodically, as each new class dedicated itself to a Brazilian definition of liberty. The need to ensure the continued belief in liberalism itself may have helped to guarantee the political system's legitimacy, but it was even more crucial to young men ready and anxious to take their lead in society.[47]

The students offered renewal in another way, not only because they were faithful to the principles of liberalism, but also because they claimed to be incorruptible. When Rui Barbosa's patron suggested that the young man avoid politics, he must have confirmed Rui's own sense of the corruption of Brazilian politics. "The country is not ready for acts of true patriotism," the older man warned Rui and characterized those who governed Brazil as "traitors" and "idiots."[48] The older man's words did not prevent Rui from embracing what was to be in the long run a notably successful political career. Nor did similar warnings lead many other young *bacharéis* to abandon the hope of a political future. Brazil had the right form of government, one student wrote in 1850. The only problem was that the morals of the current generation of leaders were bad, with politics only serving personal interests. "It is to youth that the Empire should appeal in the hope that it will be more zealous in promoting the happiness and glory of the fatherland and moral principles, thereby civilizing the great Brazilian family." Only the uncorrupted sons could save Brazilian society.[49]

The future belonged to them, and all students defined themselves in terms of the future. "We, the believers in the future" was how Conservative Party stalwart Rodrigues Alves described himself and his fellow students in his tribute to the soldiers fighting in the War of the Triple Alliance.[50] "The future will be our gospel," another student wrote a few years earlier. Because they belonged to the spirit of the age, the students would be "the irresistible force of the necessities and the legitimate aspirations of our country."[51]

In Joaquim Nabuco's first year in São Paulo he founded a newspaper to attack the Zacarias ministry that his father supported. His father asked him to stick to studying and leave journalism and politics alone (advice he would not have followed himself in his student days).[52] The sense of political independence that was so much a part of these young men's self-image (even though often compromised in actual practice) impelled them to define themselves against the politicians of their day. This was so even, and sometimes particularly, when those politicians were their fathers. The students offered a young man's purified politics, a more liberal liberalism, if you will — a liberalism of the future. This need to define themselves in opposition also played itself out in their attachment to political parties, particularly in the 1860s and 1870s.

PARTY AND IDENTITY

Until quite recently, historians have tended to dismiss the importance of party loyalties in the imperial period, despite the stability of the two-party system that arose during the Regency and consolidated itself in the 1840s.[53] Politics has been defined as "really little else than a struggle for power between factions under the leadership of prestigious families."[54] Previous generations of historians have contended that the Liberal Party represented urban interests, while the Conservative Party represented rural interests. This view has been challenged by more recent work that has demonstrated that landowners were well represented in both parties.[55] Scholars have long held that Brazil has never had strong, impersonal parties defined by ideologically consistent platforms. (In fact, it was a splinter group, the Progressive League, that produced the first political program in 1864. The Conservative Party itself never had one.[56]) The famous phrase, that there was nothing more like a Conservative than a Liberal in power, is illustrative of the lack of ideological consistency during the imperial era.

Nonetheless, Conservatives generally had a greater faith in centralized power, as well as more opportunities to wield it. Conservative cabinets governed imperial Brazil during the greater part of the Second Empire (twenty-six years to the Liberal Party's thirteen).[57] Liberals continued to advocate a looser imperial structure. At their most ideologically consistent or distinct, Liberals stood for an end to life terms for senators, direct elections in place of the electoral system, and an abolition of the emperor's moderating power.[58] In practice, however, Liberals saw the advantages of a highly centralized political system and while in power never took steps to dismantle the system.

Richard Graham has forcefully argued that the party names themselves meant nothing. Without "consistent programs," he contends, parties "simply represented momentary alliances of men in Parliament and around particular questions." Or, as one student wrote in 1856, "according to circumstances, parties adopt as many formulas, and give as many names as are necessary to designate decently, honestly, and pompously each of these great groups of combined interests and ambitions." Moreover, as Graham argues, ideological inconsistency and the lack of party discipline made it easier for government to be "an arrangement between friends." This made

possible a smoothly operating imperial political system and political stability.[59]

The descriptions of law students in the semiofficial school histories tend
to support the interpretation that party identification emphasized patronage
and family ties more than disinterested principle. "Only filial respect kept
[one student] attached to the Conservative Party," according to Bevilaqua.
Other students are described as being "Conservative by family tradition" or
a member of the Conservative Party, "like all of his relatives."[60]

Students themselves often defined the parties in nonideological terms.
"Among us, parties divide between those who want to rise and those who
don't want to fall, between the employed and those who want to be employed." Students, particularly in the 1840s and 1850s, feared that parties
posed a threat to the ideals of order and nation, as represented by the family.
"It makes us sad to see the Brazilian family divided into two groups of combatants."[61]

Yet the distinction between Conservatives and Liberals was an important
one for law students struggling to define their identities. As Judy Bieber has
recently suggested, parties "came to serve as a kind of fictive kinship that
superseded localized family loyalties."[62] Students found themselves being
recruited by local party bosses, not least of whom were members of the law
school faculties. They also found themselves making friendships and alliances with young men from across the empire who shared their partisan
affiliation. Moreover, as these young men defined themselves, they had to
come to terms with tradition and official ideology. The Conservative Party
had first defined itself as the "party of order."[63] For its younger members,
this put certain constraints on ideological inspiration. While Liberals were
no less committed to the rhetorical convention of "liberty and order," they
also had a rebellious tradition to draw upon, heroes, even martyrs who had
taken part in the regional rebellions of the 1820s through the 1840s.

These martyrs became particularly important for students from the
1860s on. Castro Alves, for example, wrote a poem in honor of Pedro Ivo,
one of the Liberal martyrs of the Praieira revolt in 1848 in Pernambuco.[64]
For Liberal Party members, national political leaders associated with the
1842 revolt, such as Teófilo Ottoni, were also considered models of appropriate political behavior. After the memories of these conflicts had begun to

fade — with all of their costs, emotional consequences, and threat to social stability — new opportunities for self-definition developed among the law students. At that point, being a young Liberal gave one a certain license to rebel and a greater latitude for political self-expression.

Moreover, there was a fundamental difference between the two law schools in terms of the configurations of political power in the provinces of Pernambuco and São Paulo. Conservative Party chief Pedro Francisco Cavalcanti de Albuquerque, the future viscount of Camaragibe and a member of an important northeastern sugar-plantation-owning family, was director of the Recife school from the year of its transfer in 1854 until 1875.[65] Although Liberal Party members did teach at the northern school, their influence was much weaker, while the São Paulo Liberals remained dominant in the southern school.

In nineteenth-century Recife, politics was dominated by the sugar planters, many of whom maintained residences in the capital city. Recife had been the site of repeated regional revolts since 1817, including the Confederation of the Equator in 1824 and the Praieira revolt in 1848. Pernambuco's Liberal Party was weakened considerably, however, by the defeat of this last rebellion. (The failure of the 1842 Liberal revolt in São Paulo, on the other hand, had a negligible impact of the fortunes of the party there.) "Nowhere in the Empire did the party suffer greater disintegration [than Pernambuco] where Liberals comprised the vanguard of revolutionary forces during the 1848 campaign," one historian has written. Liberal periodical and organizational strength were weak during the 1850s. In the 1860s, some of the largest landowners in the region helped to form the Progressive League. Among the most notable of these was the baron of Vila Bela, Domingos de Sousa Leão, the first member of the powerful Sousa Leão family to receive a law degree. The subsequent embrace of the Liberal Party by the members of the Progressive League also meant, in some respects, a further defeat for the remaining historic Liberals who had supported the failed rebellion of 1848. This conflict between historic Liberals and former Progressive Leaguers continued until the fall of the Liberal government in 1868.[66]

Conservative dominance of the northern school was exemplified by the school's stronger ties to the Catholic church. Where a certain anticlericalism was considered a fundamental component of elite male identity in much of

Brazil, in Pernambuco, conservative, even ultramontane, Catholicism was strong. When his students showed rationalist tendencies, for example, one professor chided them for not seeing that science and religion were allies in the same way as liberty and order.[67]

The Liberal Party was not wholly absent from the northern school, but it only really began to revive in the late 1860s. At that point, Recife students began to look to the Liberal Party as a "party of individuals bound together by common ideas." A member of this generation, José Mariano Carneiro da Cunha, became the dominant figure in Liberal Party politics in the late imperial period in Pernambuco. He filled this role as the editor (from 1872 to 1878) of *A Provincia*, the Liberal Party newspaper, and as the organizer of Club Popular, the "most vigorous political club in the provincial capital," which included one of the faculty members, Aprígio Guimarães, among its officers.[68]

In the southern school, the Liberal Party never lost its importance, even after its defeat in the 1842 revolt. Liberals were clearly in the majority among both students and teachers in São Paulo.[69] "Conservatism," one student wrote in 1860, "was the name adopted by the enemies of social progress."[70] Given the importance of progress as an ideal for most law students, this definition would have had a certain bite to it. Some Conservative students felt uncomfortable being in the minority in São Paulo. Others, however, exaggerated their conservative tendencies to appear more "reactionary" than they actually were, in part to shock and be noticed. To be a devout member of the Catholic church in São Paulo would gain one a certain notoriety.[71]

The period from 1860 to 1875 showed some continuity with the immediate past, but these were clearly transitional years.[72] The 1860s marked an end to Conciliation-style politics and a rebirth of partisanship.[73] The Liberal Party was reborn with an infusion of talent from Conservative ranks by way of the Progressive League. The War of the Triple Alliance, in which an entire empire struggled to subdue tiny Paraguay, made clear to many the inadequacies of Brazilian development. Moreover, many returned from the war with an awareness that the very Spanish American countries to which Brazilians habitually felt superior regarded Brazil, the slave state and monarchy, as a pariah. Abolitionism became a favorite cause among law students in this period. And the War of the Triple Alliance added to the campus unrest that led to what might be called a "false dawn" of republicanism among the student body.

In the 1860s, students at the São Paulo law school reaffirmed their liberalism in response to recurring proposals to move the law school campus to Rio de Janeiro and thereby improve centralized control. The majority of law students in the southern city were said to support the "ideas of disinterestedness and liberalism." Liberal students rejected the rule of the "party of the oligarchy, and of oppression, patronage, and scandal."[74] The student body defined itself against and measured its independence from the "oligarchy," an undefined yet potent symbol.[75] Liberals claimed to stand against the demands of the patronage system. Students began to make appeals to "the people" as a source of validation for their authority, although they made few efforts to engage popular forces directly. Instead, they addressed "the people" only to assure them that their "only hopes" lay in youth: "Only youth is pure and has the patriotism of your forefathers."[76]

The young men lamented the lack of true parties, defined by their adherence to "firm and sincere convictions."[77] In this way, they reflected the thinking of their elders, like José Thomaz Nabuco de Araujo, who throughout the early 1860s expressed similar convictions. The period was marked by a rejection of the Conciliation phase of politics and a transition to a more contentious political system. Beginning in the 1860s, the previously nonpartisan institution of the student newspaper began to be an important partisan instrument. Writing for a party newspaper could enable a student to develop valuable political connections, but it could also lead him to embrace a national, albeit partisan, and not just regional identity.[78]

For the Liberals, in São Paulo as elsewhere, 1868 was a turning point. Many students' loyalty to the imperial political system weakened notably when Dom Pedro II used his moderating power to throw out the Liberal cabinet and call for new elections to be organized by the Conservative Party. The emperor wanted to placate his Conservative military commander, whom he considered essential to winning the war against Paraguay and who refused to continue working with the Liberal ministry. As Roderick Barman has written, "The crisis had the appearance, and to a certain extent the reality, of revealing the political system of Brazil as nothing more than a puppet show manipulated from above by the emperor."[79] Rui Barbosa and other students denounced what they considered a coup d'etat and argued that the action was more typical of the Spanish American republics they disdained than the constitutional monarchy they had long supported.[80] This provoked a crisis of confidence among the largely Liberal student body in São Paulo. Joaquim Nabuco in 1869, evidently not yet converted by his reading of Bagehot, complained of the emperor's "Turkish absolutism."[81] Dom Pedro II came under increasing attack for his action, and the students' identification with him began to decline. The student body in São Paulo joined together in support of their Liberal hero, José Bonifácio, who returned to the faculty after losing his seat in the Chamber of Deputies. Nabuco held a banquet in his honor at which Rui Barbosa recited one of his few poems, which had been inspired by the "coup." Many gave speeches attacking the emperor.[82] Nabuco saluted the returning professor "in the name of youth, for they are not young who have not in their breasts the fever of liberal ideas." In this way, Nabuco clearly wrote members of the Conservative Party out of the student body. He continued, "I come to salute a man who is an idea, . . . a party that is a people, Counselor José Bonifácio, . . . the Liberal Party." By proclaiming a man an idea, Nabuco placed him above the practices of daily politics and in the pure realm of principles where idealistic youth aspired to live. By defining the Liberal Party as "a people," Nabuco offered an alternative model for the nation.

By the late 1860s, the spirit of the students was becoming not only partisan but actively republican, and thus threatened a generational split with their distant families. For example, the patron of Rui's father, Albino José Barbosa de Oliveira, a Coimbra graduate from Bahia and a magistrate linked by marriage to São Paulo coffee interests, was concerned about his young cousin's political leanings. Brazilians in the nineteenth century understood their world to be defined by obligation and obedience, but young men in the liminal stage between childhood and adulthood were constantly testing the limits of societal expectations. The students' attempts to think for themselves at times brought them into conflicts with family members. Albino tried to make Rui aware of the larger gaze of the elite male political society that he presumed Rui wanted to join. Despite their vaunted political independence, students did not live in isolation. If much of their political and literary activity followed the internal dynamic or logic of their student culture, it also was being monitored closely by family, patrons, and the political establishment as a whole.

Two men of an unidentified but high rank in government had spoken with Albino regarding the speeches Rui gave upon the death of the Paraguayan leader Francisco Solano López during the War of the Triple Alliance. In this speech, Rui had declared his preference for a republican form of government. "Think as you wish," Albino wrote. "I won't hold it against you, but I ask you to keep these opinions to yourself until after you have graduated."[83]

Rui responded to Albino that he "lamented" that Albino had been concerned about his speeches. He assured him that he never spoke anything but the truth. As for politics itself, Rui had nothing but disdain, he said, for the way it was practiced in Brazil. His own views represented "only an aspiration"; it could not possibly give the powers that be reason to fear. His political point of view, which "everyone laughs at and calls utopian," was like a "kind of inoffensive animal that scares no one, and for that reason, can not provoke hatred or a desire for revenge."[84]

The likelihood that Albino was reassured by these somewhat disingenuous remarks seems remote. Nevertheless, they do suggest that younger men were granted a large measure of political license. They were indulged because they were "idealistic youth," and thus expected to be, to some degree, independent minded. Many older elite men would have understood their students' difficult situation as part of the maturation process in Brazilian society. After all, so many of them had attended law school and knew the demands of the peer culture that the younger generation experienced.[85]

A father's concerns, nevertheless, could not be shrugged off so easily as those of a distant relative. The correspondence between Rui Barbosa and his father show that they were quite close; João Barbosa signed his letters "your father and friend."[86] Nevertheless, their letters showed signs of tension and occasions when they clearly misunderstood each other, as should hardly be surprising.

In any case, João Barbosa increasingly and strenuously expressed concern about the younger man's political activities. João Barbosa was himself a politician, although trained to be a doctor. He was always a Liberal, and in the 1860s he had aligned himself with those who chose to call themselves "progressives." The younger Barbosa's political positions had hurt him both personally and politically, as former allies in his own family shunned him. He chided Rui for misleading him about his progressive political activities. The older man was outraged that Rui was a member of a club that called itself "radical." (This was the Clube Radical Paulistano, a student association.) The father insisted that he did not want Rui to be a hypocrite but did want him to be prudent. The older man saw little sense in becoming "notorious" and was concerned by indications that Rui wanted to be seen as more progressive than his father. While João Barbosa recognized that this was, in a sense, a duty of a son, he urged Rui to consider the nature of politics. Those who were most successful politically in moving their country forward (he cited the Italian Cavour) did not announce their principles prematurely but rather led their countrymen a little at a time, hiding the direction in which they wanted to go. Others who were less prudent might be "prophets" and "apostles," but they were not politicians. The ideas that Rui expounded, and that father and son had discussed privately in numerous frank political discussions, were not yet "mature among Brazilians" and would appear when public opinion permitted.

In matters of practical politics, moreover, João Barbosa denied that Rui could possibly be more advanced than he was. The conversations in which they had imagined alternative political realities were mere theoretical fancies; being useful to one's contemporaries was something else. He further encouraged Rui to read the writings of those who had specifically rejected republicanism. He predicted that the world would teach him the error of his ways. Excessive political activism, in any case, was distracting him from his studies and hurting his "previous reputation as a good student." In the long run, João Barbosa warned, this would harm him as he tried to begin his career as a lawyer. The father grew increasingly more emphatic in his denunciation of Rui's political radicalism and warned him that his words would be used against him throughout his career, "creating hazards" and leading to "poverty."[87]

Undoubtedly, Rui's conflict with his father was mirrored in the experience of other students at the two law schools. Intergenerational conflict would become increasingly likely as the political situation in Brazil grew more ideologically charged after 1870. The removal of the Liberals from power created the conditions for the formation of a third party for those most disaffected with the imperial system. The Republican Party was founded in 1870, and a student newspaper expounding explicitly republican principles, *A Propaganda*, appeared in São Paulo in 1871. Its editors sought to reclaim a revolutionary heritage in the face of claims that Brazil lacked such traditions. "We are not totally unfamiliar with revolutions," one student wrote. "We had two that were complete and victorious, those of 1822 and 1831." (Students then and later avoided mentioning examples that both they and their elders might consider more threatening to social order, such as the Cabanagem in Pará.) The students rejected the "dominating form of monarchical government" as "an error condemned by the social nature of man." They portrayed Brazil as a nation of "two slaveries" and rejected as false an alliance between Republicans and Liberals.[88]

An alliance between Liberals and Republicans remained possible, however, from 1868 to 1878 when Liberals were eclipsed nationally. To claim common ground, Liberals often alluded to their party's past participation in rebellions.[89] Although some rejected the link between Liberals and Republicans, others found it appropriate and useful. Some students who embraced republicanism during law school never wavered from their faith and after graduation avoided political office until a republic was established in 1889. Most, however, such as Rui Barbosa himself, were more likely to run for office as Liberal Party candidates during the 1860s and 1870s. Some republicans even joined the foreign service, including Salvador de Mendonça, who served in the United States in both the imperial and republican periods.[90] By the late 1870s, some graduates of the previous decade had become active in founding and editing republican newspapers.[91] The generations of the 1860s contained many students who remained important politically after the birth of the republic in 1889. For this generation, particularly those in São Paulo, loyalty to the emperor and to the imperial political system was much weaker than it had been for the generation of the 1840s and 1850s.

In any case, the long eclipse in power of the Liberal Party, while it had the effect of weakening the loyalty of many to the monarchy, also made it possible for many others to argue that fundamental change was unnecessary. A Liberal Party true to its ideals and principles would put matters to right once it could wrest power from the Conservatives. In the meantime, abolitionism would remain a far more pressing social and political issue.

ABOLITIONISM

An important part of the mid-century political consensus had been support for the institution of slavery. Abolitionism was not a major issue on the national political scene in the 1840s and 1850s; nor was it one for the law students.[92] A reading of a classic 1850s legal text such as Pimenta Bueno's already cited *Brazilian Public Law* shows how central slavery was, at least metaphorically, to Brazilian liberals at this time. As Pimenta Bueno wrote, "Our country is not subject to arbitrary direction, to unlimited will, to slavery." In a state subject to total authority, "a man is a slave, his moral and intellectual qualities are degraded and compromised." The limitations on the emperor's power under the Brazilian constitution, Pimenta Bueno argued, guaranteed that Brazil was not a slave society. Brazilians had "a right to assert that some were not born to be slaves and others to be their masters."[93]

Students, as well, used the symbol of the enslaved to define themselves and their nation. "The sons of Santa Cruz [an early name for Brazil] can never be slaves."[94] Slavery in this sense defined not only the absence of liberty and the fear of dependence, but also identified by contradistinction those who truly belonged to the nation, who were, in fact, the true "sons of Santa Cruz." Were people of African descent born in Brazil not to be considered slaves? Or were the true sons of Santa Cruz only the young law students themselves?

Brazilian planters may not have had the same ideological commitment to slavery that their counterparts in the United States did. The gradualist approach that Brazil followed allowed for a certain philosophical laxity in this regard. Most slave owners would admit after 1850 that the institution of slavery was doomed. In his collection of Brazilian laws published in the 1850s, Teixeira de Freitas found it unnecessary to include laws relating to slavery because, he argued, slavery would eventually be abolished.[95] Abolitionist students in the 1860s were not by and large willing to wait, but they could be dismissed as impatient youth.

As part of their literary project of nation building, students in the 1850s discussed whether slaves could be appropriate subjects for literature. One student wrote in 1859: "I know that many believe that they [the slaves] can not be elevated to the stature of art."[96] If a slave could not be "elevated" to the level of artistic discourse, it was perhaps because of the presumption of some of the elite that the African also could not be elevated to the status of citizen. While the indigenous Brazilian idealized by the Indianist movement discussed in chapter 3 was not part of the students' daily lives, Brazilians of African descent were everywhere.[97] Nevertheless, although some students were reluctant to allow the slave to be a subject for literature (they were aware after all of the writings of Harriet Beecher Stowe), others began to write poems in which they adopted the voice of the slave. Generally, these poems belonged to the "melancholy slave" tradition, in which the slave longed for his African home. This was a rhetorical device that allowed poets to express their empathy for the slaves, while denying a place to them and their descendants in the Brazilian nation.

"Slavery still exists in Brazil!" one student wrote in 1856 (with an air of naiveté that is almost charming), "in our land where the air of liberty is breathed everywhere."[98] In just a few years, world events would force the issue of slavery onto the students' agenda. The abolition of slavery in the French, Portuguese, and Danish empires; the Civil War and Emancipation Proclamation in the United States; and the elimination of serfdom in Russia left Brazil isolated in the international community as one of only two remaining slave societies in the Western Hemisphere (the other being Cuba, still a colony of Spain).[99] Law students watched closely "the colossal struggle" ongoing in the United States. One wrote: "The northern states want to offer an even more beautiful model of government, becoming free of the gangrenous cancer that pollutes them."[100] The War of the Triple Alliance had an even more direct impact on attitudes toward slavery, as slaves gained their freedom by serving in the military. Although some students left to join the "Nation's Volunteers" and fight in the war, their contribution to the war effort pales in comparison.[101] The war also made Brazilians aware of how isolated their ownership of slaves made them not only in world opinion but among their continental neighbors.

Slavery now inspired dramatic rhetoric. "Death to all slave-owners, liberty for all slaves," one student wrote. "Let's put an end to this lie!"[102] Much of the emotional power of Castro Alves's poetry came from his strong commitment to abolition. For him, slavery was more than just a blot on the nation's honor. Castro Alves in his classic poem "The Slave Ship (Tragedy at Sea)" suggested a connection between slavery and the death not only of the slaves themselves but of a society and the liberties of a nation, and compares slavery to the betrayal of the nation. To abolish slavery, as far as Castro Alves was concerned, would give new life to liberty in a renewed Brazil.[103]

The students' sense of their mission to purify a corrupt society was prominent in the abolitionist movement, as it was elsewhere in their rhetoric. "As youth, the sons of reason and the gospel, we have the mission to realize great ideas," one wrote. Nowhere was the Romantic spirit more evident in their politics than in their abolitionism. As one student, Castro Alves's good friend Maciel Pinheiro, wrote, "to suffer for great causes is divine."[104] Students envisioned for themselves a central role in making Brazil a civilized nation by eliminating slavery: "We, who are the pilgrims of the future, who seek the dominion of civilization and the reign of law and virtue, protest against a fact that dishonors our country, that gives sad testimony to our backwardness and our degradation." Slavery was understood to be the principal cause of Brazil's lack of economic and technological development. Free youth had a responsibility to abolish an institution condemned by the "sentiments of the century."[105]

Slavery was universally hated among São Paulo law students, according to Joaquim Nabuco, but it was less of an issue in Pernambuco.[106] Castro Alves helped found an abolitionist society in Recife but then transferred to the southern school.[107] With his transfer in 1868, abolitionism died out in Recife. Even Joaquim Nabuco's opposite transfer from São Paulo to Recife did not revive abolitionism. Nabuco himself remained actively interested in abolitionism while a student in Pernambuco. He wrote a book-length manuscript condemning slavery as a crime and, as the basis of Brazilian society, a fundamentally corrupting influence.[108] The young law student also took on the case of a slave imprisoned for killing a man who had publicly humiliated him.[109] And he corresponded with North American abolitionists like Charles Sumner.[110]

Nevertheless, in the northeast, what one historian has called the "Traditional Planter" mentality reigned. Sugarcane planters' social and political power — indeed their identity — was linked more directly to their ownership of slaves than it was among southern coffee plantation owners.[111] Partly because of this and also the dominance of a more generally ideologically restrictive mentality in the northeast, abolitionism did not mobilize Recife students in the 1860s to the degree that it did in São Paulo.

North or south, student abolitionism consisted of more than just poetry and rhetoric, although it was largely that. In 1856, an abolitionist society in São Paulo was formed to raise funds to buy the freedom of individual slaves. Their efforts were not completely fruitless; they did, in fact, free one slave.[112] Students in 1860 decided to use the funds meant for the celebration of their graduation from law school to free a slave. As abolitionism developed more of a following in the 1860s, new organizations were more successful. An organization formed in 1863 freed an undetermined number of slaves (although Vampré in his semiofficial history of the São Paulo suggests there were many). Rodrigues Alves and Rui Barbosa, with the aid of former slave Luís Gama, transformed a masonic lodge into a public organization whose primary goal was to free slaves held illegally (as Gama himself, born free but sold into slavery by his own father, had been). This organization also succeeded in freeing a number of slaves.[113]

In the fiction they wrote while in law school, students portrayed themselves as fundamentally opposed to the values and practices of the slave owners who dominated Brazilian society. In one short story, a student visiting a coffee plantation is horrified to discover slaves being tortured. He complains to his host, "But how can you punish a man in this way?" "A man?" replied the *fazendeiro*. "I see that the little doctor is one of those who think that a Negro is equal to a white man."[114]

Their rejection of slavery brought these young men into conflict with their own families. Upon learning that Rui Barbosa had published a newspaper that his older relative Albino described as "abolitionist to an exaggerated degree," the older man invited Rui to visit his large coffee estates, "as you certainly have not yet had an occasion to see" how plantations were actually run. This "perhaps would modify your exaggerated sentiments concerning slavery, when you saw the humanity with which these people, so in need of tutelage, are treated."[115] In this letter, age condescended to youth, as age often does, and appealed to the young man's lack of experience of the "real world." I have no evidence to indicate whether the younger man ever responded directly to Albino on the issue of slavery. Most likely, he maintained a discreet silence. It is interesting to note, however, that in the larger context of society (and undoubtedly in terms of his own economic interests), the older man clearly saw that it was Rui's abolitionism rather than his republicanism that was more of a threat and merited correcting.

In trying to master the hegemonic discourse of liberalism, students also lived out its contradictions. European liberalism could not simply be grafted onto a slave society without some cognitive dissonance. As they tried out the dominant discourse, they were better able to see the lack of fit between the ideals and the reality that others had learned to live with. Students, experiencing in the *repúblicas* their own first taste of freedom distant from their fathers, came to resent the chains imposed on others through slavery and on themselves through patronage. Their student culture was the expression of the ambivalence young men feel when they come together to prepare for their future role as leaders. The few private writings we have of these young men suggest their uncertainty about these roles and whether they fit or ought to fit into them. In their public writings and their public speeches, they often did not let this uncertainty show. The need for patronage was a double-edged sword and threatened the autonomy prized by "independent youth." Students expressed apprehension over their vulnerability to seduction by the "backward" forces governing Brazil.[116]

Having left the family home and established themselves, in their own minds, at least, as independent agents, the students stood at an important turning point. The peer culture provided its own set of criteria for success, but the outside world they would soon join had a rather different set. These competing loyalties and desires created a certain degree of emotional conflict for the young men at the law schools. Family ties conflicted at times with current friendships, while future aspirations could call for the young men to curb their present political inclinations. Yet by embracing abolitionism, they were expressing most clearly their uncertainty about participating fully in the Brazilian society whose leaders they would become. Brazilian elites have been criticized for imitating European political trends. Many have suggested that these men were alienated from their society and therefore unable to address its real problems. Their interest in abolitionism, however, suggests a desire to have Brazilian society live up to the best of its liberal precepts.[117]

After the 1860s, a commitment to the abolition of slavery became part of the Brazilian law student ideal. It signified independence and fidelity to liberal principles and represented a break with the ties that bound the young men to their patrons and families. As part of the law students' mission, abolitionism conferred on them a renewed moral authority to accompany their long-standing claims to authority based on control over language. By calling for the end of slavery, students sought to show that the language they employed was not mere rhetoric, but indicative of their idealistic commitment to the creation of a transformed Brazil.

And yet one has to keep in mind that the abolitionist ideal of the student years was often just that, an ideal appropriate for a special time in a student's life. Rui Barbosa himself was a slave owner in 1884 — more than a decade after he graduated — when he "reconverted to abolitionism" along with other members of the Liberal Party. He then set free his slave Lia, whom he had inherited from his family.[118]

The example of Gaspar Silveira Martins, stalwart of the Rio Grande do Sul Liberal Party, is particularly noteworthy in its illustration of the lack of fit between student aspirations and social realities. When in the middle of his law school career he transferred from Recife to the São Paulo school, his father gave him one of the family house slaves, a shy and obedient slave nicknamed Moleque or "street urchin" Tancredo. On the journey to São Paulo, Silveira Martins told Tancredo that he was now free and that he would pay him a certain portion of his monthly allowance to be his servant. He did not require him to do any heavy tasks and primarily employed him as a private messenger. When Silveira Martins's roommates asked Tancredo to do a task that he felt was beneath him, Tancredo replied that he was the special servant of his "doctor." The formerly timid slave now acted as if he was the owner of the república, according to Silveira Martins's biographer, and began to treat Silveira Martins's roommates familiarly. When his roommates complained about this, Silveira Martins defended his servant. Nevertheless, when the time came for Silveira Martins to return to the family ranch after graduation, the "lordly" servant, accustomed to being the trusted companion of a "doctor," was forced to go to work in the fields, a slave of Silveira Martins's father once again.[119]

After the passage of the Free Birth Law in 1871 (which granted freedom, in the long run at least, to slaves born after its passage), the issue of abolition was put on hold. The first half of the 1870s was a period of apathy and stagnation for students at both schools. In the late 1860s, the War of the Triple Alliance had agitated the law school spirit. It raised the issues of slavery and republicanism to a new level. Similarly, the deposition of the Liberal government in 1868 had, momentarily at least, a radicalizing effect on the student body (and, in the long run, a corrosive impact on the legitimacy of the imperial political system). For a time it even seemed as if Republicans and Liberals had reason to make common cause. While republicanism began to gain ground among some in the province of São Paulo, it tended to die out among the law students. In São Paulo, the years between 1871 and 1876 were depicted as a period of "silence and obscurantism."[120] Only with the return to power of the Liberal Party in 1878, and its subsequent failure to live up to its ideas, would a powerful new formulation of Brazilian liberalism — an anti-monarchical, positivist republicanism — be born. This took place within the context of important transformations in Brazilian society and changes in the law schools themselves.

6

REFORM, REDEFINITION,
AND DECLINE

Historians have frequently identified 1870 as a starting point for the on-set of "modernization" in Brazil. As in the rest of Latin America, the im-portance of this date stems from the acceleration of export-led economic growth. In Brazil, as well, 1870 is particularly significant; it was the year in which the War of the Triple Alliance was won and the Republican Party was founded. In the following year the Law of Free Birth was passed, guarantee-ing the eventual extinction of slavery. In the 1870s, new intellectual trends began to take hold, most notably in the Brazilian case (as in many other Latin American countries), positivism.[1] One intellectual historian has even gone so far as to argue that, as far as the history of ideas is concerned, the empire ended not in 1889, but in 1870.[2]

In 1872, Brazil's emperor returned from his first European trip and thereafter began to show signs that he would not be able to adapt to chang-ing times. Dom Pedro II was aging prematurely, in part because of the stress of the recently concluded war. He was unable to see the need for serious modifications in the political system. Instead, he became increasingly cau-tious and overly concerned with detail at a time in which the administration of government was becoming more complicated with each passing year, es-pecially as new technologies enhanced communications. At the same time, he was seemingly incapable of doing what was necessary to guarantee the survival of the monarchy itself. Lacking a male heir, the emperor's preju-dices regarding women's capacities kept him from encouraging Princess Is-abel to prepare to take the reins, even though she served as regent during his trips abroad. By the 1880s, the monarch, once the savior of Brazilian unity, was no longer the indispensable man.[3]

As Brazilian society was undergoing dramatic, if uneven, change, the students faced a "crisis of hegemony." Their traditional leadership roles were coming into question, and patronage networks bent under the weight of an oversupply of law school graduates.[4] Socioeconomic change was also undermining the patriarchal order within which and against which students had defined themselves. By the later 1870s, the law schools themselves were being transformed both in the way they were run and in the types of identities that were formed there. Changes in school rules and regulations that were intended to improve the quality of instruction weakened the students' sense of community even as they provided expanded opportunities to explore new identities and ideological commitments. Students sought an identity that would fit the needs of a society undergoing a slow transition from slave to free labor.[5] This chapter will address such questions as, to what extent was the students' sense of mission changing? Where would they look for a new source of the cultural authority they had previously found primarily in literature? How would their understanding of the nation and the state be redefined? Would they turn against the imperial system altogether?

The young men at the law schools, and chiefly in more economically dynamic São Paulo, enthusiastically embraced new philosophies. Some emphasized the role of evolution; "order and progress" was the motto derived from the French founder of positivism and sociology, Auguste Comte. The students sought to replace the traditional emphasis on literary skills as the defining characteristic of young elite manhood and intellectual endeavor with a new orientation toward the analytical skills of social science. Many argued that the centralized monarchical system the *bacharéis* had served for generations had to be replaced by a decentralized republic that would be more responsive to Brazil's changing economy and society. Given the elite's fear of social disorder, these changes at times posed risks. The students' crisis of hegemony, an identity crisis, if you will, was only resolved with the fall of the empire in 1889. In this chapter, I will explore the changes taking place in Brazilian society, the efforts made to reform the law schools themselves, and the adoption of republicanism, positivism, and social science as the political and intellectual underpinnings of a new elite identity.

SOCIAL TRANSFORMATION AND THE DECAY OF THE OLD ORDER

In the 1870s and 1880s, Brazilian society was undergoing significant transformation. These changes, particularly in the urban and public settings in

which the law students had held a privileged space, would have major ramifications for the young men's long-standing domination of that society. The
construction of railroads, for example, expanded dramatically in the latter
decade, particularly in southeastern Brazil, a region that was continuing to
grow economically as new areas were opened to coffee production.[6] In contrast, the northeast was continuing to decline. Students lamented the "dec-
adence of abandoned agriculture" in Pernambuco.[7] New industries were
also overwhelmingly located in the southern regions of Brazil. There were
roughly 175, mostly small-scale factories in 1874; by 1884, their number had
increased to six hundred.[8] The expansion of the railroads and the birth of industry, moreover, suggested to some that Brazil now needed technical skills
that law students did not possess.[9]

The Brazilian population also was growing and changing. From ten million people in 1872 Brazil had grown to fourteen million by 1889. Slaves
who had represented one-third of the population at the time of independence in 1822 had declined to only 15 percent in 1872. The slave population
had moved south since 1850 as well, as declining sugar interests were forced
to sell their slaves to the rising coffee interests of the south. The process of
emancipation quickened in the 1880s, particularly after 1885 as abolitionists encouraged slaves to flee plantations. Slaves, certain now of a more sympathetic reception in the cities, left by the thousands. In the city of São Paulo
itself, the slave population was no more than 9 percent by 1887.[10] On the eve
of abolition one year later, only 5 percent of the total Brazilian population
was enslaved.[11]

Accompanying the transition from slave to free labor was increasing economic inequality between regions. For that reason, the economic interests
of the Brazilian ruling class were increasingly diverging.[12] Nowhere was the
pace of economic change quicker than in the province of São Paulo, particularly in its western part. From no railroad track in 1860 and only 139 kilometers of it in 1870, São Paulo expanded to 1,212 kilometers of railway by
1880. This followed a dramatic growth in the number of coffee bushes as
well, from 26.8 million in 1860 to 60 million in 1870, 69 million in 1880,
and 106 million by 1890.[13] Decades of intermittent and largely unsuccessful
efforts to attract European immigration finally bore fruit, as thousands of

Italians, in particular, came to Brazil to work on the coffee plantations, first in a steady stream after 1882 and then in a "flood" beginning in 1887.[14]

The city of São Paulo in particular was expanding dramatically during the 1870s; by the 1880s it would no longer be the college town that the law students had so easily dominated. With only roughly twenty thousand residents in 1872 (the year of the first national census), the city more than doubled (forty-four thousand by 1886) and then grew to sixty-four thousand in the year after the establishment of the republic.[15] The proliferation of railroads throughout the coffee regions in the province made it possible for large landowners to live in the capital city itself. Their greater presence further lessened the social importance of the students in city life. The presence of a large immigrant population as well, though it was hardly socially or politically dominant, transformed the setting in which the young men at the law schools had once reigned supreme.

Public spaces, once the almost exclusive realm of slaves, the working poor, and the law students themselves, were now filled with people on foot or riding in streetcars.[16] Women of the middle and upper classes, once hidden away in the patriarchal homes or carried in sedan chairs by slaves, were now increasingly mobile and visible. In part, this was due to improved conditions in São Paulo, where, as in other Brazilian cities, streets were now paved and illuminated by gaslight, garbage was collected, and underground sewers took other wastes away. Most important for women's new urban presence was the proliferation of streetcar lines in all of the major cities.[17] This further lessened the monopoly over public space that elite young men had traditionally enjoyed, diminishing their once awesome prestige.

The larger transformations in Brazilian society were also reflected in the elimination of the male stranglehold on access to the professions. Women began to enter the professions, albeit on a small scale.[18] The first Brazilian woman doctor graduated from New York Medical College in 1881. The first woman graduate of a Brazilian medical school graduated from the Bahia Medical School in 1887. With little fanfare, the first female students were admitted to the law schools, and the first three, all from the province of Pernambuco, graduated from Recife in 1888. The most prominent of these three, Maria Fragoso, became a translator and writer on social questions as well as the spouse and intellectual partner of a fellow law school graduate, the intellectual and politician Artur Orlando.[19] Publications by, and not just for, women were increasing, as literacy was perceived less and less as an exclusively male attribute.[20] Perhaps not surprisingly, not all law students reacted sympathetically to calls for further emancipation of women.[21] In small but significant and cumulative ways, these young men's monopoly over social and political power was being called into question. Generally, historians have argued that the socioeconomic changes after 1870 undermined the traditional Brazilian patriarchy within which the young men had sought not only recognition as adult males and independent social and political actors but an ultimate role as reigning patriarchs themselves.[22]

Public criticism of the law schools increased. Critics charged that they were nothing more than factories of *bacharéis*, producing too many students with degrees they had not earned. The students responded that they "were, are, and will always be the hope of the country, and sooner or later, also will govern the destinies of the country," but still the criticisms clearly stung. Moreover, the attacks came from new and increasingly prestigious sectors of the society.[23] By the 1870s, the literary ideal that had been popular among students since the 1840s was being challenged by people representing new economic interests. A new organization called the Industrial Association criticized the law schools for producing men of letters when the nation needed technically trained men.[24] A British character in a play from the late imperial period noted the law students' failure to acquire knowledge that would be useful to society. "When doctors of law are trained, do they study navigation, learn to plant potatoes and coffee, and do they read up on military matters?" The answer was clearly "no." And who to ask the question more provocatively than a representative of the industrializing world, in comparison with which Brazil was falling behind?[25]

It has been commonplace to see the rise of new class interests in the late imperial period as a product of the economic transformations of Brazilian society and to contrast "progressive" urban interests with "traditional" rural interests. If, as some have suggested, reformers hailed from a rising middle class in response to changing economic and social realities, one would still have to explain why so many of them came from within the ranks of the political class, the state agents in training at the law schools, who were hardly outsiders.[26] The rise in law school enrollment in the late imperial period reflected new opportunities for young men like Antônio Silva Jardim, the son of a small farmer and schoolmaster, and Anibal Falcão, whose father worked as a stenographer in the Pernambuco provincial assembly.[27] Yet the law school republicans of the late imperial period were frequently sons of the imperial nobility, as well. Young men at the law schools, sensitive as always to world historical trends and to a loss in their traditional prerogatives, sought a way to maintain their own relevance in, and hegemony over, social and political power. Moreover, they had to do so in a time when the institution of the law school itself, centrally controlled and resistant to reform, was undergoing important changes.

REFORMING THE LAW SCHOOLS

Major reforms transformed the law schools in 1879.[28] From this point on, the schools offered two degrees, one in the traditional juridical sciences and one in social sciences. Although the differences between the content of the two degrees was less than one might imagine, the emerging social sciences had an undeniably stronger presence in the curriculum. This had important ramifications for the students' understanding of themselves, as we will see. Further reforms in 1885 added four natural sciences to the list of subjects tested on the entrance examinations.[29] To address the long-standing problem of professorial absenteeism, instructors were forbidden to hold political or administrative office while employed as teachers. (Not surprisingly, this particular reform was honored mostly in the breach.)

The most fundamental change, however, was that students would no longer be required to attend classes. The fear of flunking a year after missing forty classes no longer hung over students' heads. If they chose, students could even take exams without attending any classes. Without required attendance, it was argued, "professors who teach more and better" would attract more students, and teachers would be encouraged to improve the quality of their instruction. Professors were themselves freed from teaching the state-mandated textbooks and therefore, theoretically at least, would be able to adapt more quickly to developments in their field.[30] Reformers maintained that this "free market" of ideas, laissez-faire attendance policy, and greater competition for teaching positions would lead to a new dedication to learning previously absent at the law schools. Central control would be limited to "necessary inspections to guarantee conditions of morality and hygiene."[31]

The reforms soon drew criticism from both faculty and students. By 1882, one professor argued in the São Paulo school's annual report, the schools were in an advanced state of decline.[32] Attendance at classes, never particularly high, as we have seen, was dramatically reduced by as much as 50 percent overall. On some days, no more than one-third of the student body was in attendance. In July 1888, almost a decade after the reforms had been enacted, many classes had to be canceled because not a single student showed up.[33] Students, one professor remarked, were now free to "travel, to hunt, to do anything other than attend classes in which they are enrolled and do the required studying." Professors regretted that the "free attendance" policies had left students with more time to engage in the activities that the faculty had previously often scorned, such as editing newspapers and trying "to correct the errors of humanity with the mature knowledge gained by those between the ages of 16 and 20."[34] Given the opportunity, many students, sometimes as many as one hundred at a time, did take final exams without attending classes. The Recife school seems to have been particularly lax in this regard because ninety-four students transferred from São Paulo to Recife in one year alone, attracted, critics charged, by the notorious "complacency" of the examiners in the north.[35] The professors in São Paulo also responded to the new reforms by displaying ever more "excessive benevolence" during the examinations, which led to further grade inflation.[36]

Professors argued that the reforms had been misguided, allowing young men too much autonomy. "Why do we not let a blind man lead us by the hand?" one asked. What are our students but men "blind with passion, with inexperience, with youth?" Will not a blind man "lead himself to the abyss?" Just so, "enthusiastic and inexperienced youth doesn't know what its own interests are."[37] Professors noted that they were less equipped than ever to pass judgment on the moral or civic conduct of their students. Some teachers argued that the new attendance policies made this aspect of their duties impossible to execute.[38] The reforms had virtually eliminated the last vestiges of authority the professors possessed and created opportunities for a further expansion of the importance of the peer culture's role in student life. This fostered new possibilities for self-definition in changing times, but it in no way improved the pedagogical function of the law schools.

The reforms had other ramifications as well. They changed the process of socialization I have described in earlier chapters. Students no longer were required to make the long journey to Recife or São Paulo to take the entrance examinations. They needed only to travel to the capitals of their respective provinces. They no longer had to spend a year or more so far away from home living with peers before their first day of classes. By spending less time away from their homes, the ties that bound them to their families and traditional patronage networks and local concerns were not weakened to the degree they had been previously. Students had less time to develop ties with the national community that the law student body represented. This came at a time when economic differentiation among Brazil's regions was already creating divisions between the interests of particular regions. The result was that it was even more difficult for a more national outlook to develop among the law students and less likely that students would come to identify with a centrally controlled state.[39]

In other ways, too, by lessening the academic standards the reforms also inadvertently weakened the bonds within the student body itself. The elimination of the traditional Saturday sessions in which students had to expound upon a particular point of law decreased opportunities for them to practice public speaking.[40] Moreover, it lessened the "reciprocal dependence," one professor noted, "the strongest link that cements student solidarity." Students no longer had to spend as much time together outside of class preparing for these special Saturday classes and no longer had to rely on each other for advice on improving their performance.[41]

The elimination of the attendance policy, whatever the good intentions behind it, seems to have helped undercut students' group identity in the 1880s.[42] Students complained about the loss of "fraternity" and "unity" and looked back to the decades of the 1840s through 1860s as the golden age of student life.[43] "There no longer exists that collectivity, that solidarity that turned all into only one and one into everyone."[44] The law students were a group in decline. São Paulo's chronicler Richard Morse has argued that the law students there, lost in bohemianism and aimless acts of vandalism, were no longer responsible "for marking out horizons of national life."[45]

While there is no evidence that the law students were suddenly irrelevant in the late imperial period, they themselves felt that something fundamental had changed. "The collective soul of youth," Silva Jardim, a student at the southern school, wrote in 1879, "has fragmented."[46] Despite the accompanying losses, students rejected suggestions that "free attendance" be revoked.[47] The expansion of their autonomy, once granted, became a privilege they understood as a right and a further symbol of their highly prized independence. The fragmentation of student identity, however, could not be reversed. It was a reflection both of the recent reforms and the diverging interests of the elite as a whole.

While the reforms contributed to changes in the ways in which identities were formed at the law schools, other social changes, particularly in São Paulo, were transforming the setting in which the young men were socialized. As the city of São Paulo grew, even the *república* itself, which had been central for decades to students' self-image, was losing its preeminence as the student dwelling. Instead of living in a microcosm of the student community, students now often lived more anonymously in large rooming houses with other young men from more varied social backgrounds and oriented toward other purposes. Roommates now included those engaged in commerce or employed as office workers, young men previously dismissed as "others."[48]

The fragmentation of student identity is illustrated by the increasing partisanship in the student press, which reached a new peak beginning in the late 1870s. The Republican Party had a new visibility among the São Paulo students beginning in 1877. Abolitionism, which had been dormant as a national and a student issue after the Free Birth Law was passed in 1871, was reborn in the late 1870s as well. Newspapers representing the interests of Catholic students appeared at the southern school where previously they had been a rarity.[49] One newspaper provided the following tongue-in-cheek list of parties "sheltered in the shade of the old temple of science": "the Ultramontane Conservative Party, the non-Ultramontane Conservative Party, the Ultramontane Liberal Party, the Pure (Reformist or Revolutionary) Liberal Party, the Radical or Radical Liberal Party, the Moderate Liberal Party, the Philosophic Party, the Eclectic Party, the Pure, Moderate or Hybrid Republican Party, and the Slippery or All-Flags Party."[50]

Moreover, students and professors both were clearly concerned about the number of new students matriculating since the reforms of 1879. They viewed it as a threat to the law school's traditional status as the domain of gentlemen. A newspaper reported in 1885 that a "coachman" from Rio Grande do Norte had entered the Recife school. "If the government doesn't open its eyes," one student warned, albeit somewhat facetiously, "we will soon have tailors, shoemakers, cigar-makers, and *tutti quante.*"[51] Others expressed concern that many students from the poorest of Brazilian provinces were passing the entrance exams. Reportedly eighty students from the same poor northeastern state of Rio Grande do Norte alone had passed the 1885 tests. One reason for the tremendous increase in enrollment during these years was that the number of secondary schools had increased dramatically; the primary function of many of them was to prepare students to take the entrance exams. And while fears of the threat of the popular classes gaining access to social and political power through the law schools was clearly exaggerated, the enrollment of more and more students clearly was taking its toll on the imperial political system.[52]

Furthermore, the acceptance of what had been seen as natural hierarchies within the student body was coming into question as well. In his first year at the southern school, self-described "iconoclast" Silva Jardim rejected the rule that *caloiros* should only listen at club meetings and public gatherings. He attempted to speak at a gathering of student republicans in the São José Theater. When his fellow students realized that the young man so insistent on making his opinions known was a *caloiro*, they hooted resoundingly, even after the club president, Afonso Celso Junior, had asked that the rule barring first-year students from speaking be abolished. Silva Jardim left the republican club immediately after this incident, arguing that the rule against freshmen speaking was a remnant of Portuguese authoritarian traditions. As such, it was incompatible with republican aspirations as well as the student ideals of unity and fraternity.[53] Silva Jardim's rhetoric recalls the heady days of the late 1820s and 1830s, when identities were still in flux and much about Brazilian politics and elite male identity was still open to question.

The faculty itself was changing during this period as well. Professors who had formerly been role models for Liberal Party youth were retiring. Stepping down in 1881, for example, was José Bonifácio, who had been a hero for generations because of his ability to function as an integral party of the imperial political system while seeming idealistically apart from it.[54] Furthermore, some who joined the faculty in the late imperial period were less wedded ideologically to monarchical government. Some even had republican tendencies and abstained from politics before the establishment of the republic. Others, such as Brasílio Rodrigues dos Santos, a member of the São Paulo class of 1877 who joined the faculty in 1883, made no secret of their republican inclinations.[55]

The transformation of the law schools and of Brazilian society at large raised new questions as well about student identity and about what types of political arrangements best suited Brazil. Despite the good intentions of the reformers, however, the reforms had done little to improve educational quality at the two law schools. Instead, they accelerated a process of fragmentation of the student community, which made it easier for them to question the very type of political system they were being trained to serve. Within the expanded autonomy created by the reforms, many students in the late imperial period — particularly in São Paulo — opted for a republican solution to what they perceived as Brazil's backwardness.

THE ADVENT OF REPUBLICANISM

Part of the crisis of identity that I have described centered on law students' large-scale disaffection with the imperial political system in the late 1870s and 1880s. While it had not been unknown for students to embrace at least mildly antiestablishment political positions in the past, particularly, as we have seen, over the issue of slavery in the 1860s, the disaffection with the political system they expressed from the late 1870s on bears special consideration.[56] What explains the timing of the rise of republicanism among the law students? Why were they so disaffected with a political system that had benefited the *bacharéis* more than any other social group? Did their embrace of republicanism also suggest a change in their relationship with the Brazilian population as a whole? What dangers did other students see in the call for the establishment of a republic?

Roderick and Jean Barman have suggested that the adoption of republicanism as a creed during this period was a result of the overproduction of law graduates and the inability of the centralized political system to adapt to accommodate this oversupply. The numbers seem to speak for themselves: in the 1870s, the average number of students graduating from the São Paulo law school was thirty; in the 1880s, the average had soared to seventy-six. This clearly made it difficult for many more men with law degrees to find jobs. And, indeed, this urgency among place seekers seems to be reflected in one of the first changes made once the new republican government was founded on 15 November 1889: states (as the imperial provinces were now called) were granted the responsibility for determining how many political and judicial positions there should be.[57] But the turn toward republicanism must have been more than just a response to decreased employment opportunities. Otherwise, republicanism would have been even stronger in Recife, where the number of graduates was much higher (63 *bacharéis* a year in the 1870s and 123 a year on average in the 1880s). Moreover, presumably, frustrations with the existing patronage network's ability to deliver the goods, so to speak, would have run much deeper, too. In fact, republicanism never gained much of a following in the northeast in general, and one must therefore consider again the diverging economic trajectories of the regions in which the law schools were located.[58]

One of the major reasons why republicanism gained more adherents in the southern school was that the centralized political system had been put in place in the 1820s when southern Brazil was still relatively undeveloped economically and politically. By the late imperial period, representation at the national level reflected political realities of a bygone era. Northeastern states whose economies had been relatively stagnant for decades had more representatives in the Senate and Chamber of Deputies than states like São Paulo and Rio Grande do Sul, whose economies and populations were expanding (and from which many of the major student republican leaders hailed). A more flexible political system could have adjusted to fit these new realities and would have expanded substantially the political and bureaucratic opportunities at the expense of the north.[59]

It is not surprising, therefore, that students in Recife, who tended to come from the provinces that benefited most politically from the status quo, should be less likely to join the ranks of republicans. Even with the overproduction of law graduates, they still had more to gain from keeping the system as it was. Students in Recife would also undergo a process of redefinition of their own, but their solution to the crisis of hegemony would be more philosophical than political.

In any case, the timing of the rise of student republicanism is also significant. Although republican student organizations were founded in São Paulo beginning in 1876, republicanism became increasingly popular among students after 1878, the year in which the Liberal Party returned to power.[60] In their ten-year absence from power, the Liberals had been known as "the martyr party" suffering "political ostracism."[61] Once back in power, however, they failed to carry out significant reforms. Some idealistic students, frustrated over the lack of reform, turned to republicanism.[62] Student republican disdain was often greater for the Liberal Party than for the Conservatives; they scorned Liberal "inertia and atrophy."[63] The long-term social transformation Brazil was undergoing was fundamental. However, the embrace of republicanism was, at least in part, a political response to a political problem.

As student identification with the Liberal Party was breaking down, so was the reverence for the ultimate national symbols: the imperial family and particularly the aging emperor himself. It is certainly worth speculating whether the emperor could really fill his role as the ultimate patron when the patronage networks as a whole were undergoing such strain. Portrayals of the emperor in the student press turned increasingly harsh. Students joked about the need to "make anatomical studies of the monarchical body because it seems unique; [although dead] it still remains standing."[64] Republicans organized against a third empire that would, they feared, follow the death of Dom Pedro II, presumably in the not too distant future.[65] This tactic may have been made easier by the emperor's failure to produce a male heir who lived to adulthood and by Princess Isabel's politically unwise choice of a French count as a husband. Student republicans charged that the Conde d'Eu would be the real ruler "because the individuality of the wife, no matter who she is, is absorbed and annihilated by her husband." The princess herself, as a woman known for her deep religious convictions, moreover, was a favorite target of republican propaganda.[66]

As national symbols were spent and conventional partisan identifications weakened, student republicans offered a new understanding of the nation itself, one that placed diverging regional interests over an overriding national interest. A turn to a decentralized form of government meant a move away from the idea that the nation-state was the highest good.[67] Students looked back to the regional rebellions of the 1830s (before the centralized imperial system had been fully established) for inspiration. Some of those most committed to republicanism were from the southernmost province of Rio Grande do Sul. They gathered together to form the Twentieth of September Club to study and celebrate the Farroupilha, the separatist revolt that took place in the province from 1835 to 1845. (This club continued to be important throughout the 1880s.)[68] One student, Joaquim Francisco de Assis Brasil, a rancher's son, wrote an account of the Farrapo rebellion at the request of his fellow club members. Assis Brasil would be a major figure in his home state's Republican Party in the years immediately following graduation and even more important after the establishment of the republic. In his history, he blamed the centralized imperial administration for ignoring the needs of the province and stifling local initiative. In 1835, he wrote, the general population in Rio Grande do Sul had seen little value in a central government that took everything and gave nothing in return. The parallel with the current situation he thought would be obvious to his readers. A federal system, he maintained, was the only one consistent with liberty.[69]

A decentralized government also seemed more in keeping with the interests of the more dynamic south. Southerners protested "the predominance that the north undoubtedly exercises over the south." There was a need for "self-government," a phrase used in English in student writings. The provinces received a disproportionate return from the central government, students complained.[70] Southern students described the federalist form of government as "not only the form of government most consistent with the principles of liberty and equality, but also the one that is best adapted to the integral and harmonious development of all the progressive forces of our society."[71]

On the national level, by the mid-1880s Liberal Party members had begun to respond, at least rhetorically, to the appeal of federalism for fear of losing the support of coffee plantation owners in western São Paulo.[72] In practice, however, the Liberal Party in power was no more inclined to adopt federal principles than the Conservative Party. Conservative students justified centralized power as not only necessary but popular. "The Brazilian people love central power," one student wrote. "What doesn't come from the imperial government doesn't have much authority."[73] Furthermore, a republic "would be an organism without a motor, . . . without a driving force to help it function with regularity."[74]

As students weighed in on the debate over imperial versus regional power, national ideals were reformulated in other ways. Federalism was justified because it was necessary for "order and progress." This slogan had been adopted from the French positivist thinker Auguste Comte and was introduced into the student vocabulary by student republicans.[75] "Order and progress is the republic," wrote Júlio de Castilhos, a student at the São Paulo school in the late 1870s and a future governor of his home state of Rio Grande do Sul under the Republican regime of the 1890s. "Order and progress is the objective of that part of our contemporary generation that is not consumed by a life of inertia and sterility."[76]

The slogan soon dominated student discourse, and members of all three parties represented in the law student body sought to lay claim to it. "Order and progress are the two principles of the Liberal Party," one student proclaimed.[77] Conservatives, for their part, rejected the right of either Liberals or Republicans to claim to stand for either order or progress, the former because they stood for "reform or revolution" and the latter because they were followers of the "bloody revolution of 1789." Order for the Conservatives did not mean "motionlessness," one student argued, but rather "harmony, complete equilibrium, a systematic and harmonious whole." "Without true order, one cannot have progress. Once you have order, progress will naturally follow."[78] Nevertheless, some Conservatives thought that even adopting a new slogan could pose risks. "Order and liberty are the two poles of the determined law of orbit within whose limits the Conservative Party moves, outside of which nothing is certain and true and everything is dangerous." Conservatives should content themselves with the "study of physical laws and calm reflection, a slow march without hurry."[79]

The refashioning of what we would now call a "usable past" was an important part of republican discourse. Certainly many students, Francophilic as ever, evoked the French Revolution and wrote poems celebrating its important leaders. (It should be noted, after all, that the republican ideal in France itself had only triumphed definitively in the 1870s.)[80] But the need to find Brazilian precedents for republican aspirations was even more pressing. One São Paulo newspaper editor stressed the "urgent necessity . . . of rehabilitating our historic traditions, that have been so evilly and nauseatingly appropriated by the adulators of the monarchy."[81] We have already seen how students from Rio Grande do Sul, as well as other student republicans, looked to the Farroupilha of the 1830s and 1840s. Student republicans also reclaimed heroes such as Tiradentes, martyred hero of a conspiracy nipped in the bud in colonial Minas Gerais. The students liked to remind their readers that Tiradentes had been "ordered decapitated by the great-grandmother of the current Emperor of Brazil." "We are your sons, Tiradentes," the students claimed, in contrast with their own fathers who had listened "to the throne's perfidious counsels."[82] In this respect, student republicanism represented in part a generational rebellion and reflected the recurrent need for each generation to present itself as the idealistic vanguard. "Youth," one republican student addressed his fellow students, "you are always first in the grand struggles."[83]

In arguments over the past, however, both monarchists and republicans could lay claim to an understanding of the lessons of history. Conservative students took pride in their party's claim to have "saved the Empire from general anarchy, and perhaps from dissolution" in the 1830s. Republicans, Conservative students charged, were in danger of encouraging social anarchy.[84] "Revolutionaries will never obtain the voluntary and peaceful submission of the inferior classes to the superior classes," argued one Conservative student, clearly aware of his political class's traditional hegemony over Brazilian society.[85]

Like the liberals of mid-century, however, the majority of student republicans continued to stress caution and moderation in their discourse. In fact, republicans contended that the republic represented a "perfect equilibrium of elements of order and progress, a just harmony between authority and liberty."[86] Perhaps because of the republican emphasis on order, there is little evidence of increasing political conflict between faculty and students in the late imperial period, despite many students' turn to the left. Adorno claims that there was a "politicization of indiscipline" at the São Paulo school beginning in 1871. For evidence, however, he offers only the incident in 1871 itself, when changes in the ways examinations were administered led to the

destruction of school property. The incident had no larger political ramifications and in no way did it mark a turning point at the school.[87]

Even the emperor Dom Pedro II himself seemed unperturbed by the law
students' republican tendencies. When a law professor tried to have a student punished for publicly criticizing him in print, the emperor pardoned
him, noting "I have good will towards this young man." Somewhat surprisingly, the student had once sent the monarch two copies of a pamphlet in
verse in which he ridiculed him. The young man had even sent his publication via registered mail.[88] The emperor himself claimed not to consider
monarchy inherently superior to the republic, although it has been argued
that he did not take Brazilian republicans all that seriously. "For him," his
biographer Roderick Barman notes, "its supporters rather resembled children playing at being adults, a fantasy to be permitted and indulged but not
to be confused with the realities of life."[89] The ideological laxity of the
powers that be guaranteed that student rebellion had few costs. And proclaiming oneself a republican could have real benefits among one's fellow
students.

Given the rhetorical emphasis on order, to what degree did republicanism represent a new orientation toward the popular classes? There were
hints of a new political style developing in Brazilian cities, particularly in
the renewed campaign for abolition after 1878. A new style was also evident
in the efforts to organize for a republic, both of which involved giving
speeches in public squares. Sandra Lauderdale Graham has suggested that
Brazilian political culture was transformed during this period because of a
riot in Rio de Janeiro over a decision to impose a tax on the use of the city's
tramways. Although the riot was short lived, Lauderdale Graham has suggested that this popular protest, the first of its kind in forty years, created
the possibilities for "redefining the actors, audience, and stage-setting of political culture." Politics, previously viewed as an elite activity consisting of
speeches given before a select audience in congressional auditoriums, was
never the same again. Republicans and abolitionists, and even mainstream
politicians, began to use public spaces to organize popular support through
direct appeals to urban interests.[90] Even the student press showed evidence
of a new relation to "the people." A student newspaper in Recife, for example, set its price low so it could be sold to the popular classes.[91] Viewed from

the perspective of later developments in Brazilian history, particularly twentieth-century populism, the shift Lauderdale Graham argues for seems relatively slight. Nevertheless, to the politicians of the day it seemed highly significant and threatening.

Student republicans were in the forefront of calls to organize "conferences in the public squares."[92] Students disagreed, however, over the degree to which the Brazilian population at large was ready for the republic and how much effort was needed to change popular attitudes regarding the monarchy itself. Few student republicans doubted that it was their role to "educate the people and show the way to follow."[93] "In the circumstances in which we find our country," one student wrote, what was needed was "a slow and peaceful propaganda, demonstrating the scientifically incontestable and evident historical legitimacy of the republic in Brazil." Another student, on the other hand, confidently argued in 1882 that "Catholicism no longer exercises considerable influence over the spirit of the people." Since "the religious spirit" had long been a powerful support of monarchies that granted the Crown political legitimacy, it would now be relatively easy for a new republican order to be established. Some saw (or claimed to see) evidence that republicanism was "the fertile idea that is penetrating the brain of the Brazilian people, agitating it, impelling it, electrifying it."[94] Nevertheless, most saw a need, at the least, for a long-term educational process for the Brazilian people. The need for an active tutelary role signified a change, if hardly a complete break with the past. Instead of relying upon an assumed deference from the poor, republicans argued for a more active relationship with them, one, however, that continued to assume the law students' superiority.

Both on a national level and in the law student body, Republicans were split between evolutionary and revolutionary wings, though most students belonged to the former. Others, however, satirized the evolutionists as the "ideal form of republicans. With folded arms they await the coming of the republic, and while the republic does not materialize, the republicans are ministers, deputies, senators, and councilors of state."[95]

Conservative students certainly felt threatened by the proposed alliances with the popular classes, however unequal that relationship might be. Conservative Party members took pride in the fact that they would never be misled by what they termed the "unthinking applause of the masses." "Whoever adulates the people," one student wrote, "runs the risk of having to submit to its excesses." One should not "shout" in the public square for "too much liberty." Down that road lay anarchy. Conservatives saw themselves as "sleeping atop a volcano." A republic would create conditions in which "a citizen certainly would be obliged to defend the honor of his family by force of arms."[96]

As far as popular aspirations went, Republicans on the national level proved to be less idealistic than their student counterparts by demonstrating a willingness to temporize on the issue of abolition in order to gain the support of large landowners.[97] Students, not surprisingly, were often less willing to compromise on abolition merely to gain adherents to a particular party in elections. A new generation of abolitionists among the law student body portrayed landowners in no uncertain terms as the enemy of idealistic youth.[98] With the revival of the national debate over abolition in the late 1870s, students actively began forming commissions again to agitate for abolition and to create organizations that would purchase the liberty of particular slaves. One student wrote that as landowners' sons who had benefited financially from the labor of slaves, they had a responsibility to pay their debt to slaves. A belief in abolitionism, however, often went hand in hand with a tendency to blame the slaves themselves, rather than the institution of slavery itself, for Brazil's lack of technical progress. Student abolitionists, like their elders, called for more efforts to attract northern European, particularly German, workers.[99]

With the abolition of slavery on 13 May 1888, the monarchy gained a new popularity among the popular classes, particularly in Rio de Janeiro. One Rio newspaper chided the Republicans for their failure to understand this: "The apparent crime of counter-revolution which they [the popular classes] appear to perpetrate is natural and arises logically from their own interests, demonstrating that the intuition of the masses had greater value than the science of the *bacharéis* — not knowing how to read, they are not deluded by paper promises. All they see is the monopolists of the land, those who only yesterday were beating and whipping them. Their own reason will tell them that the exploiters of the past will be those who will always exploit them in the future."[100]

As this critic of actually existing republicanism suggested, the limits of the republican message should not be forgotten. Neither student Republicans nor the relatively few men in Rio and other southern cities who were calling for the establishment of a new form of government were particularly radical. For many students, republicanism was merely part of a larger search for new forms of identity that would ensure their continued authority over Brazilian society at large. Both Republicans and their student critics sought to redefine national ideals, giving renewed emphasis to the concept of progress and making claims for their ability to achieve that objective. Order remained a paramount goal for elite students. In the long run, republicanism primarily would involve making political power more congruent with new economic interests.

A NEW STUDENT IDEAL

Republicanism was less of an issue in the north, where the economy was stagnating and the larger setting of Recife was ill suited for ideological experimentation. But even among students in São Paulo, where the economy was booming and new ideas were in the air, republicanism was hardly universally accepted, as the critics quoted in the preceding section make clear. Nevertheless, new identities and ideologies were being explored in both places. If the student political ideal of the late 1870s and 1880s politically was to be a republican, intellectually it was to be a positivist. If the ideal student of this period wrote literature, he was supposed to be a realist rather than a Romantic — assuming he did not abandon literature altogether for social science.

Many students to be sure continued to pursue the older student ideal of the literary man. In many ways, however, a young man like Júlio de Castilhos, who would thrive in the first decade of the republic, represented a distinctively different style of Brazilian elite manhood, one that emphasized political activism and sociological analysis over poetic inspiration. Castilhos was neither a poet nor an orator. Even when he overcame his stuttering problems, he never grew fond of public speaking, but his political writings were among the sharpest of his time.[101]

Older Republicans expected the younger students to understand that republicanism implied both a new ideology and a new style. In the 5 October 1885 issue of *Revista Republicana*, an editor criticized a student Republican (who happened to be the son of Quintino Bocayuva, an important evolutionary Republican propagandist) for writing poetry in the style of Romantic poet Casimiro de Abreu and other poets "that made Brazil shed tears endlessly some forty years ago." A "Republican orator needs vigor, a certain masculine coloration, that enlightens and persuades," he chided. Republicanism required, therefore, not only an ideology that placed the good of the province over the nation-state, but also what was now considered a more manly man.

Although literature remained important, its character had altered significantly. Many student Republicans linked political reform with a new style of more socially conscious literature. Literature no longer would have the personal character that had distinguished it for decades. "The novel," one student wrote, "as well as the drama and the poetry of our time, should be inspired principally by the duties of man as a citizen and by the larger problems that agitate society, always seeking to characterize these problems truthfully and with feeling."[102] The Romanticism of a previous generation was to be replaced with a new realism whose aim was achieving "documentary fidelity."[103] "Dark Romanticism died / the night before / expiring like a vagrant / in a bed of stolen water," proclaimed one Recife student.[104] The influence of French authors continued to be important to this new generation; instead of Victor Hugo, however, the new model was Emile Zola. Literature was now understood less as the creation of individual genius and more as a product of social relations.

The new generation defined itself as anti-Romantic. Student literary theorists called for a style that was clearer and simpler, not so burdened with the Romantic "rhetorical flowers" that disguised "immoralities." This change in literary style involved a move from "subjective" intuition to "objective" knowledge and from "pastoral" and lyrical verses to "scientific" poetry.[105] The "end of subjectivity" was declared. Romantic ideals of intuition and inspiration were to be replaced by observation and the testing of general theories. As science came to be seen as the "only valid and useful form of knowledge," literature should now adapt its methods.[106] The Indianismo of the Romantics was rejected as well. Instead, one can see the embrace of the new "scientific racism," in which Brazil's experience of miscegenation was now understood to have been a principal reason for the nation's failure to develop.[107]

It is debatable, however, to what degree the writers of this generation escaped the pull of Romanticism in practice. Their anti-Romantic poses were imbued with a Romantic attitude. Even law students with more time on their hands than previous generations did not devote themselves to crafting novels in which the analysis of society could bear fruit. Such social science fiction remained an aspiration more than a reality. Students continued to write poetry, although more of it would have a political and social orientation. A decade after his death, Castro Alves remained the student ideal of the engaged poet. "Besides everything else" that one could admire about him, one student wrote, "he was not an individualist poet."[108] Whether socially engaged or not, many regarded the poets of the late imperial period as of a much lower caliber than the best of previous generations, such as Álvares de Azevedo and Castro Alves.[109]

In any case, many had begun to reject the literary ideal altogether. "It is not with words that we have to construct the great building that is called Brazil," one student wrote, in pointed rebuke to the aspirations of previous generations.[110] "Literature," ardent republican Silva Jardim noted, "finds itself abandoned by the most talented."[111] Certainly, the desire to replace the literary ideal with a new one more oriented around science could seem threatening, and many saw the need to find a new ideal that would not consign them to irrelevance in the eyes of the larger society.

The new students needed an ideology and a new source of cultural authority. They found the former in positivism and evolutionary thought generally and the latter in social science.[112] Although some have argued that the influence of positivism was overstated, even its opponents argued that it was the dominant creed among their law school colleagues.[113] Many student republicans derived their politics from theories of evolution being promulgated in the North Atlantic cultures by such thinkers as Herbert Spencer.[114] An important newspaper from this period was titled simply *Evolution*. The lessons that evolution taught were simple; one student dismissed those "who imprudently persist in not comprehending that historic laws are irresistible." For Júlio de Castilhos, developments seemed to follow these laws as "mathematical . . . , infallible . . . , and invariable." The "inexorable logic of events" demonstrated that the monarchy was "agonizing in the throes of death."[115] (The emphasis on irresistibility, infallibility, invariability, and inexorability suggest the type of authoritarian personality Castilhos would demonstrate in the 1890s as governor of Rio Grande do Sul.)

Many students declared themselves to be followers of the founder of positivism, Auguste Comte. Student newspapers occasionally even employed the positivist calendar.[116] Although Comte died in 1857, his ideas did not gain currency in Brazil until the mid-1870s. As an ideology that placed a premium on order, positivism was particularly attractive to Brazilian elites.[117] A Comtean understanding of the world involved dividing world history into distinct phases through which all societies passed. Brazil, still languishing in the "theological-metaphysical" phase, would have to move forward to the new industrial, "positive" phase. The evidence that Brazil needed to move beyond an agricultural society was clear to those with their eyes on the North Atlantic world. The railroads, both a sign and tool of Brazil's technological and economic development, required skilled workers, which Brazil had to import. Even the names of law student newspapers indicated the new scientific and technological orientation (*The Embryo* and *Locomotive*, for example, in São Paulo).[118] To some extent, the new, almost technocratic ideal was regional, even provincial. The "verses of a Paulista," it was said, were "good roads, machines, agriculture, improvements."[119]

How did the law students themselves fit into this new understanding of historical development? How could they avoid becoming irrelevant? They no longer seemed to be in the vanguard of society. Comte himself had been trained as an engineer; Spencer quite explicitly rejected domination by the literati.

The answer to this conundrum was to portray themselves, of course, as scientists of a particular type: ones who studied society. The slogan of the new generation, "order and progress," was, after all, "the sociological dogma."[120] The students' new role was to study the unchanging laws of social change, diagnose society's ills, and prescribe a cure.[121] The editors of *A República* declared that they were "all followers of modern sociological principles."[122] While a previous generation had specifically emphasized the development of a national literature as their calling, one Republican newspaper in 1880 wrote of the "need . . . to study social and political questions in a more rational, scientific way to provide solutions in accordance with the evolving march of society."[123] "Instead of the novel, of poetry, this transitory

. . . literature without any practical use, the new generation devotes itself to the study of economic questions [and] sociology."[124] Students saw themselves as studying "positively" the questions that were taught metaphysically in law school. Social science was seen as "indispensable for the salvation of our country."[125]

In defending his doctoral thesis in Recife, Sílvio Romero, later one of the foremost social and literary theorists of his day, exemplified the intellectual arrogance of the positivists (and of youth) who felt they understood the laws governing society and disdained all who did not share his ideas. He informed his examining committee that "metaphysics doesn't exist anymore, in case you didn't know it." When one of the professors responded that he had not known this, Romero retorted, "Then go study and learn." "Was it you that killed metaphysics?" one professor then inquired. "It was progress and civilization," Romero replied. Then he left the room after declaring, "I am not here to [respond to] this mob of ignorant people who know nothing."[126]

Although less attracted to republicanism, students in Pernambuco were no less engaged in trying to define a new understanding of themselves in changing times. Recife partisans have argued that the northern school, located as it was on the coast, had more access to cutting-edge European ideas than the land-locked southern school, although by the late nineteenth century this interpretation seems more than a bit anachronistic. In any case, most point to the so-called Recife School and its guiding light, Tobias Barreto.[127] He has been called "the most notable professor that the Brazilian law schools ever had." Moreover, it has been argued, his influence on his students was particularly great. "The young men who had him for a teacher became his fanatical followers."[128] His popularity with the young law students of Recife stemmed not only from his openness to new ideas but also from his habit of spending his leisure time in the same cafés, theaters, and taverns that his students did.[129] This man of modest background spent his years after law school practicing law and studying German, and even, as we have seen, publishing newspapers in German in a provincial town where no one else spoke the language. He sought to lessen the influence of French thinkers in Brazil and hoped to replace the rampant Francophilia with a reverence for German accomplishments and ideas. Like others of his time, Barreto emphasized the development of law as a social product as well as the role of evolution in his philosophical and scientific writings. Students saw in him the promise of reconciling the increasingly fragmented identities at the law school. As a poet, one student wrote, Barreto spoke as a man of science, and as a man of science, he improvised as a poet. Moreover, despite the fact that he was not a particularly political person, he was said to have "an intensely democratic and profoundly republican temperament."[130]

The importance of Tobias Barreto at the Recife law school has been exaggerated, however. He was isolated on the faculty and actively opposed by professors who still taught the divine origin of laws; he was not able to help a candidate supportive of his ideas get a job there in 1885. (Barreto's isolation was, in part, a result of his personality. Even an instructor more attuned to Barreto's way of thinking might find himself the object of his scorn because while Barreto followed German evolutionists such as Rudolf von Jhering, his colleague admired Spencer.)[131] In any case, Barreto did not even get a regular teaching position until 1887, after five years as a substitute. His promotion did not necessarily suggest that his colleagues now adhered to his ideas. He was promoted because, as the rule of seniority required, he had been a substitute longer than anyone else. Moreover, his poor health in the last three years of his life limited his effectiveness as a teacher and his ability to transform the northern school. He died in June 1889.[132]

Barreto was more of a scholar than an activist and perhaps more of a bohemian than either. The students' admiration for him did not signify that they had a greater interest in learning than the students of previous generations, though some did go on to make important contributions to Brazil's intellectual life. Most liked his openness and his willingness to challenge the reigning orthodoxies at the northern school. His example further legitimized their effort to redefine themselves.

To what extent did the law students' exploration of new identities imply firm ideological commitments on their part? One student, who pseudonymously published his memoirs of his student days after graduating in 1882, was skeptical equally of the political trend toward republicanism, the intellectual inclination toward positivism, and the literary bent toward realism. He considered his colleagues to be little more than opportunists and did not take their ideological commitments all that seriously. The students, however, were clearly opportunistic only to the extent that their republicanism represented a desire to gain a reputation among their colleagues. As the memoirist himself noted, his fellow students would soon discover that poetry and republicanism did not go together, especially once they found themselves after graduation working in their "sinecures, the Siberia of all ardent aspirations."[133]

For many, of course, the interest in positivism or republicanism may have been no more than a passing fad, part of youth's process of exploring new roles and identities. The twentieth-century phenomenon of "radical student, conservative graduate" undoubtedly was commonplace in late imperial Brazil. After all, republican aspirations, while they were undoubtedly popular among one's fellow students, did not go far in the outside world. A good example of the failure to live up to student ideals was Afonso Celso. An ardent republican during his student days (he edited the newspaper *A República*), this son of the Viscount of Ouro Preto forsook his republicanism immediately after graduating in 1881 when his father arranged for him to represent a remote, drought-prone part of his native province of Minas Gerais in the imperial legislature. The former republican was not yet twenty-two when he took his seat in the Chamber of Deputies; he represented the same district until the fall of the empire in 1889. Afonso Celso later rejected the charge that his entrance into national politics at such an early age represented a "characteristic example of monarchical corruption."[134] Yet, for many students, his election perfectly exemplified the closed political system of patronage and nepotism against which student republicans claimed to be fighting. In the student press to which he had recently contributed, Celso was accused of apostasy.[135] Others complained that the government was generally composed of mediocre men when it should have been open to those who exhibit "talent, patriotism, and civic duty."[136] Clearly, these calls for the establishment of a true meritocracy must have had special resonance at a time when jobs were becoming harder to come by.

Nevertheless, opportunities were increasing for those who wanted to make a living while remaining true to their aspirations. For example, despite his marriage to the daughter of a professor and Liberal Party stalwart, Silva Jardim continued to represent the revolutionary wing of Republicanism after graduation by traveling around the country encouraging opposition to the monarchy.[137] Castilhos, after his graduation, became an editor of *A Feder-*

ação, a Porto Alegre newspaper founded by a member of the pivotal class of 1868.[138] By the late 1870s, many Republican newspapers were being founded in southern provinces, often by people who made their daily living as lawyers. As lawyers, they could continue to be politically active without sacrificing their ideology by joining the Liberal Party. Some, like Borges de Medeiros, Castilhos's successor as Rio Grande do Sul's strongman, spent more time during their working hours recruiting converts to the cause than preparing legal briefs.[139] A Republican party was founded in Rio Grande do Sul in 1882. Assis Brasil himself became the first Republican elected to the provincial assembly in 1886. By the fall of the empire, Republicans outnumbered Conservatives in the southernmost province, but they were still a minority compared to members of the traditionally strong Liberal Party. In São Paulo, as well, there were as many Republicans as Conservatives in 1889, but there were still twice as many members of the Liberal Party.[140] In Recife, a "Republican Center" was founded in 1886, but its importance was much less than that of Republican clubs in the south.[141] Most of the Republican newspapers and an even larger percentage of the Republican clubs were concentrated in three provinces: São Paulo, Rio Grande do Sul, and Rio de Janeiro.[142]

In any event, it was the military, and not the law students or *bacharéis*, who overthrew the empire on 15 November 1889. In the early years of the republic it would be decided whether the military would be able to replace the traditional elite male identity with one modeled after their own technocratic and positivistic inclinations. Some have claimed that a new elite arose after 1870.[143] I have argued, however, that while Brazil was changing, the law students remained key players in the discussion of who had the right to rule over Brazil. Many Brazilian law students continued to embrace the long-standing literary ideal. Others, however, found a new justification for their role in society by embracing a new philosophy in positivism, a new source of cultural authority in social science, and a new definition of the nation as a decentralized republic instead of a centralized constitutional monarchy. The new student ideal was of a man in tune with historic laws of evolution and inspired more by sociology than by literature, but still the idealistic vanguard in a corrupt society. Time would tell whether that ideal could continue to guarantee the *bacharéis* their hegemony over Brazilian society.

CONCLUSION

Say what they like, do what they may, whatever happens, whether in the name of the

people or the army, . . . Brazil will always be governed by men of letters, by the pen and

the word — by the bacharéis, *in short — because they were, are, and will always be the*

elite of the nation. **Estevão Leão Borroul,** *Não* (1890)

The simple faith of Estevão Leão Borroul, an ordinary *bacharel*, that he had the right to lead Brazilian society, had been shared by generations of law students. This was the crucial lesson learned at law school. It was not taught primarily by teachers. Although professors could also use this language, particularly on important occasions like the Eleventh of August celebrations, they resented the young men's attitude that they were already prepared to take up the reins of leadership, a conviction that made them frequently unteachable. The lesson was one that society taught law students in their daily interactions and relationships and one they taught each other in their active extracurricular lives. It was a message embedded in their student culture. The law school experience was certainly in part an indoctrination into the attitude and values of the ruling class, although that indoctrination inhered more in the whole process of socialization than in the formal teaching.

Moreover, the students' self-understanding changed over time. The first generation of law students tried to define themselves against their Portuguese heritage, saw themselves as liberals, and gradually decided that the regional revolts of the 1830s suggested the need to find ways to harness the explosive potential of liberalism in a slave society. These students did not necessarily know they would be the dominant force in politics and were taught even less effectively than subsequent generations. Nevertheless, they became the most loyal of all imperial bureaucrats and politicians. The imperial system gave them a central role to play in Brazilian politics and opened up opportunities for leadership on a national level at a time when the number of legally trained young men was still quite small. By the 1840s, students were more conscious of themselves as a ruling class, and they sought sources of cultural authority outside of the political realm to justify their social dominance. Literature became a means to an end: to define a particular identity and mission that gave a special justification to their continued rule even when liberalism itself had become problematic.

For this generation, the memories of the regional revolts were still fresh. Nevertheless, the troublesome liberal discourse never stopped being a central part of student identity. The law students sought to redefine the liberal discourse to fit Brazilian society as they wanted it to continue to be, politically stable and hierarchical. By the 1860s, international events, like the Civil War in the United States, and domestic political trends, like the rebirth of partisanship after a generation of political tranquility, opened up new opportunities for self-definition. The ability to manipulate language continued to play a central role in their identity. Students sought, however, to stake a claim to being the class that was truest to the ideals of liberalism and therefore best able to transform Brazil along the lines of the models they most admired, those of England and France. For this reason, the generation of the 1860s, particularly during the War of the Triple Alliance, embraced abolitionism as a central part of its student identity. By the late imperial period, the young men at the law schools, under attack from new social and economic interests, began to search for a new justification for their continued dominant role in Brazilian society. They found it in positivism and social science, and many turned against the monarchy itself and embraced republicanism.

One of the reasons the students felt a need in the late 1870s and 1880s to remake themselves was that they had new rivals for cultural authority. A particularly important one was the military. It had long been a force in Spanish American politics, but it had been effectively kept out of the political arena under the Brazilian imperial system (with the notable exception of the "coup" of 1868, in which the military commander forced the emperor to turn out the Liberal government). After the abdication of Dom Pedro I in 1831, as we have seen, landowners sought to downsize the armed forces and created the National Guard, which was under their own control. (The law students themselves supported the creation of the National Guard.) Sons of the land-owning class did not view the military as an attractive career path. Military commanders were under the authority of provincial presidents (as the incident between the military and the São Paulo law students described in chapter 3 makes clear). These presidents were, themselves of course, largely law school graduates. Civilian politicians abused their authority to draft political rivals or their clients into the military so as to remove them from the scene at election time.[1]

The military's lack of prestige relative to the law school graduates began to change somewhat with the War of the Triple Alliance, in which Brazil was embarrassed by the length of time it took to subdue such a small country as Paraguay. By the end of the war, an estimated 111,000 Brazilians had served in the military. The ordeal of the war suggested the need for a new, professionalized military that would be strong enough to live up to the country's aspirations to regional leadership. The experience of the war had also helped establish a greater sense of corporate identity among the military and a new belief that they had a role to play in transforming the nation.[2]

Although military schools predated the law schools, the Academia Real Militar having been founded in 1810, they were relatively insignificant institutions, politically speaking, during the following decades when the law schools became dominant.[3] Even within the armed services themselves, education at the military academies was not necessary for promotion within the ranks. Over the course of the imperial period, the armed forces became more open to talent, regardless of social background, than the rest of Brazilian society. Military men were acutely conscious of the ways the imperial system benefited a political class that was defined largely by birth and connections. At the same time, from 1850 on, the military officer corps gradually became more professional, and officers were more likely to have been educated at the military academies.[4]

After the war was over, both military men and civilians called for change in the military academies.[5] The reformed schools created an institutional framework for producing an alternate hegemonic male identity to that inculcated in the law schools. The Escola Militar provided training in engineering from its founding in 1838 to 1859. Educational opportunities in engineering expanded with the founding in 1859 of the Escola Central, a civilian engineering school whose activities were under the authority of the minister of war until 1874. Reformed and renamed the Escola Politécnica in 1874, the school, now under the minister of the interior, opened up new possibilities for young men interested in employment on the railroads.

The military academies, however, remained the main provider of technical education in the country.[6] Beginning in the mid-1870s, students at the military academies could take a course in military engineering in their final years, instead of having to study with civilians. More mathematics and physical science courses were added to the military curriculum, as well, because of the strong influence of positivists among the faculty. A military education, with its emphasis on technical training at government expense, became more attractive for sons of the middle class.[7] As Angel Rama suggests, the increasing valorization of training in engineering and the sciences that accompanied the rise of positivist ideas "tempered" the "hegemony of law."[8] The students, as we have seen, were quick to respond to this threat to their authority.

Before the 1880s, the military was a relatively insignificant force in political terms, a fact that law students frequently noted as proof of the superiority of Brazil's imperial political system over that of its neighbors. Military men had been influential only to the degree that they had ties to important political patrons. (Officers had far fewer opportunities to become powerful patrons in their own right.) Beginning in the 1880s, however, young reform-minded members of the military began to function more as a pressure group to voice their own interests. They published their own newspapers (crucial, as we have seen, to the formation of a corporate identity). Military men even began to run for political office after the reform of 1881 established direct elections in place of the previous electoral system. The Military Club, founded in 1887 in Rio de Janeiro, became an effective forum for military grievances and aided the creation of both a group and a politicized military identity. In a popular political move, the club passed a resolution in November of that year promising that they would no longer take part in the retrieval of fugitive slaves. Students at the military academy in Rio de Janeiro, for their part, also became increasingly politically active.[9]

Military men began to see themselves as a force for political change in the nation. The refusal of civilian politicians to take their concerns seriously was galling. Salaries set in 1857, for example, were not granted until 1887, despite a further pay increase passed by the imperial legislature in 1873. After its return to power in 1878, the Liberal Party, in particular, had sought to reduce appropriations for the military (no doubt in part because of bitter memories of its experience in 1868). Military men also grew resentful when they were punished for attempting to defend the "honor" of the military class from attacks in the civilian press.[10]

Military men began to reject what they saw as the corruption of the civilian politicians, whom they referred to disdainfully as *casacas*, or "suits." As technically trained men, moreover, they began to see themselves as the ones with the skills to transform Brazilian society. While their disdain for the literary elite and the civilian politicians grew, however, they were also being courted by some republican *bacharéis* who sought their aid in plotting to overthrow the monarch after 1886. Civilian republicans were divided over the wisdom of this course of action. The evolutionary republicans argued that the transition to the republic would come in time and so opposed this strategy.[11] Not surprisingly, many civilians were uneasy about seeking the aid of the military to foment a coup.

As Celso Castro helpfully reminds us, it was a "small and specific" "group of military men," and not the military as a monolith, that brought down the monarchy in November 1889. Of particular importance was a group that included junior officers and military academy students, most of whom were generally thought to have been influenced by the positivist teachings of the Escola Militar's math professor, Benjamin Constant Botelho de Magalhães.[12] No military leader, even those who had long been loyal to the emperor, took the initiative to lead a defense of the imperial system, largely because military concerns had been neglected for decades. As the monarchist Eduardo Prado remarked, "The divorce of the emperor from military matters . . . was what saved Brazilian civilization, but it was what made [Dom Pedro II] lose the monarchy."[13]

The republican regime that resulted showed signs of change as well as continuity with the old regime. Some military men hoped that the establishment of the republic would also mean an end to the political power of the graduates of the law schools. In fact, however, the republic did not usher in either a technocracy (this would have to wait until the military coup of 1964) or what might be called a "socioligarchy." Nevertheless, the literary elite's monopoly over political power was broken. The republic provided opportunities for political power and cultural authority for men with more diverse educational backgrounds.

During the Old Republic (1889–1930), men with more diverse educational backgrounds, such as degrees in engineering and agronomy, pursued careers in politics.[14] Antonio Francisco de Paula de Souza, for example, was the grandson of early proponents of Brazilian independence and the son of a coffee plantation owner in São Paulo. He studied engineering in Europe in the 1860s and became a republican after his return to Brazil. He worked on railroads in both the United States and Brazil. With the coming of the republic, he served as superintendent of public works in São Paulo as well as in the ministries of foreign affairs and agriculture under President Floriano Peixoto. Elected to his home state assembly, he introduced a bill to create a technical school modeled after those he had experienced in Germany.[15] In terms of cultural production, as well, a man like Euclydes da Cunha, trained as an engineer and the "epitome of the new scientific professional," could take a leading role. He wrote perhaps the literary masterpiece of the Old Republic, *Os Sertões* (published in English as *Rebellion in the Backlands*), an account of the republican government's war against a millenarian movement in Bahia as well as a meditation on national identity.[16] Public health officials also gained a new cultural prestige, largely because of their successful efforts to eliminate epidemic diseases at the turn of the century. Students in the health professions even began to outnumber law students in the early twentieth century. One intellectual suggested that Brazil should "get rid of the Bachelor of Arts, of the '*Traitema Baccalaureatus*,' and hand all power to the hygienists for them to 'sanitize' the country." Medical doctors sought to provide "scientific orientation that would ensure the execution of appropriate laws and give stability and purposefulness to the best plans for the progress and enrichment of the country." They gave particular attention to racial issues.[17]

The importance of some of the new intellectual trends in the late imperial period bore greater fruit under the republic. Positivists gained political power; eighteen served as governors in eleven states, although their influence was strongest in the state of Rio Grande do Sul.[18] The republic employed many positivist symbols, but the fundamental revisions of the national ideal were completed by liberal federalists from São Paulo.[19] In any case, civilians, such as Rui Barbosa, had continued to play a major role in the early republican cabinets. The military's "fragile unity" in 1889 could not survive the fractionalization that often accompanies power.[20] By 1894, the military had become fearful of the corrupting impact of political participation on their professional identity and of increasing divisions within their ranks. They consequently returned to the barracks and eventually ceded power to the São Paulo land-owning elite, although some individuals continued to be "politically active."[21] Only one more military man would be elected president during the remaining years of the Old Republic. Civilian supremacy had been reaffirmed and that meant that law school graduates would continue to play the dominant political role.

The dream of a decentralized federal government held by so many law students in the late imperial period redounded in practice to the advantage of representatives of Brazil's new economic forces, particularly those in São Paulo. By and large, the Old Republic was run by and for the western São Paulo coffee interests, and the southern law school continued to have more than a provincial importance. Most of the Brazilian presidents after 1894 (six of nine) were graduates of the São Paulo law school.

Law schools themselves continued to be centers for the production of the most important state agents. The number of schools, in fact, increased exponentially with the coming of the republic. Many states created their own law schools to create their own cadres of what they in turn hoped would be politicians and bureaucrats loyal to state interests. This had a limited impact on the São Paulo school, as their state's national prominence guaranteed them a continued influence. The Recife law school, however, declined dramatically in national importance with the fall of the empire. Local leaders continued to graduate from there, but the school lost influence even in regional terms. By and large, the proliferation of law schools helped ensure that the politicians of the republican period were much more tied to their home states than their imperial counterparts had been. The republican leaders were, in this sense and perhaps in others, more provincial.[22]

With the republic, the extracurricular life of the students lost its traditional vigor. In Recife, an official law school publication was created that was dominated by the faculty and administration rather than the students themselves.[23] The inevitable decline of São Paulo's college-town flavor accelerated in the Old Republic as the city grew and industrialized. The daily press expanded dramatically. Daily newspapers such as *O Estado de São Paulo* were by now far more important than student papers.[24] Moreover, the student press ceased to serve an important function as one of the molders of national identity. This was because in the decentralized political system of the Old Republic a national elite male identity was a goal neither of administrative overseers nor even of the students themselves. As the student press became moribund, so too did other symbols of collective identity and locations where significant socialization experiences had formerly occurred. The *repúblicas*, already in decline in the late imperial period, were virtually extinct as an institution by the early 1900s.[25]

Professors at both law schools had quickly adjusted to the new political situation. On 19 November 1889, faculty members on both campuses convened to discuss recent events. Not long before, teachers had celebrated Dom Pedro II's evident return to good health and expressed a faith that with his recovery the empire would last for many years. Now, they declared their loyalty to the republic. The forms of address changed from "God save your excellency" in the opening months of 1889 to "Health and Fraternity" by the end of the year. The minister in charge of education for the provisional government (Aristides Lobo, himself a member of the Recife class of 1859) was called "Citizen Minister." As members of the Constituent Assembly, law school faculty members were involved in the drafting of the new republican constitution.[26]

For some *bacharéis*, the transition from the imperial to the republican system was not easy. Sons of prominent politicians under the empire like Joaquim Nabuco and Afonso Celso abandoned political careers after 1889. Both looked back on the imperial period with strong nostalgia. Nabuco finally accepted an offer of a diplomatic posting in 1900 in order to become reconciled to the nation.[27] Some of the law students in the first generation of the Old Republic also found it difficult to adjust to the new situation, and by the mid-1890s some were quite active as members of a monarchist party. The student monarchists were particularly concerned about the new political role of the military, which *bacharéis* of the old school complained made Brazil more like Spanish America. Monarchists as a group revered tradition and idealized the empire as a "model of civic virtue and conservative religiosity" (although on this latter point the students must have had particularly short memories).[28]

For many other *bacharéis*, however, the transition to the new form of government went as smoothly as that of the professors. Campos Sales, who had seen his political ambitions stunted under the imperial political system and had long hoped for the establishment of a republic, rose to the presidency. Others like Rodrigues Alves, who had actively repressed republicans as an official in the imperial period, adjusted just as quickly and went on to serve as president of the republic as well.[29]

The centralized imperial political system was replaced by a decentralized government. Crucially for the *bacharéis*, local states were able to make their own policies (as long as they did not adversely affect the fortunes of the coffee interests). Presidents of what were now states were able to create jobs, fill them, and set salaries. States in the center-south flourished under this system, particularly São Paulo, while the decline of northeastern states continued to accelerate.[30]

Part of the problem was the northeastern states' inability to develop strong party structures. The relative underdevelopment of republicanism among the northern law students had ramifications for the political developments of the early republican period. In Pernambuco, where a republican party (as opposed to a club) had failed to develop before the fall of the empire, those sympathetic to republicanism lost out to adaptable, former monarchists. Pernambuco was weak in Congress because of factionalism and because of its large illiterate population, who were denied the right to vote. Under the federal system, Pernambuco continued to stagnate economically and found itself unable to defend its own interests. In Bahia, as well, the imperial republican clubs were unable to transform themselves into a dominant republican party.[31] Although the republicans in Minas Gerais were disorganized in 1889, the *bacharéis* in the Mineiro Republican Party became the bulwark of congressional support for the republic's division of power between São Paulo and Minas (the so-called coffee- with-milk alliance). Both the Mineiros and the Paulistas made their peace with many former monarchists, but the Paulistas were able to organize something that fell between what Joseph Love has called a "functionally or ideologically cohesive party and a vertically organized clientele network."[32] In Rio Grande do Sul, the Republicans were able to organize Brazil's most ideologically cohesive party under the direction of positivist Júlio de Castilhos, though they had to survive a bloody civil war to do so. Castilhos was no democrat. Nor was he, as we have seen, a traditional *bacharel*, fond of poetry or florid speeches. He was a gifted polemicist, however, and unlike many of his contemporaries he had a program.[33]

Despite these changes in student life, the new role of the military, and greater competition for political and cultural authority, the law students' attempt to guarantee their hegemony over the political system succeeded. At times, they regretted the greater political role for the military that some of them had helped bring about, but by and large politics continued to be their domain. The emphasis on a literary education remained, although it came increasingly under attack. Technical education did not get off the ground until the 1930s when a graduate of the law school in Rio Grande do Sul, Getúlio Vargas, came to power in Brazil. When he became dictator in 1937, he had all of the state flags burned. This symbolically ended the provincialism of the republican period and began a new era of national political and economic development, in which Vargas would rule with strong support from like-minded military men until 1945. For the Vargas regime, public primary and secondary education would play a greater role in redefining and modernizing Brazil, thereby providing psychologists, public health officials, sociologists, and statisticians with opportunities to exercise new authority over Brazil's citizenry.[34]

In the course of the twentieth century, Brazil became increasingly urban and industrialized. While landowners continued to be prominent politically in more traditional areas, authority became much more diffuse and divided, although hardly equally. Scholars who follow me in this line of inquiry will have to range more widely to answer similar questions about schooling, politics, and society in a changing historical environment. In the twentieth century, there were clearly no longer two schools in which a political class was formed as there had been in the nineteenth. Only 44 percent of the top leaders had a legal education in the period from 1930 to 1983, according to one study. Undoubtedly, attention will have to be paid to a more complex educational environment in Brazil itself as well as to the experience of Brazilians educated abroad. And the more complex political climate after 1945 will also have to be taken into account. Populist politicians, with their tendency to speak the language of the popular classes, transformed political dynamics after World War II, particularly in the more dynamic southern parts of Brazil.

The Cold War gave the military new opportunities to once again develop confidence in its own potential for political leadership, particularly in schools developed with U.S. help and training. By 1964, the populist appeal seemed threatening enough in the wake of the Cuban Revolution that the military seized power and kept it for more than twenty years. This marked a fundamental change in Brazilian civil-military relations.[35] The experience of military rule from 1964 to 1985 inhibited the rise of civilians to the highest positions in government, although the controlled political system continued to function (ab)normally with professional politicians in a rubber-stamp Congress. Those with technical training had expanded opportunities in the military bureaucracy, while the legally trained increasingly were confined to the judicial bureaucracy. Professional organizations that had begun to thrive under Vargas's paternalist state began to assert a greater professional independence.[36]

Brazil witnessed dramatic changes beginning with Vargas's programs of industrialization and the acceleration of social and economic transformation in subsequent decades. Nevertheless, the legacy of the imperial period remains important for Brazilian politics, not least of all in terms of Brazilians' expectations of what a politician should be. Liberalism, even in its late-twentieth-century guise, remains an awkward fit in Brazilian society. Moreover, the link between language and power has not been broken. It should hardly be surprising that a figure like Paulo Freire, the developing world's leading theorist on literacy training for adults, came out of the poorer and more traditional Brazilian northeast. Nor should we be surprised that he suffered exile from his native land for his attempt to transform the dynamic between power and education. Moreover, in three presidential elections since the return of civilian rule, the founder of the Workers' Party, Luís Inácio da Silva, Lula, has been lambasted in the press for his grammatical lapses.

This suggests that for many Brazilians his inability to speak flawless Portuguese still indicates an incapacity to lead. The legacy of the nineteenth-century literary elite lives on. But the legacy of the "socioligarchy" lives on, as well, because the man who defeated Lula in the 1994 and 1998 elections was Fernando Henrique Cardoso, one of the foremost sociologists and intellectuals of his generation.

NOTES

INTRODUCTION

1. Antônio Baptista Pereira, "Crônica," manuscript edition in the Arquivo Histórico do Rio Grande do Sul, Lata 40, Maço 1, p. 6.

2. Loveman, *For la Patria*, pp. 7–9, 14–16.

3. See Lanning, *Academic Culture in the Spanish Colonies*, pp. 5–8; Addy, *Enlightenment in the University of Salamanca*, pp. 48–52; Burkholder, "Honor and Honors in Colonial Spanish America," p. 37.

4. See Chasteen, *Heroes on Horseback*, pp. 2–7, 177–81; Lynch, *Caudillos in Spanish America*.

5. Camp, *Political Recruitment across Two Centuries*, pp. 59–65, 124–27.

6. López-Alves, *State Formation and Democracy*, p. 2.

7. See Uribe-Uran, *Honorable Lives*, particularly pp. 9–11, 15–19, 24–25, 28–29, 49–51, 58–59, 71–75, 88, 116–17, 158–59.

8. López-Alves, *State Formation and Democracy*, pp. 2, 12, 15, 21, 31–32, 69–73, 80–95, 122–39, 171–92, 195–99, 203–6. See also Loveman, *For La Patria*, pp. 32–33, 38–39. For Domingo Sarmiento's complaints regarding the lack of deference among the popular classes in the era of the Argentine *caudillo* Juan Manuel de Rosas, see *Life in the Argentine Republic*, p. 70. See also Halperín Donghi, Jaksić, Kirkpatrick, and Masiello, *Sarmiento: Author of a Nation*, pp. 27–28.

9. Beattie, "Transforming Enlisted Army Service," p. 51.

10. See Raymond Aron's careful discussion of the distinction between "Social Class, Political Class, Ruling Class," in *Power, Modernity, and Sociology*, pp. 107–26.

11. The centrality of the law school graduate was proven by Brazilian political scientist José Murilo de Carvalho in his Stanford University doctoral dissertation, "Elite and State-Building in Imperial Brazil," in 1975. In English, his main article on this subject is "Political Elites and State Building,"

387–99. The dissertation has been published in two parts in Portuguese as *A Construção da Ordem* (1980) and *O Teatro de Sombras: A Política Imperial* (1988). See also Pang and Seckinger, "Mandarins of Imperial Brazil," 215–44; Barman and Barman, "Role of the Law Graduate," 423–48; Morse, *Community to Metropolis* (1974) highlights the important role of the students in shaping the character of the city in the nineteenth century. The official and semiofficial histories of the schools provide a wealth of information on the operations of the schools and the activities of the law students but are generally weak on interpretation. See particularly Almeida Nogueria, *A Academia de São Paulo*; Vampré, *Memórias para a História da Academia de São Paulo*; Bevilaqua, *História da Faculdade de Direito do Recife*; Nestor, *Faculdade do Recife*; Veiga, *História das Idéias*. The Almeida Nogueira book, a massive collection of "alumni notes," is particularly useful for historians seeking information on career patterns, and it also offers a wealth of anecdotes about student life. Vampré relies heavily on Almeida Nogueira and primarily arranges his information in a more useful chronological manner. None of the books on the Pernambuco school is as rich as Almeida Nogueira's. Howard Craig Hendricks completed a doctoral dissertation on the Recife law school in 1977 at the State University of New York at Stony Brook, which remains unpublished. Hendricks's dissertation focuses on the period when the law school was in decline, even as a regional institution. See Hendricks, "Education and Maintenance of the Social Structure." See also his article, "Role of Brazilian Law Schools." My study is the first to look at both schools and analyze the changes in student life and thought over the entire imperial period.

12. For a discussion of the Jesuits' contribution to Brazilian culture, particularly education, see Azevedo, *Brazilian Culture*, pp. 145–46, 155, 170, 355. For a discussion of the motivations behind the expulsion of the Jesuits, see Hemming, *Red Gold*, pp. 451–82, and Maxwell, *Pombal*, pp. 57–59, 84–86.

13. See pp. 383–88 of Carvalho's article, "Political Elites and State-Building."

14. See Maciel de Barros, *Ilustração Brasileira*.

15. Coelho, *As Profissões Imperiais*, pp. 90, 94–95, 120–21, 128–29. Telles, *História da Engenharia no Brasil*, pp. 458, 467. Guilherme Schuch de (the Baron of) Capanema received his undergraduate training in engineering in Vienna and his doctorate from the Escola Militar in Rio.

16. Coelho, *Profissões Imperiais*, pp. 76–77, 92–93, 172–73. There was even a certain disdain for the practice of law itself among those with a law degree, according to Coelho. Alberto Venâncio Filho discusses the repeated and relatively unproductive attempts to found a professional organization for lawyers in this period in *Notícia Histórica dos Advogados do Brasil*, pp. 11–20.

17. For a discussion of the ways in which Anglo-American models have tended to distort the historical study of professions, see Rothblatt, "How Professional Are the Professions?"

18. For an analysis of the historical shifts in dominance among professions in the United States, see Kimball, *"True Professional Ideal,"* particularly, pp. 12–14, 16, 19–25, 43–54, 80–126, 149–97, 200–30,, 277–325.

19. See Serbin, "Priests, Celibacy, and Social Conflict," pp. 22–23, 25, 39–41, 69–80, 95–98, 110.

20. Freyre, *Mansions and Shanties*, particularly pp. 19–20, 24, 57–72, 72, 94, 354–99.

21. Martins, *Patriarca e Bacharel*, particularly pp. 103–7, 127–38, 150–55, 168–73.

22. Barman, *Citizen Emperor*; Schwarcz, *As Barbas do Imperador*.

23. See, particularly, Martins, *Patriarca e Bacharel*, p. 27.

24. In this, I am extending, although she might argue that I am exaggerating, Emilia Viotti da Costa's own emphasis on ambivalence in *The Brazilian Empire*, pp. 196–98. I think that her emphasis on the alienation of intellectuals in the late imperial period is misplaced. The student republicans and positivists of the 1870s and 1880s were, I argue, trying to establish a new basis for their authority.

25. Faoro, *Os Donos do Poder*, p. 226. See also Buarque de Holanda, *Raizes do Brasil*, p. 104.

26. Pang, *In Pursuit of Honor and Power*, p. 268. For his larger discussion of "who ruled the Empire," see pp. 189–235.

27. Graham, *Patronage and Politics*, pp. 4–6.

28. See Graham, *Patronage and Politics*.

29. See Barman, "Brazilians in France," pp. 23–39.

30. Adorno, *Os Aprendizes do Poder*; Venâncio Filho, *Arcadas ao Bacharelismo*.

31. My understanding of identity formation is both directly and indirectly influenced by the writings of Erik H. Erikson. See his *Identity: Youth and Crisis*, particularly pp. 29–30, 160–61, 208–12, 240–49, 256–60. For an excellent study of how Chilean political identities changed over the past several decades, see Hite, "Formation and Transformation."

32. Bourdieu, "Rites of Institution," in *Language and Symbolic Power*, pp. 117–26.

33. Two of the most useful studies of student culture are Willis, *Learning to Labor*, and Holland and Eisenhart, *Educated in Romance*. For a study of student culture in a Latin American context, see Levinson, " 'Todos Somos Iguales.' " Two excellent studies of Brazilian military student culture (discovered only after the original dissertation itself was completed, thanks to Peter Beattie) were written by Castro, *O Espírito Militar*, and *Militares e República*, particularly pp. 33–51. Historians have been less interested in examining these issues, but I found the following three works encouraging early on: Horowitz, *Campus Life*; Gleason, *Young Russia*, particularly pp. 114–59, and Lincoln, *In the Vanguard of Reform*, particularly pp. 41–76.

34. My understanding of these issues is influenced by Stepan, *Military in Politics*; Suleiman, *Elites in French Society*, particularly pp. 11, 17–30, 126–27; Rozbick, *Complete Colonial Gentleman*, pp. 4, 25; and Bourdieu, *State Nobility*; Levinson, Foley, and Holland, *Cultural Production of the Educated Person*.

35. The best study of the limitations of the São Paulo students' liberalism is Adorno, *Os Aprendizes do Poder*. Its primary weakness is its failure to address the changing meanings of liberalism in the imperial period.

1: PORTUGUESE LEGACIES, LIBERAL ASPIRATIONS

1. Schwartz, *Sovereignty and Society*, pp. xii–xiv, 14, 15. See also Carvalho's discussion of Coimbra and its role in forming a homogeneous elite in *Construção da Ordem*, pp. 29–30, 38. For general discussions of the role of *letrados* in Iberia and Latin America, see Kagan, *Students and Society*, and Rama, *Lettered City*.

2. Schwartz, *Sovereignty and Society*, pp. 5–6.

3. Barman, *Brazil: Forging of a Nation*, pp. 27–28, 119–23.

4. Schwartz, *Sovereignty and Society*, pp. 72–77, 361–62.

5. Lamy, *Académia de Coimbra*, pp. 22, 27, 624, 689.

6. Arquivo Nacional Microfilm 006.0–76, "Criação do Curso Jurídico no Brasil." See also Flory, *Judge and Jury*, p. 40.

7. See the discussion in "Criação do Curso," particularly the comments of Estevão Ribeiro de Rezende, 2 January 1825. Maciel de Barros, *Ilustração Brasileira*, pp. 14–16.

8. See the comments of the Viscount of Cachoeira in his "Projecto de Regulamento ou Estatutos para o Curso Jurídico Mandado Crear n'esta Corte pelo Conselheiro D'Estado Visconde de Cachoeira e Apresentado em Março de 1825" (Rio de Janeiro: Typographia Imperial e Nacional, 1826), p. 3 in 1E354, MI, Curso Jurídico de São Paulo, Arquivo Nacional. Hereafter, Ministério do Império will be abbreviated as MI.

9. Vampré, *Memórias*, 1:5, 12.

10. Vampré, *Memórias*, 1:7.

11. Quoted in Barman, *Brazil: Forging of a Nation*, p. 138.

12. Cachoeira, "Projecto ou Estatutos," p. 4.

13. Vampré, *Memórias*, 1: 20.

14. Schwartz, *Sovereignty and Society*, p. 74, and Carvalho, "Political Elite and State-Building," pp. 386–87. For a discussion of the role of Roman law in the rise of absolutism in Europe, see Anderson, *Lineages of the Absolutist State*, pp. 24–25 and 27, although Anderson mentions Portugal only in passing. See also Davidson, "Brazilian Heritage of Roman law," particularly pp. 59 and 63; Morse, *O Espelho de Prospero*, p. 44. Brandão and d'Almeida, *Universidade de Coimbra*, p. 57.

15. See Vampré, *Memórias*, 1: 15, 17–18, 22, 35.

16. See Vampré, *Memórias*, 1:6. For a discussion of the importance of political economy in the curriculum of the law school during the early years, see Adorno, *Os Aprendizes do Poder*, p. 96.

17. Vampré, *Memórias*, 1:32–34, 150, and Almeida Nogueira, *Academia de São Paulo*, 4:39. Say and Adam Smith became mainstays of the law school curriculum in Colombia in the 1830s, as well. See Uribe, "Rebellion of the Young 'Mandarins'," pp. 351–52.

18. Vampré, *Memórias*, 1:6–7, 10–11. See also Bevilaqua, *Faculdade do Recife*, pp. 13, 14.

19. Freyre, *Olinda, Segunda Guia Prática*, pp. 39, 58–59. Carvalho, "Elite

and State Building," p. 68. See also the discussion of the liberal bishop in Barreto, *Ideologia Liberal*, pp. 882–86.

20. Vampré, *Memórias*, 1:82–86.

21. Vampré, *Memórias*, 1:86–87, 306, and Almeida Nogueira, *Academia de São Paulo*, 2:16, 25, 28–30. Bandecchi, "Libero Badaró," p. 105.

22. Macaulay, *Dom Pedro I*, particularly ix–xi.

23. Flory, *Judge and Jury*, pp. 8, 31, 51.

24. Carvalho, "Political Elites and State-Building."

25. See any issue of *O Olindense* or *O Eco D'Olinda*, published at the northern school in the early years and available at the Biblioteca Nacional, Seção de Obras Raras, in Rio de Janeiro.

26. "Curso Jurídico," *O Olindense*, 17 May 1831, p. 19.

27. Bandecchi, "Libero Badaró," p. 104.

28. Almeida Nogueira, *Academia de São Paulo*, 2:6; 4:68, 5:82. The class of 1832 was the first class of students educated solely at the São Paulo law school. See 5:1–2. See also Barman and Barman, "Role of the Law Graduate," p. 435. Students at Coimbra who opposed Dom Miguel even killed a number of professors who supported him. See Brandão and d'Almeida, *Universidade de Coimbra*, p. 125, and Lamy, *Academia de Coimbra*, pp. 66–73.

29. See, for example, the discussion of José Maria Frederico de Souza Pinto in Vampré, *Memórias*, 1:168–69.

30. A. de Toledo Piza, quoted in Almeida Nogueira, *Academia de São Paulo*, 4:22.

31. Reinhart, "Political History," pp. 3–4.

32. Nabuco, *Estadista do Império*, p. 53.

33. "Prospecto," *O Olindense*, 29 July 1831, p. 123.

34. Nabuco, *Estadista do Império*, pp. 49, 53.

35. See Castelo Branco, *Esteio da Liberdade na Corte*, pp. 5, 21–23.

36. Werneck Sodré, *História da Imprensa no Brasil*, p. 101.

37. See Vampré, *Memórias*, 1:72.

38. For a discussion of events following the death of Badaró, see Almeida Nogueira, *Academia de São Paulo*, 5:9–10, 14–16. See also the discussion of Badaró student ally, José Augusto Gomes de Menezes, in Vampré, *Memórias*, 1:172.

39. Bandecchi, "Libero Badaró," pp. 107–8, 111, 112–13.

40. Morse, *Community to Metropolis*, pp. 67–68.

41. See, for example, the theoretical discussions of free labor in *O Olindense*, 21 June 1831, p. 70.

42. Amaral, "Jornalismo Acadêmico," p. 14.

43. "Interior," *O Olindense*, 17 May 1831, p. 17.

44. Letter of 11 June 1838 by Toledo Rendon in 1E351, MI, Curso Jurídico de São Paulo, Arquivo Nacional. See also Veiga, *Idéias*, 3:336.

45. Vampré, *Memórias*, 1:339.

46. See one student's letter, published significantly by the typographer of the liberal newspaper *O Farol Paulistano* in 1830, available in 1E351, MI, Curso Jurídico São Paulo, Arquivo Nacional. For examples of similar behavior in the North American context, see Novak, *Rights of Youth*, particularly pp. 38–57.

47. "Interior," *O Olindense*, 27 May 1831, p. 31. See also the translation of Benjamin Constant, "Da Liberdade Individual," in *O Amigo das Letras*, 18 April 1830, p. 37; see the translation of Vicesimus Knox, "A Aversão Decidida ao Despotismo e o Ardente Amor da Liberdade," *O Amigo das Letras*, 25 July 1830, pp. 186–92. See Berreto, *Ideologia Liberal*, p. 30, on the distinction between "responsible" and "arbitrary" government.

48. See documents contained in 1E351, MI, Curso Jurídico São Paulo, Arquivo Nacional.

49. Arquivo Nacional 1E353, MI, CJSP, ROD. "Indifferentismo Político," *O Argos Olindense*, 4 August 1838, p. 3.

50. "Indifferentismo Político: continuado do n. antecedente," *O Argos Olindense*, 11 August 1838, p. 4.

51. "Curso Jurídico," *O Olindense*, 17 May 1831, pp. 19–20. For a discussion of the treatment of first-year students in Coimbra, see Lamy, *Academia de Coimbra*, pp. 430–31. See also pp. 414–15 for a discussion of hierarchies among the student body.

52. See, for example, the discussions of federalism in *O Eco d'Olinda*, 3 March 1832, p. 79, and 17 March 1832, pp. 87–88, and "Communicado: Diálogo entre dois federalistas do Já e do Logo," 31 March 1832, pp. 93–94. See also "Interior," *O Olindense*, 23 August 1831, pp. 159–61, and other discussion in the following issues of *O Olindense*: 23 August 1831, pp. 223–24; 25 October 1831, pp. 237–39; and 16 March 1832, pp. 393–94.

192 ■ *Notes to Pages 30–32*

53. Da Costa, *Brazilian Empire*, pp. 53–77. For a general overview, see Santos, "Liberalism in Brazil." Barreto also argues that "independence and its later consolidation correspond to the maturity of the liberal ideal in Brazil." See *Ideologia Liberal*, p. 18.

54. Flory, *Judge and Jury*, p. 5.

55. For a discussion of the major regional revolts, see Bethell and de Carvalho, "1822–1850," and Carvalho, *Teatro de Sombras*, pp. 12–16. See also Chasteen, "*Cabanos* and *Farrapos*," pp. 32 and 34, and Mosher, "Pernambuco and the Construction of the Brazilian Nation-State," particularly pp. 3, 12–13, 33–37, 150–246.

56. Carvalho, "Political Elites and State-Building," p. 391.

57. Almeida Nogueira, *Academia de São Paulo*, 5:68–72. For the situation in Pernambuco, see Andrade, *Movimentos Nativistas*, pp. 58–62, and Mosher, "Pernambuco and the Construction of the Brazilian Nation-State," p. 31.

58. The best single study of the Setembrizada is Andrade, *Movimentos Nativistas*, particularly pp. 75–100. See also Bethell and Carvalho, "1822–1850," p. 59; Bevilaqua, *Faculdade do Recife*, pp. 98, 298; and Mosher, "Pernambuco and the Construction of the Brazilian Nation-State," pp. 33–37, 52–53. For a contemporary description in the student press, see "Interior. Pernambuco," *O Olindense*, 20 September 1831, pp. 187–88. See the letter from the students to the president of the province of Pernambuco regarding the necessity for "obedience . . . to constituted authority" in *O Olindense*, 22 September 1831, p. 192.

59. "Interior. Artigo Communicado." *O Olindense*, 22 September 1831, p. 191.

60. Beattie, "Transforming Enlisted Army Service," pp. 59–60.

61. "Interior. Dia 7 de April," *O Olindense*, 10 April 1832, p. 425.

62. "Interior. Artigo Communicado." *O Olindense*, 22 September 1831, pp. 191–92; "Interior," *O Olindense*, 28 October 1831, pp. 241–42; "Interior," *O Olindense*, 27 September 1831, p. 199. For information on the formation of the National Guard, see Uricoechea, *Patrimonial Foundations*, pp. 64–69.

63. Nabuco, *Estadista do Império*, pp. 53, 54, 56.

64. Flory's discussion of the turn away from liberalism by the political class in general is particularly good. See *Judge and Jury*, p. 141.

65. "Interior," *O Olindense*, 27 May 1831, p. 32. See also "Interior," *O Olindense*, 26 August 1831, pp. 165–66, and "Interior. Artigo Communicado." *O Olindense*, 22 September 1831, pp. 191–92; *O Olindense*, 28 October 1831, p. 33. See the list of newspapers that support "order" in "Interior. Communicado." *O Olindense*, 28 October 1831, p. 244.

66. "Pernambuco," *O Olindense*, 17 May 1831, p. 18.

67. *O Olindense* devoted much space to coverage of the association's activities. See, for example, "Sociedade Patriótica Armonizadora" in the 3 June 1831 issue, p. 43, and "Interior" in the 26 July 1831 issue, p. 118.

68. See Correio de Andrade, *Movimentos Nativistas*, pp. 63–64.

69. "Interior," *O Olindense*, 3 December 1831, p. 277. See also Chasteen's discussion of the role of the press in *"Cabanos and Farrapos,"* p. 35.

70. "Interior," *O Olindense*, 3 December 1831, pp. 277–78, and 23 March 1832, p. 404.

71. *Eco D'Olinda*, 17 March 1832, p. 87.

72. "Interior," *O Olindense*, 3 December 1831, p. 277.

73. "Interior," *O Olindense*, 16 March 1832, p. 393.

74. "Pará," *Eco D'Olinda*, 17 March 1832, p. 88.

75. "Interior. Rio de Janeiro," *O Olindense*, 2 August 1831, p. 128, and *O Olindense*, 22 July 1831, p. 114.

76. Adorno, *Os Aprendizes do Poder*, pp. 49–50.

77. Vampré, *Memórias*, 1:303.

78. Veiga, *Idéias*, 3:329–35.

79. "Prospecto," *O Argos Olindense*, 4 August 1838, p. 1; "Rio Grande do Sul," *O Argos Olindense*, 11 August 1838, p. 1; "O Espírito de Partido Não Tem Remorsos," *O Argos Olindense*, 22 August 1838, pp. 1–2; "Interior," *O Argos Olindense*, 5 September 1838, pp. 1–2; and "O Governo Actual," *O Argos Olindense*, 28 August 1838, p. 1. See also Chasteen *"Cabanos and Farrapos,"* p. 44, for his description of how the Farrapos were seen as "erring but redeemable subjects of the Empire who were eligible for a negotiated peace."

80. Almeida Nogueira, *Academia de São Paulo*, 4:150–51. See also Mendonça, *Diplomata na Corte*, pp. 23–24.

81. See Mosher, "Pernambuco and the Construction of the Brazilian Nation-State," pp. 150–253.

82. For a more recent and nuanced analysis of the key alliances between old and new economic interests in the Rio (port and province)-Minas Gerais region, see Needell, "Party Formation and State-Making." Needell argues that the Regresso begins with "older, more established sugar and slaving families and interests of port and lowlands, from which many of the Paraiba coffee families emerged themselves."

83. Weffort, *Por Que Democracia?*, p. 84; see also Mattos, *Tempo Saquarema*, pp. 133, 163.

84. Adorno, *Os Aprendizes do Poder*, pp. 73, 223. See also De Mattos, *Tempo Saquarema*, pp. 113–15.

85. Adorno, *Os Aprendizes do Poder*, p. 73.

86. *O Olindense*, 17 May 1831, p. 17. For a discussion of slavery and liberalism, see Barreto, *Ideologia Liberal*, pp. 142–45; for other examples of the use of slave metaphors, see "Interior," *O Olindense*, 27 May 1831, p. 31, where Dom Pedro I's appointees are called slaves.

87. "Interior. Communicado." *O Olindense*, 13 May 1831, p. 39; see also Da Mattos, *Tempo Saquarema*, p. 133.

88. Adorno, *Os Aprendizes do Poder*, pp. 21–25, 75, 77, 89, 127–37, 234.

89. I fundamentally disagree with Flory that Brazilian elites abandoned liberalism (at least, as a fundamental component of their self-conception) for the very same reason he himself notes. See *Judge and Jury*, pp. 89, 148, 205.

90. One of the most important studies of Latin American Liberalism from a historical perspective is Hale, *Mexican Liberalism*; see p. 39. See also Safford, "Politics, Ideology, and Society," p. 352.

91. Barman and Barman, "Role of the Law Graduate," p. 440; see also Vampré, *Memórias*, 1:303.

92. The best survey of student newspapers in São Paulo is Amaral, "Jornalismo Acadêmico."

93. See the 2 May 1842, and 4 June 1842, letters of José Antônio Saraiva to Henrique Garces Pinto de Madureira in the Instituto Histórico e Geográfico Brasileiro Coleção Henrique Garcez, Lata 553, Pasta 26. See also Vampré, *Memórias*, 1:344.

94. IHGN, Coleção Henrique Garcez, Lata 553, Pasta 26, Letters from José Antônio Saraiva, 29 March 1845 and 13 May 1845.

95. Barreto, *Ideologia Liberal*, pp. 104–5, 120–21, 129–30; Flory, *Judge and Jury*, pp. 9–11, 133–34.

96. Bethell and Carvalho, "1822–1850," p. 80.

97. Flory, *Judge and Jury*, pp. 133–34, 151–52, 164, 172, 191–92, 194. See also Barman, *Brazil: Forging of a Nation*, pp. 193, 213.

98. Barman, *Brazil: Forging of a Nation*, p. 194; Needell, *Tropical Belle Époque*, pp. 54–58.

99. Barman and Barman, "Role of the Law Graduate," p. 435.

100. Renato Mendonça, *Diplomata na Corte*, pp. 43–44.

101. Carvalho, "Elite and State Building," p. 90.

2: LANGUAGE AND POWER

1. An early version of this chapter was published as Kirkendall, "Orators and Poets."

2. Azevedo, *Brazilian Culture*, pp. 155, 166, 194, 339.

3. Schwartz, *Sovereignty and Society*, p. 72.

4. The early statutes are contained in Cacheoira, "Projecto ou Estatutos," pp. 12–13. See also Almeida Nogueria, *Academia de São Paulo*, 4:69.

5. For entrance requirements, see Arquivo Nacional Microfilm 006.0–076, "Criação do Curso Jurídico."

6. Vampré, *Memórias*, 1:10; Alencastro, "Vida Privada e Ordem Privada no Império," in Alencastro, *História da Vida Privada no Brasil*, pp. 30–35.

7. Vampré, *Memórias*, 1:86–97, 306; Almeida Nogueira, *Academia de São Paulo*, 2:16, 25, 28–30.

8. Bevilaqua, *Faculdade do Recife*, p. 308.

9. Quoted in Bevilaqua, *Faculdade do Recife*, p. 44; for the original, see Arquivo Nacional 1E367, MI, Curso Jurídico de Olinda, Relatórios e Ofíicios do Diretor.

10. Quoted in Bevilaqua, *Faculdade do Recife*, p. 50.

11. Nabuco, *Estadista do Império*, p. 53. Nabuco, himself a politicized student in literary times, labeled this excessive interest in literary matters a "false preoccupation." He had largely abandoned his own literary aspirations while in high school, although he did publish a book on the Portu-

guese poet Camões and otherwise dabbled in literary pursuits while his political ambitions were blocked in the years following graduation. See Carolina Nabuco, *Life of Joaquim Nabuco*, pp. 11, 22–30.

12. Note that months go by before *O Olindense* published a single poem, despite the fact that it referred to itself as a literary and political newspaper. See also the conspicuous lack of poetry in *O Argos Olindense*.

13. See Paulino José Soares de Souza, "Discurso Proferido na Sessão de 25 de Agôsto de 1870," *Annaes do Senado* (1870), p. 7, and *Annaes do Senado*, "Sessão em 7 de Agôsto, 1875," p. 104.

14. Amaral, "Jornalismo Acadêmico," p. 17.

15. Almeida Nogueira, *Academia de São Paulo*, 4:55–61, 5:83. Veiga, *Idéias*, 2:295–98.

16. Vampré, *Memórias*, 1:113–14.

17. Vampré, *Memórias*, 1:192, and Almeida Nogueira, *Academia de São Paulo*, 4:56.

18. See correspondence from 1829 to 1830 in 1E361, M1, Curso Jurídico de São Paulo, Arquivo Nacional, as well as Almeida Nogueira, *Academia de São Paulo*, 4:55.

19. For the discussion of the "linguistic turn" during the reign of Dom Pedro II, see Bevilaqua, *Faculdade do Recife*, p. 44. See also Rama, *Lettered City*, p. 24.

20. Bourdieu, *Language and Symbolic Power*, pp. 51, 55–57, 64–65, 70–71, 99–102.

21. See, for example, Rotundo, *American Manhood*, pp. 240–44; Leloudis, *Schooling the New South*, pp. 67–68. Bledstein, *Culture of Professionalism*, pp. 248–59. For an earlier generation's emphasis on literature in the United States, see Leloudis, *Schooling the New South*, pp. 46–48. In the United States, the collegiate interest in sports accelerated after the 1860s.

22. *A Legenda*, 1 July 1860, p. 1; see also Américo Pinto's similar sentiments in "Discurso," *O Atheneu Pernambucano* (April 1860): 7.

23. *Ensaios Litterários* (August 1849): 26.

24. See, for example, *Kaleidoscópio*, 27 July 1860, and *O Sete de Setembro*, 7 April 1865. See self-descriptions as poets, orators, and philosophers in *Atheneu Pernambucano* (August 1856): 89. Note the confidence with which Almeida Nogueira lists the best orator, poet, and so on of certain years in, for

example, *Academia de São Paulo*, 1:97. For a description of linguistic competition in a similar setting, see Spitzer, *French Generation of 1820*, p. 221.

25. Antônio Simplício de Salles, "Physiognomias Acadêmicas," *A Legenda*, 11 October 1860, p. 92.

26. Lears, "Concept of Cultural Hegemony."

27. For a discussion of the priest's privileged access to language, see Goody, *Logic of Writing*, pp. 16- 17. See also Ong, *Orality and Literacy*, and Kimball, *Orators and Philosophers*. For an interpretation similar to my own in a broader Latin American context, see Rama, *Lettered City*, particularly pp. 24, 29–30. See also Adorno, *Os Aprendizes do Poder*, pp. 170–71, 240. For a classic critique of the Brazilian *bacharel*, published in 1928, see *Retrato do Brasil* by Paulo Prado, a member of the last graduating class of the São Paulo law school during the imperial period. See particularly pp. 145–46.

28. Grossberg, "Institutionalizing Masculinity."

29. M. de S. Bueno, "Chrônica da Academia de São Paulo," *Memórias da Associação Culto á Sciencia*, 10 May 1859, p. 5.

30. Gilmore, *Manhood in the Making*, pp. 4, 25, 37, 38, 122, 220.

31. Williams, *Dom Pedro, the Magnanimous*, pp. 244, 250.

32. Vampré, *Memórias*, 1:359.

33. Recife professor Joaquim Vilella encouraged this orientation in *Atheneu Pernambucano* (August 1856): 76. A "literary gazette," he wrote, "is always a useful diversion when compared with those acrimonious discussions that only serve to discredit the country, in the state of demoralization that unfortunately the press has reached among us through the personal battle of parties." See *A Estréa*, no. 1, 1854, for a discussion of why literature is more important than politics. See also *Aurora* (May 1849): 35.

34. Moreira Brandão, "Introducção," *Aurora* (May 1849): 5.

35. Vampré, *Memórias*, 2:193.

36. "Chrônica Litterária," *Ensaios Litterários* (May 1849): 18, and "Introducção," *Ensaios Litterários* (May 1850): 2.

37. Manuel Pereira de Sousa Arouca, "Chrônica," *Memórias da Associação Culto á Sciencia*, 31 May 1859, p. 9.

38. "Introducção," *Ensaios da Sociedade Brazilia*, 15 October 1859, p. 1.

39. Rangel Pestana, "As Lettras, Sciencias e Artes no Brasil," *Memórias da Associação Culto á Sciencia* (April 1860): 44.

40. See Magalhães Junior, *José de Alencar*, pp. 137–38, 191, 212, 223. See Sommer's discussion in *Foundational Fictions*, pp. 138–71.

41. Morse, "Language in America," in *New World Soundings*, p. 17.

42. Cunha, *Lingua, Nação, Alienação*, p. 21.

43. See Pimenta Bueno, *Direito Público Brasileiro*, p. 22.

44. Cândido, *Formação*, pp. 18–22, and Guimarães, *Alencar*, p. 35.

45. Barbosa Lima Sobrinho, *Lingua Portuguesa*, pp. 77, 78, 80.

46. M. A. Machado, "O Canto do Índio," *O Album dos Acadêmicos Olindenses* (June 1850): 157–58.

47. José M. de Freitas, "O Sertanejo," *Atheneu Pernambucano* (May 1857), p. 30.

48. Hobsbawm and Ranger, *Invention of Tradition*.

49. See *O Brado da Indignação*, 3 September 1850, p. 3. See also "Sandices em Guisa de Crítica, Pelo Senhor Figueira," *O Brado da Indignação* (October 1850), p. 21.

50. See Schwarcz's discussion of "The Importing of the Novel to Brazil and its Contradictions in the Work of Alencar," in his *Misplaced Ideas*. See also Maciel de Barros, *Signifição Educativa*, pp. xvi–xvii. See also Haddad, *Romantismo Brasileiro*, particularly pp. 66–100.

51. See, for example, Guimarães, *Rosaura*, pp. 41, 261, 264.

52. Quoted in Martins, "Byron e *O Guarani*."

53. "Esboço Crítico-Litterários," *O Clarim Litterário* (May 1856): 4.

54. See information on Alencar's reading habits during his student days in Magalhães, *Alencar*, pp. 31, 34.

55. Haberly, "Mystery of the Bailiff's List," 10–12.

56. João Capistrano Bandeira de Mello, "Memória Histórica Acadêmica," (Recife: Typographia Universal, 1861), pp. 21–22. This can be found in the Recife Law School Library.

57. On the mission of the Romantic poet, see Maciel de Barros, *Significação Educativa*, pp. 84–87.

58. "Reflexôes sobre a Poesia Brasileira," *Ensaios Litterários* (August 1849): p. 37. "Complex relations exist between liberalism and Romanticism," says Ubiritan Borges de Macedo, *Liberdade no Império*, p. 31; see also pp. 30, 52–54. Oliveira Torres notes that the "ultimate ideological basis of everything" during the empire was Romanticism. See *Democracia Coroada*,

pp. 471–72. Victor Hugo himself said that Romanticism was "liberalism applied to literature." For a discussion of the complex relationship between Romanticism and politics in France, see Schamber, *Artist as Politician*, particularly pp. 5, 10, 40–50, 96–98, 127. See also the discussion of Romanticism in Bloom, *Ringer in the Tower.*

59. Domingos José Gonçalves de Magalhães, *Suspiros Poéticos e Saudades* (Paris: Dauvin et Fontaine, 1836).

60. Prado, *Retrato do Brasil*, p. 145. Maciel de Barros, *Significação Educativa*, p. 246.

61. Carvalho, *O Cantor dos Escravos*, pp. 89–96.

62. For a discussion of the student poets of the 1840s, see Almeida Nogueira, *Academia de São Paulo*, 3:19–22. For parallels with the old South in the United States, see Faust, *James Henry Hammond*, pp. 11–12, 17. Poetry was of secondary importance in relation to oratory at the South Carolina College, an institution in many ways comparable to the Brazilian law schools as a training ground for the political elite in a slave society.

63. "Chrônica," *Atheneu Pernambucano* (April 1863): p. 20.

64. "Sobre um Esboço da História Literária na Academia," *Revista da Academia* (May 1852): p. 255. A collection titled "Lyre of the Twenty-year-old," by Manuel Antônio Álvares de Azevedo, was published at this time in São Paulo. See Vampré, *Memórias*, 1:358, and the list of books of poetry by students in 2:70. See the horrified response to a student's public promise never to write a poem again in P. de Calasans, "Sabbatina," *O Clarim Litterário* (July 1856): 8.

65. Viana Filho, *Vida de Rui Barbosa*, p. 27, and Almeida Nogueira, *Academia de São Paulo*, 4:162.

66. Cândido in *Formação*, 2:198.

67. See, for example, the comments regarding Martim Francisco Ribeiro de Andrada in "Sobre um Esboço da História Litterária na Academia," *Revista da Academia* (May 1852): p. 289, as well as the pseudonymous Hinckmar's reviews of collection of poems by students in *Cinco Annos n'uma Academia, 1878–1882* (São Paulo: Seckler, 1882).

68. See, for example, Almeida Nogueira, *Academia de São Paulo*, 2:338.

69. Carvalho, *Cantor dos Escravos*, pp. 78, 117–18, 121; see also Vampré,

Memórias, 2:170, 172. The question is from Carolina Nabuco, *Life of Joaquim Nabuco*, p. 14.

70. Haberly, "Eugênia Câmara."

71. Sommer, *Foundational Fictions*, pp. 6, 15, 33.

72. See, for example, Santos Lopes, "Lá se Foi," and Vieira de Mattos, "Cabellos Loiros," *Ensaios Litterários do Atheneu Paulistano* (September 1852): 79–80.

73. See, P. de Calasan's review of J. D. R. da Cunha's *Cantos e Prantos* in "Sabbatina," *O Clarim Litterário* (July 1856): p. 7.

74. *Ensaios Litterários* (May 1849): p. 1.

75. See, for example, F. F. Correa, "O Túmulo d'uma Virgem," and L. F. Veiga, "O Que Eu Amo," in *O Atheneu Pernambucano* (August 1856): 61; Leonel M. de Alencar, "Uma Virgem," and F. C. Varvalho, "Virgem," in *Ensaios Litterários*, 8 October 1850, pp. 70–72.

76. See Haddad, *Poemas de Amor*, pp. 6–7. For examples of this idealization and the way some students mocked it, see "Traços da Minha Vida de Estudante," *Ensaios Litterários* (May 1848): 66.

77. Cândido's comment about Álvares de Azevedo could be extended to many others. See *Formação*, 2:184.

78. G. B., "A Virgem Dormindo," *Revista da Academia* (April 1859): 119–21.

79. Critics have developed Mario de Andrade's suggestion that Álvares de Azevedo had a "phobia of sexual love." See Soares, *Ressonâncias Veladas da Lira*, p. 71, and Haddad, *Poemas do Amor*, pp. 2–3. I am grateful to John D. French for insight into the interpretation of this poem.

80. Silva Nunes Junior, "Untitled," *O Constitucional*, 11 August 1883; Vicente de Carvalho, "Dea," *O Constitucional*, 19 May 1883; Wenceslão de Queiroz, "Untitled," *O Constitucional*, 13 June 1883.

81. See Tolman, "Castro Alves," 242–43.

82. "Introducção," *A Estrea* (1854), p. 4. On the cult of the dead poet, see Freyre, *Mansions and Shanties*, pp. 70–71. For examples of dead poets, see Salvador de Mendonça, "Claudio Manuel," and Pedro Luiz, "O Poeta," *A Legenda*, 11 August 1860, pp. 47–48; "A Morte de Feliciano Coelho Duarte," *Ensaios Litterários*, 8 October 1850, pp. 47–48; Bevilaqua, *Faculdade do Recife*, pp. 87–88; and Cândido, *Formação*, 2:149–51.

83. See Almeida Nogueira, *Academia de São Paulo*, 2:106–7, and Vampré,

Memórias, 1:365–66. On the Christ imagery, see "Introducção," *A Estréa* (1854), p. 4.

84. Vampré, *Memórias*, 1:365–66; see also Almeida Nogueira, *Academia de São Paulo*, 7:106–7; Magalhães Junior, *Poesia e Vida*, pp. 14–15. For an evocation of him, see J. A. de Passos, "Escuta," *O Atheneu Pernambucano* (April 1863): p. 18.

85. Kelsall, *Byron's Politics*, pp. 1, 2.

86. See Cândido's discussion of Castro Alves in *Formação*, 2:268–83.

87. See Haberly's discussion of the Romantic artist in "Eugenia Câmara," pp. 167–70.

88. P. de Calasans, "A Gonçalves Dias," *O Clarim Litterário* (May 1856): p. 5.

89. "Introducção," *A Estréa* (1854), p. 3.

90. See Cândido, *Formação*, 2:26, 28, 178, 184, 284. For a discussion of how the literati replaced the priestly class in the nineteenth century in terms of cultural authority in Latin America, see Rama, *Lettered City*, pp. 36–37, 43. For a discussion of Romanticism and youth, see Schmitt, *Political Romanticism*, p. 153, and Schamber, *Artist as Politician*, p. 11.

91. See, for example, *Revista da Academia*, May 1859, p. 266. For descriptions of particularly prominent student orators, see Vampré, *Memórias*, 1:390–91, and Almeida Nogueira, *Academia de São Paulo*, 1:97, 4:146. Most student newspapers provide examples of speeches. For a discussion of oratory in the imperial period, see Souza, *Império da Eloqüencia*, pp. 29–37, 91–94. For a useful comparison with the importance of oratory in the Old South, see Wyatt-Brown, *Southern Honor*, particularly p. 47. For a general treatment of the importance of oratory in the history of education, see Kimball, *Orators and Philosophers*, pp. 24–37, 53.

92. Almeida Nogueira, *Academia de São Paulo*, 3:287, 4:182.

93. See Szuchman, "Middle Period," p. 1. It could be suggested that only in the twentieth century has oratory begun to lose its transcendent importance as a form of verbal expression in many parts of the world. See Ong, *Orality and Literacy*, pp. 109, 111.

94. See Adorno, *Os Aprendizes do Poder*, pp. 244–46. For a discussion of how formality helps to restrict access, see Fairclough, *Language and Power*, pp. 65, 66. See also Bourdieu, *Language and Symbolic Power*, pp. 74–75.

95. See, for example, *Revista do Club Acadêmico* (April-May 1869): p. 31.

96. See, for example, M. de S. Bueno, "Chrônica da Academia de São Paulo," *Memórias da Associação Culto á Sciencia*, 10 May 1859, p. 8, and "Chrônica da Academia de São Paulo," *A Propaganda*, 14 April 1871, p. 4. See also Almeida Nogueira's discussion of one student's insatiable love of discussion in *Academia de São Paulo*, 7:192.

97. Quoted in Dornas Filho, *Silva Jardim*, p. 32. See also Graham, *Patronage and Politics*, p. 186.

98. For a complaint about student orators' frequent "abuse of metaphors," see Almeida Nogueira, *Academia de São Paulo*, 7:87. See also 3:104 and 7:202–3, for descriptions of academic style.

99. Almeida Nogueira, *Academia de São Paulo*, 1:87. See Rama's discussion of the use of formal language in *Lettered City*, pp. 31, 33, 35.

100. Almeida Nogueira, *Academia de São Paulo*, 1:140, 197, 198, 213.

101. C. De Mendonça, *Revista do Club Acadêmico* (August-September 1869). Medonça seemed convinced that women had never attended the Eleventh of August celebrations but "Sessão Magna," in *O Atheneu Pernambucano* (August 1856, p. 33) clearly indicates that women had attended the northern school's celebrations more than ten years earlier. In any case, their participation was no less mute in 1856 than it was in 1869.

102. The best single contemporary source on the Brazilian student newspaper during its heyday is Pessanha Povoa, *Annos Acadêmicos, 1860–1864* (Rio de Janeiro: Typographia Perserverança, 1870), particularly pp. 29–34, 60–66, 95–99, 152–60.

103. J. Campos, "Sabbatina," *O Clarim Litterário* (May 1856): 8.

104. *O Atheneu Pernambucano* (June 1858): 1.

105. For a discussion of "indifference," see Moreira Brandão, "Introducção," *Aurora* (May 1849): p. 1; *Memórias da Associação Culto á Sciencia*, 19 May 1859, p. 1, and *Ensaios Litterários do Atheneu Paulistano* (August 1852): p. 2. For information on the growth of associations, see chapter 3.

106. Adorno, *Os Aprendizes do Poder*, pp. 154–55, 226, 234.

107. Witrúvio, "Introducção," *O Bello Sexo* (1850), p. 4. It is significant that it is described as a literary and a "recreational" newspaper, but not a scientific one. See also the descriptions of *A Violeta* in Vampré, *Memórias*, 1:363–64.

108. See, for example, *A Estréa* 1, no. 3, 1854.

109. "Introducção," *Ensaios Litterários* (May 1850): 1. See also Almeida Perreira Filho, "Chrônica Litterária," *Ensaios Litterários* (May 1849): p. 17.

110. *Ensaios Litterários* (May 1850): p. 1, and "Introducção," *Ensaios Litterários* (September 1847): p. 1.

111. J. Campos, "Introducção," *O Clarim Litterários* (May 1856): p. 1.

112. See, for example, U. Corioloano de S. L., "A Liberdade da Imprensa," *O Atheneu Pernambucano* (August 1856): 44–48.

113. Almeida Pereira Filho, "A Imprensa," *Ensaios Litterários* (May 1849): p. 7.

114. See also "Introducção," *Ensaios Litterários* (September 1847): p. 1.

115. Zaluar, *Peregrinção pela Provincia*, pp. 127–28.

116. See the discussion of the death of one newspaper after another sixteen issues in 1856 in "Sabbatina," *O Clarim Litterário* (September 1856): p. 8, and the discussion of the failure of several mid-1840s' newspapers in Moreira Brandão, "Introducção," *Aurora* (May 1849): p. 3.

117. J. Campos, "Introducção," *O Clarim Litterário* (May 1856): p. 1; "Introducção," *Ensaios Litterários* (May 1850): p. 2.

118. See the discussion of this issue in Santos Filho, "Martim Cabral."

119. Carlos Ferreira, "Chrônica," *Revista do Club Acadêmico* (June–July 1869): 42–43.

120. "Sanduice em Guisa da Crítica, pelo Senhor Figueira," *O Brado da Indignação*, 3 September 1850, p. 7.

121. "Programma," *O Publicador Paulistano*, 25 July 1857, p. 1.

122. Antônio Simplício de Salles, "Antônio Ferreira Vianna," *A Legenda*, 21 October 1860, p. 93.

123. See, for example, the literary representations of student encounters with a daughter of the nouveau riche in Bernardo Guimarães, *Rosaura* (originally published in the 1870s and set in the São Paulo of the 1840s when the author was a student there), pp. 20–22. See also the depictions of law students on pp. 3 and 111 of Cardoso de Oliveira, *Dois Metros e Cinco* (Rio de Janeiro, 1905), set in Recife and Bahia in the late 1880s, when the author was a student.

124. Cardoso de Oliveira, *Dois Metros*, p. 1.

125. Guimarães, *Rosaura*, pp. 22, 24, 28, 30, 31–32, 41, 47, 94. Women played an important role as consumers of literature in nineteenth-century

Brazil, almost never as producers. See Zilberman, "Mulher Educável," 138. Nísia Floresta, a recently rediscovered woman author, spent much of her life in Europe, and many of her works were unpublished at the time of her death and/or available only in French and Italian. See Bezarra Mariz, *Nísia Floresta Brasileira Augusta.*

126. *O Brado da Indigação*, 3 September 1850, p. 2.

127. Cunha, *Lingua, Nação, Alienação*, p. 21.

128. Quoted in Da Costa, *Brazilian Empire*, p. 197.

129. Rama, *Lettered City*, p. 77.

130. For a discussion of the persistence of "gentlemanly" values in a North American context, see Haber, *Quest for Authority and Honor*, pp. ix–x, 4, 5.

131. Adorno, *Os Aprendizes do Poder*, pp. 92, 158, 170–71.

132. See, for example, Maximiano Bueno, "Chrônica da Academia," *Memórias da Associação Culto á Sciencia* (April 1860): p. 35.

133. Lins, *Rio-Branco*, p. 39; Buarque de Holanda, *Raízes do Brasil*, pp. 120–21.

3: PEERS, PATRONS, FAMILY, AND COMMUNITY

1. See, for example, Pang and Seckinger, "Mandarins of Imperial Brazil," pp. 221–22, and Adorno, *Os Aprendizes do Poder*, p. 235.

2. My understanding of identity formation is influenced by Anderson, *Imagined Communities*, as well as Martin, "Choices of Identities."

3. For a discussion of the importance of the journey in the creation of national identities, see Anderson, *Imagined Communities*, pp. 55–61.

4. See Lewin's discussion, which builds on the arguments of Oliveira Vianna, in *Politics and Parantela*, pp. 11, 17.

5. See Borges's discussion of Sérgio Buarque de Holanda's work on p. 235 of *Family in Bahia.*

6. Freyre, *Order and Progress*, p. 115.

7. See, for example, Almeida Nogueira, *Academia de São Paulo*, 2:125, and Evaldo Cabral de Mello, "O Fim das Casas-Grandes," in *História da Vida Privada*, 2:408. Lewin argues that marriage between cousins declined over the course of the nineteenth century in the northeastern state of Paraiba (al-

though it is not unknown even today in the northeast). See *Politics and Parentela*, pp. 147–60, and Borges, *Family in Bahia*, pp. 241–42.

8. Metcalf, *Family and Frontier*, pp. 6, 96.

9. Nazarri, *Disappearance of the Dowry*, pp. xix, 5, 14.

10. Graham, *Patronage and Politics*, p. 17.

11. Antônio Simplício de Salles, "Physionomias Acadêmicas," *A Legenda*, 21 October 1860, p. 92.

12. Borges, *Family in Bahia*, pp. 37–38, 76–77.

13. See the 6 August 1867 letter from Joaquim José Guedes to Barbosa in Barbosa, *Correspondência*, p. 69.

14. Quoted in Carolina Nabuco, *Life of Joaquim Nabuco*, p. 21.

15. Viana Filho, *Vida de Rui Barbosa*, p. 20.

16. See Martins, *Patriarca e Bacharel*, p. 28. See Magalhães Junior's description of the relationship between Álvares de Azevedo and his correspondent, the Baron of Iguape, in *Poesia e Vida*, p. 69. See also Almeida Nogueira, *Academia de São Paulo*, 8:199. For a fictional representation, see Guimarães, *Rosaura*, p. 34. For information on a Brazilian student's relationship with his correspondent during his years at Coimbra in the colonial period, see Russell-Wood, "Antônio Álvares Pereira," pp. 193, 198–200.

17. Calmon, *Vidas e Amores*, pp. 83–85.

18. Rothblatt, *Revolution of the Dons*, pp. 183, 229; Calmon, *Vidas e Amores*, pp. 83–85; Viana Filho, *Vida de Rui Barbosa*, p. 77.

19. Szuchman, *Order, Family, and Community*, pp. 103–4.

20. For descriptions of particular *repúblicas*, see Magalhães, *Alencar*, p. 28; Almeida Nogueira, *Academia de São Paulo*, 2:196; Magalhães Junior, *Poesia e Vida*, p. 63; Rocha, *Álvares de Azevedo*, pp. xxviii, xliii; Carolina Nabuco, *Life of Joaquim Nabuco*, p. 12; Vampré, *Memórias*, 2:51; Carvalho, *Cantor dos Escravos*, pp. 61, 121. Calmon, *Vida e Amores*, p. 51. See the brief description of a typical "poorly furnished" student dwelling in Joaquim Angêlico Bessoni de Almeida's play, "Neste Caso Eu Me Caso; ou Os Estudantes do Recife" (Recife: Typographia Universal, 1862), p. 17 (this play is available in the Biblioteca Pública Estadual, Recife, Pernambuco). For an interesting contrast of a more "suspect social space," see Beattie's discussion of military barracks in "The House, The Street, and the Barracks."

21. Leeds, "Brazilian Careers and Social Structure," 1330. For a discus-

sion of old-boy networks and career patterns in Mexico, see Camp, *Political Recruitment*, pp. 13–19, 41–46, 96–99.

22. See the list of the first students to matriculate in IE350, MI, Curso Jurídico de São Paulo, Arquivo Nacional.

23. Joaquim Nabuco, *Minha Formação*, p. 37.

24. Carolina Nabuco, *Life of Joaquim Nabuco*, p. 12. See Kett's useful discussion of the move from dependence to semidependence to independence in *Rites of Passage*, pp. 14–37.

25. J. V. Couto de Magalhães, *Revista de Academia* (April 1859): 40–41.

26. See, for example, *O Constitucional*, 11 August 1882.

27. See A. Witruvio Pinto Bandeira e Accioli de Vasconcellos's extended celebration of friendship (dedicated to several of his classmates) in "A Amizade," *O Album dos Academicos Olindenses*, 30 June 1850, pp. 120–23 (misnumbered 125). The importance of examining friendship historically was first made clear by Smith-Rosenberg, "Female World of Love and Rituals." See also Rotundo's discussion of friendship in *American Manhood*, pp. 34, 38–39, 43, 75–76.

28. See Almeida Nogueira, *Academia de São Paulo*, 1:137, 182, 219, 2:205–16, 245; 3:266; 7:174–75, 296–97. Students, of course, also had colleagues who were cousins as well. See 2:243.

29. Cardoso e Oliveira, *Dois Metros e Cinco*, pp. 2 and 24–25.

30. See Bessoni de Almeida, "Neste Caso Eu Me Caso," where it is the *caloiro's* responsibility to make breakfast.

31. For information on the internal workings of *repúblicas*, see Almeida Nogueira, *Academia de São Paulo*, 3:212, 4:190.

32. See, for example, the letters of recent graduate J. A. Ribeiro da Silva to Rui Barbosa in Barbosa, *Correspondência*, pp. 126–27.

33. Almeida Nogueira, *Academia de São Paulo*, 1:243, 3:298–99.

34. See the discussion in Rio-Branco, *Reminiscências*, pp. 30–33.

35. Zaluar, *Peregrinação*, pp. 126–27.

36. Guimarães, *Rosaura*, p. 262.

37. Rio-Branco, *Reminiscências*, pp. 30–33; Viana, *Vida de Rui Barbosa*, p. 20; Almeida Nogueira, *Academia de São Paulo*, 4:152, 219.

38. Almeida Nogueira, *Academia de São Paulo*, 4:152, 219.

39. See the discussion of the centrality of the future Baron of Rio

Branco's student home in Lins, *Rio-Branco*, p. 39; See also Debes, *Campos Sales*, pp. 30–32.

40. See, for example, Almeida Nogueira, *Academia de São Paulo*, 4:209, 8:169–70.

41. See Almeida Nogueira, *Academia de São Paulo*, 1:221.

42. Almeida Nogueira, *Academia de São Paulo*, 2:247–51.

43. For a brief discussion of the Sociedade Philomática, see Vampré, *Memórias*, 1:256.

44. For information on these organizations, see, for example, F. C. de Abreu e Silva, *Memórias da Associação Culto á Sciencia*, 30 July 1859, pp. 38–41; Bevilaqua, *Faculdade do Recife*, pp. 301–2; Vampré, *Memórias*, 2:65, 117–18. For a historical look at male youth organizations of various types, see Rotundo, *American Manhood*, pp. 62–65. For a discussion of literary societies in their heyday in the United States, see McLachlan, "Choice of Hercules."

45. Vampré, *Memórias*, 1:376.

46. Joaquim Vilela de Castro Tavares, "Discurso," *Atheneu Pernambucano (Supplemento)* (August 1856): p. 75.

47. See Cândido, *Formação*, 2:151.

48. See the discussion of this organization in Morse, *Community to Metropolis*, pp. 87–88, as well as Vampré, *Memórias*, 1:351.

49. See Melo Franco, *Rodrigues Alves*, pp. 25–32, particularly the list of members on p. 28; Viana, *Vida de Rui Barbosa*, p. 30. See also Haddad, *Romantismo Brasileiro*, pp. 63–66, 82–110.

50. *Atheneu Pernambucano* (April 1863): p. 21; "O Que Há de Novo?" *Imprensa Acadêmica*, 28 April 1864, p. 2.

51. Viana, *Vida de Rui Barbosa*, pp. 20–21.

52. This was a common theme in inaugural issues of student newspapers. See, for example, "Introducção," *Ensaios Litterários do Atheneu Paulistano* (August 1852): p. 2; "Introducção," *Memórias da Associação Culto á Sciencia*, 10 May 1859, p. 1.

53. See, for example, "Introducção," *Aurora* (May 1849): p. 4; *Memórias da Associação Culto á Sciencia*, 10 May 1859, p. 2. See the use of the term *zoilo* in Bessoni de Almeida, "Neste Caso Eu Me Caso," p. 22.

54. "Necrologia pelo Senhor Figueira," *O Brado da Indignação*, 3 September 1850, p. 4.

55. F. Quirino dos Santos, "Chrônica da Academia," *Memórias da Associação Culto á Sciencia* (June 1860): p. 98.

56. See Leeds, "Brazilian Careers and Social Structure," p. 1331, for a discussion of twentieth-century Brazilian student associations.

57. See, for example, M. de S. Bueno, "Chrônica," *Memórias da Associação Culto á Sciencia*, 10 May 1859, p. 6.

58. See the letter of one student to his colleague Rui Barbosa, expressing his gratitude for being invited to join the Clube Radical Paulistano in Barbosa, *Correspondência*, pp. 84–85.

59. Dealy, *The Public Man*, particularly pp. 4, 7, 12–13, 19. Almeida Nogueira, *Academia de São Paulo*, 7:91, 8:241.

60. C. F. Guedes Alcôforado, "Discurso," *Ensaios Litterários*, 11 August 1849, p. 32.

61. F. Rangel Pestana, "Chrônica da Academia," *Memórias da Associação Culto á Sciencia* (July 1860): p. 114.

62. For information on the founding of this student society, see M. de S. Bueno, "Chrônica," *Memórias da Associação Culto á Sciencia*, 10 May 1859, p. 6, and Vampré, *Memórias*, 2:295.

63. "O Que Há de Novo?" *Imprensa Acadêmica*, 28 April 1864, p. 2.

64. See, for example, "Boletim," *A Legenda*, 21 August 1860, p. 47.

65. J. Campos, "Faculdade de Direito," *O Atheneu Pernambucano* (June 1858): p. 20; José Antônio de Figueiredo, "Memória Histórica Acadêmica" (Recife: n. p., 1857), p. 8; Antônio de Vasconcellos Menezes de Drummond, "Memória Histórica Acadêmica" (Recife: Typographia de Manoel Figueiredo de Faria e Filho, 1864.

66. See, for example, Almeida Nogueira, *Academia de São Paulo*, 1:227; 2:336; and 3:266.

67. Calmon, *Vida e Amores*, p. 61. For a discussion of modern-day "trotes" in a military school, see Castro, *Espírito Militar*, pp. 26–31. See also Castro, *Militares e República*, pp. 34–36.

68. See, for example, the description in *Ensaios Litterários* (September 1848): p. 40.

69. See, for example, "Boletim," *O Futuro*, 28 June 1862, p. 32, and "Boletim," *O Futuro*, 16 August 1862, p. 60; Dr. J. A. de Figueiredo, "Intro-

ducção," *O Atheneu Pernambucano* (April 1863): p. 1; Affonso Guimarães Junior, "Relatório," *Revista da Associação Recréio Instructivo* (July 1861): p. 4.

70. See the character Alberto's comment that "I don't admit that between students and colleagues there should be disharmony" in Bessoni da Almeida, "Neste Caso Eu Me Caso," p. 21.

71. Barman, *Brazil: Forging of a Nation*, pp. 218–19, 237.

72. J. J. Monte Junior, "Relatório," *O Atheneu Pernambucano* (April 1863): p. 2.

73. M. A. Duarte de Azevedo, "Discurso," *Ensaios Litterários do Atheneu Pernambucano* (September 1852): 34–35; Ferreira Vianna, "Atheneu Paulistano," *Ensaios Litterários do Atheneu Paulistano* (September 1852): p. 72.

74. See, for example, C. F. Guedes Alcôforado, "Discurso," *Ensaios Litterários*, 11 August 1849, p. 30; F. Alves de Carvalho, "Discurso," *O Atheneu Pernambucano* (August 1856): p. 77.

75. Francisco de Paula Baptista, "Memória Histórica dos Acontecimentos Mais Notáveis do Anno Findo" (Recife: n. p., 1858), pp. 6–7.

76. Guimarães, *Rosaura*, pp. 8–9, 74–75, 81, 84–85. On the identities on which characters in the novel were based see, Álvares de Azevedo, *Cartas de Álvares*, pp. 235–36.

77. See, for example, Viana, *Vida de Rui Barbosa*, pp. 20–21.

78. Bevilaqua, *Faculdade do Recife*, p. 296. For a discussion of hierarchies in a military academy, see Castro, *Espírito Militar*, pp. 15–31, 52–53.

79. See, for example, Franklin Tàvora, "Chrônica," *O Atheneu Pernambucano* (September 1862): p. 19, and "Chrônica," *A Propaganda*, 14 April 1871, p. 4.

80. Bevilaqua, *Faculdade do Recife*, p. 296.

81. Almeida Nogueira, *Academia de São Paulo*, 1:263–65, 3:217; Vampré, *Memórias*, 1:386–87.

82. Graham, *Patronage and Politics*, p. 30.

83. For a discussion of how student culture often replicates social hierarchies, see Farnham, *Education of the Southern Belle*, p. 4.

84. Bevilaqua, *Faculdade do Recife*, p. 31.

85. *O Olindense*, 17 May 1831, pp. 19–20.

86. Vampré, *Memórias*, 1:387.

87. See Vampré, *Memórias*, 1:114–15, 121, 182–83.

88. See the depiction of the backlander father in Bussoni de Almeida, "Neste Caso Eu Me Caso," pp. 59–60, whose inability to speak Portuguese well, like that of other nonstudent characters in the play, is also played for laughs.

89. Almeida Nogueira, *Academia de São Paulo*, 1:213; 2:247, 293; 3:288, 298. For descriptions of Rio Branco, see 3:294, and Lins, *Rio Branco*, p. 18.

90. Adorno, *Os Aprendizes do Poder*, p. 155. See also Graham's discussion of the style of the imperial politician in *Patronage and Politics*, pp. 179, 255–56.

91. P. de Calasans, "Sabbatina," *O Clarim Litterário* (July 1856): p. 8; J. Campos, "Sabbatina," *O Clarim Litterário* (July 1856): p. 8. On the Colégio Dom Pedro II uniform, see Needell, *Tropical Belle Époque*, p. 54.

92. Almeida Nogueira, *Academia de São Paulo*, 1:125; 2:48, 258; and 3: 244; Vampré, *Memórias*, 2:51. See also Carolina Nabuco, *Life of Joaquim Nabuco*, pp. 14–15, for a description of a particular "dandy" who was in great demand at society dances. See also Graham's discussion of the importance of dress in *Patronage and Politics*, pp. 68–69, and Needell's discussion of the continuing importance of these matters in the republican period in *Tropical Belle Époque*, pp. 166–68. See Yeager's discussion of the clothes worn by the fictional character Martín Rivas, a Chilean type similar to the *bacharel*, in "Elite Education," 101–2.

93. Freyre, *Mansions and Shanties*, pp. 177–78.

94. Bourdieu, "Rites of Institution." See also Adorno, *Os Aprendizes do Poder*, pp. 28–29.

95. Bevilaqua, *Faculdade do Recife*, p. 300.

96. L. N. Fagundes Varella's poem is cited in Debes, *Campos Salles*, p. 30.

97. Aurélio Buarque de Hollanda Ferreira, *Pequeno Dicionário Brasileira da Lingua Portuguesa*, 11th ed. (Rio de Janeiro: Editora Civilização Brasileira, 1983), p. 581; Castro looks at "others" in the military school context in *Espírito Militar*, pp. 38–45, 147–62.

98. See Yeager's discussion of this issue in "Elite Education," p. 98.

99. Almeida Nogueira, *Academia de São Paulo*, 4:74.

100. See, for example, "Boletim," *O Futuro*, 30 August 1862, p. 68.

101. Quoted in Vampré, *Memórias*, 1:112.

102. Almeida Nogueira, *Academia de São Paulo*, 4:120–21.

103. Sette, *Arruar*, pp. 7–8. See also DeFreitas, *Tradições*, p. 51; Freyre, *Mansions and Shanties*, p. 36; Dias, *Power and Everyday Life*, pp. 52–59. See also the increasingly abundant literature on the Brazilian distinction between the private world of the "house" and the public world of the "street." See particularly Da Matta, *Casa e Rua*, pp. 39–54; Lauderdale Graham, *House and Street*, pp. 4, 10, 15–18, 42–46.

104. Haberly, "Câmara," p. 165.

105. Freyre, *Order and Progress*, pp. 35–36, 89, 116; Calmon, *Vida e Amores*, pp. 101–2.

106. See Vampré, *Memórias*, 1:468.

107. Debes, "Alguns Aspectos," 332–35.

108. Junius, *Em São Paulo*, pp. 35–36.

109. Pedro Affonso Jr., *O Evolucionista*, 28 May 1887.

110. Almeida Nogueira, *Academia de São Paulo*, 4:74.

111. Freyre, *Order and Progress*, p. 114, and *Mansions and Shanties*, pp. 177–78. See also Morse, *Community to Metropolis*, pp. 135–36.

112. Almeida Nogueira, *Academia de São Paulo*, 9:124.

113. Almeida Nogueira, *Academia de São Paulo*, 4:77–91; Vampré, *Memórias*, 1:455–56.

114. *A Actualidade*, 5 October 1863.

115. Bevilaqua, *Faculdade do Recife*, p. 118.

116. Lins, *Rio Branco*, p. 17.

117. For information on the history of Recife, see Freyre, *O Recife, Sim!*, pp. 61, 83.

118. De Freitas, *Tradições e Reminscências*, pp. 21, 27.

119. Lins, *Rio Branco*, pp. 26–27.

120. Zaluar, *Peregrinação*, p. 123. See also Manuel Antônio Álvares de Azevedo's complaints in *Cartas*, p. 110.

121. Almeida Nogueira, *Academia de São Paulo*, 2:221–22; Rio-Branco, *Reminiscências*, p. 31.

122. Almeida Nogueira, *Academia de São Paulo*, 8:213–15.

123. Quoted in Elazaria, "Lazer e Vida Urbana," pp. 144–45.

124. Almeida Nogueira, *Academia de São Paulo*, 4:75.

125. Guimarães, *Rosaura*, pp. 9, 273–74.

126. Cardoso de Oliveira, *Dois Metros e Cinco*, pp. 1, 3, 7, 9, 21–27, 32–35.

127. Quoted in Calmon, *Vida e Amores*, p. 151.

128. Mosher, "Pernambuco and the Construction of the Brazilian Nation-State," p. 21.

129. Bevilaqua, *Faculdade do Recife*, pp. 55–56, 69.

130. Bevilaqua, *Faculdade do Recife*, p. 73.

131. Nestor, *Faculdade do Recife*, p. 25.

132. See, for example, *A Legenda*, 1 October 1860, pp. 73, 75.

133. *O Kaleidoscópio*, 7 April 1860; "Chrônica," *Atheneu Pernambucano* (April 1863): p. 19.

134. Pimenta Bueno, *Direito Público Brasileiro*, pp. 53, 191.

135. See Lúcio de Mendonça's poem, "A Mocidade Brasileira," in the *Revista do Club Acadêmico* (August-September 1869): 28–29, and *A Independência*, 2 May 1868.

136. "A Mocidade e os Regrogrados," *O Futuro*, 12 July 1862, p. 38.

137. "Introducção," *Ensaios Litterários* (September 1847): p. 4; see also C. F. Guedes Alcôforado, "Discurso," *Ensaios Litterários*, 11 August 1849, p. 31; M. P. de Lacerda Werneck, "Discurso," *Atheneu Pernambucano* (August 1856): p. 82; Joaquim Antunes de Figueiredo, "Discurso," *Revista da Academia Litterária* (July 1863): p. 168. For a discussion of how identities are constructed through narratives, see Martin, "Choices of Identities," pp. 7–8, 16.

138. M. P. de Lacerda Werneck, "Discurso," *O Atheneu Pernambucano* (August 1856): p. 66.

139. "Introducção," *Ensaios Litterários do Atheneu Paulistano* (August 1852): p. 2.

140. Antônio Simplício de Salles, "Physiognomias Acadêmicas," *A Legenda*, 21 October 1860, p. 92.

141. Graham, *Patronage and Politics*, particularly pp. 1–3, 79–85, 93–98. See also Da Costa's sophisticated discussion of this issue in *Brazilian Empire*, pp. 55, 61, 75, 185, 188–90.

142. Freyre, *Mansions and Shanties*, pp. 354–68.

143. Quoted in Graham, *Patronage and Politics*, p. 67. See Prudente de Morais's attempts to enlist the aid of the son of another prominent politi-

cian, Teófilo Ottoni, in getting a position for his older brother in "Alguns Aspectos," p. 341.

144. See the 2 July 1869, 24 July 1869, and 29 May 1870 letters from João José Barbosa de Oliveira to Rui Barbosa in *Correspondência*, pp. 86, 88, 125.

145. Guimarães, *Rosaura*, pp. 58, 72, 112, 152–54.

146. Almeida Nogueira, *Academia de São Paulo*, 1:142–43. For examples of other students who received financial aid from more affluent families, see 1:250.

147. Almeida Nogueira, *Academia de São Paulo*, 2:230.

148. Graham, *Patronage and Politics*, p. 178. On the historical impact of parental status on career patterns in Mexico, see Camp, *Political Recruitment*, pp. 180–82.

149. See, for example, "Duas Palavras ao Público," *Atheneu Pernabucano* (June 1857): p. 64, and "Actas da Sessão Magna," *Memórias da Associação Culto á Sciencia*, 30 August 1859, p. 53.

150. See, for example, "Introducção," *A Estréa* (May 1854): p. 6.

151. "Sabbatina," *O Clarim Litterário* (August 1856): p. 7. See Prudente de Morais's discussion with his brother in "Alguns Aspectos," pp. 334.

152. See, for example, F. Rangel Pestana, "Chrônica da Academia," *Memórias da Associação Culto á Sciencia* (July 1860): p. 114.

153. M. de S. Bueno, "Chrônica da Academia," *Memórias da Associação Culto á Sciencia*, 10 May 1859, pp. 6–7.

154. See, for example, Zaluar, *Peregrinação*, p. 128. See *Memórias da Associação Culto á Sciencia*, 31 May 1859, p. 24, and M. P. Sousa Arouca, "Chrônica," from the same newspaper, 31 August 1859, p. 55.

155. Vampré, *Memórias*, 1:393.

156. Vampré, *Memórias*, 2:68–69.

157. See letters from Rui Barbosa (14 October 1868 and 6 April 1869) to Albino José Barbosa de Oliveira and (28 November 1868) to João Ferreira de Moura in *Correspondência: Primeiros Tempos*, pp. 71, 72, 76.

158. See Rui Barbosa's letter of 28 November 1868 to Ferreira de Moura in *Correspondência: Primeiros Tempos*, pp. 71–72.

159. See Sancho de Barros Pimental's letter to Joaquim Nabuco, 23 January 1872, available in the Fundação Joaquim Nabuco, Instituto de Documen-

tação, CEHIBRA-DOTEX, Cppi, doc.15.3. On career patterns generally, see Pang, *In Pursuit of Honor and Power*, pp. 206–35.

160. See, for example, Almeida Nogueira, *Academia de São Paulo*, 2:112.

161. Barman, *Brazil: Forging of a Nation*, p. 237. See the letter of Candido Drummond Furtado de Mendonça from 1873 in Martins, *Patriarca e Bacharel*, pp. 217–18.

162. Almeida Nogueira, *Academia de São Paulo*, 2:254, 259.

163. Pang and Seckinger, "Mandarins of Imperial Brazil," pp. 223–26.

4: TEACHERS AND STUDENTS

1. For historical and anthropological treatments of teacher/student relations that have influenced this discussion, see Horowitz, *Campus Life*; Willis, *Learning to Labor*; Kagan, *Students and Society*; Levinson, " 'Todos Somos Iguales,' " particularly pp. 279–300.

2. Here I depart from Carvalho, *Construção da Ordem*, pp. 21, 29, 51, 72. Carvalho did not examine the internal workings of the schools as such.

3. See Santos, "Liberalism in Brazil," p. 37, on the function of the educational system in Brazil. See also Maciel de Barros, *Ilustração Brasileira*, pp. 207–27.

4. Bevilaqua, *Faculdade do Recife*, p. 23.

5. Freyre, *Olinda, Segunda Guía Prática*, p. 132.

6. Vampré, *Memórias*, 1:308–9, 314.

7. See, for example, Bevilaqua, *Faculdade do Recife*, pp. 42, 44.

8. For information on absent and negligent teachers in São Paulo, see Vampré, *Memórias*, 1:207, 279, 310–11, 333, 341; and Almeida Nogueira, *Academia de São Paulo*, 2:8.

9. Bevilaqua, *Faculdade do Recife*, p. 45.

10. Bevilaqua, *Faculdade do Recife*, p. 61.

11. Vampré, *Memórias*, 1:355.

12. For a discussion of the continuing problem of missing teachers in later years, see Vampré, *Memórias*, 2:135. For congressional criticism, see 1:399. Regarding professors teaching courses on subjects on which they were ill informed, see Joaquim Vilella de Castro Tavares, "Memórias Históricas" (Recife: n. p., 1856), p. 6.

13. See, for example, Almeida Nogueira's description of Martim Francisco in *Academia de São Paulo*, 2:303.

14. Francisco Leandro de Toledo, "Relatório dos Dias que Deixou de Haver Aula nas Diferentes Aulas em 1868," 17 October 1868, in 1E360, MI, Faculdade de Direito de São Paulo, Arquivo Nacional.

15. See, for example, the comments in *O Constitucional*, 17 November 1863, in Coleção Tavares Bastos, Biblioteca Nacional, Seção dos Manuscritos, I-3, 33.5 no. 18.

16. Bevilaqua, *Faculdade do Recife*, p. 44. For the original, see Sacramento Lopes Gama, "Relatório," 19 December 1837, in 1E367, MI, Curso Jurídico do Olinda, Arquivo Nacional.

17. Afonso Arinos de Melo Franco, *Rodrigues Alves*, 1:14–15. See also Graham, *Patronage and Politics*, p. 222.

18. For examples of professors leaving, see Bevilaqua, *Faculdade do Recife*, pp. 38, 39. On leave policy, see pp. 43–45. For complaints about poor salaries, see comments on p. 38 regarding the failure of teachers to wear appropriate attire during examinations, which the director attributed to their alleged poverty. They wore an overcoat and canvas pants to what was supposed to be a "solemn public act: the conferring of a degree."

19. See package 1456 in the archive of the Faculdade de Direito do Recife.

20. Bevilaqua, *Faculdade do Recife*, pp. 32, 36.

21. See Adorno, *Os Aprendizes do Poder*, pp. 26–27, 103–6.

22. Lamy, *Academia de Coimbra*, p. 49; for a discussion of reforms enacted at Coimbra under Pombal by a defender, see Lemos, *Relação Geral*, pp. 11, 46, 52–53, 61.

23. "Curso Jurídico," *O Olindense*, 31 May 1831, p. 40, and "Correspondência," 3 June 1831, p. 46; see also Vampré, *Memórias*, 2:296.

24. Almeida Nogueira, *Academia de São Paulo*, 4:301.

25. Almeida Nogueira, *Academia de São Paulo*, 1:262.

26. See Almeida Nogueira's description of a particularly good teacher, Chrispiniano Soares, *Academia de São Paulo*, 3:215.

27. This was considered an urgent reason to transfer the northern school to Recife. See Bevilaqua, *Faculdade do Recife*, p. 55.

28. Nabuco, *Estadista do Império*, p. 51.

29. Bevilaqua, *Faculdade do Recife*, p. 308; Carvalho, "Elite and State Building," p. 82.

30. Almeida Nogueira, *Academia de São Paulo*, 1:265.

31. See, for example, Barreto, *Questão Acadêmica em 1871*, pp. 5–6.

32. Miguel do Sacramento Lopes Gama, "Relatório 20/September/1844," 1E368, MI, Curso Jurídico do Olinda, Arquivo Nacional. See also Bevilaqua, *Faculdade do Recife*, pp. 97–98, and Auler, "Dom Pedro II," p. 70. For a discussion of the emperor's visits to schools, see Barman, *Citizen Emperor*, pp. 184–85.

33. Almeida Nogueira, *Academia de São Paulo*, 4:15, 47, 53.

34. Vicente Pires da Motta, "Relatório, 4/December/1874," p. 7, in 1E363, MI, Faculdade de Direito de São Paulo, Arquivo Nacional.

35. See "Quadro Estatístico, 1836" in 1E367, MI, Curso Jurídico do Olinda, Arquivo Nacional; "Quadro Estatístico, 1844" in 1E368, MI, Curso Jurídico do Olinda, Arquivo Nacional, 1844–1847. Only 5 of the 273 students received less than the highest grades. See "Quadro Estatístico, 1851," 1E357, MI, Faculdade de Direito de São Paulo, Arquivo Nacional. See 1E369, MI, Curso Jurídico de São Paulo, Arquivo Nacional, 1855–1858; "Quadro Estatístico, 1859," 1E371, MI, Curso Jurídico do Recife, Arquivo Nacional, 1860–1867; "Quadro Estatístico, 1855," in 1E358, MI, Curso Jurídico de São Paulo, Arquivo Nacional, 1855–1858; "Quadro Estatístico, 1870," in 1E361, MI, Faculdade de Direito de São Paulo, Arquivo Nacional, 1869–1870.

36. See, for example, Netto Machado's "Relatório" of 13 December 1869 in 1E361, MI, Curso Jurídico da Faculdade de Direito de São Paulo, Arquivo Nacional, 1869–1870, and Auler, "Dom Pedro II," p. 72.

37. See Avellar Brotero's "Relatório" of 30 January 1845 in 1E356, MI, Curso Jurídico de São Paulo, Arquivo Nacional.

38. See, for example, Almeida Nogueira, *Academia de São Paulo*, 4:94.

39. Vampré, *Memórias*, 2:193.

40. Almeida Nogueira, *Academia de São Paulo*, 7:148.

41. See *O Ypiranga*, 23 November 1867.

42. Rangel Pestana, "As Lettras, Sciencias, e Artes no Brazil," *Memórias da Associação Culto A Sciencia* (April 1860): p. 45. See Avellar Brotero's "Relatório" of 30 January 1845 in 1E356, MI, Curso Jurídico de São Paulo, Arquivo Nacional.

43. Almeida Nogueira, *Academia de São Paulo*, 8:124, 131.

44. Almeida Nogueira, *Academia de São Paulo*, 4:153, 154.

45. "Curso Jurídico," *O Olindense*, 31 May 1831, p. 41.

46. Vampré, *Memórias*, 1:215, and the 1 August 1835 report in 1E353, MI, Curso Jurídico de Olinda, Arquivo Nacional.

47. Calmon, *Vida e Amores*, p. 163.

48. See Graham, *Patronage and Politics*, pp. 67, 222.

49. Vampré, *Memórias*, 1:335.

50. Almeida Nogueira, *Academia de São Paulo*, 4:107.

51. Vampré, *Memórias*, 2:14.

52. Bruno Jansen Pereira, "Duas Palavras aos meus Collegas por Occasião da Colleção do Grau de Bacharel no Dia 1 de Dezembro de 1865," (Recife: Typographia Commercial de Gerald Henrique de Mira, 1866) in Folder 2056, Arquivo da Faculdade de Direito do Recife.

53. Letter from Pedro Autran to José Antônio Saraiva, 14 April 1861, 1E371, Curso Jurídico do Recife, Arquivo Nacional, 1860–1867.

54. Carolina Nabuco, *Life of Joaquim Nabuco*, pp. 16–17.

55. Bevilaqua, *Faculdade do Recife*, p. 103. Teachers in the Old South, for example, had much more authority over student life. See Leloudis, *Schooling the Old South*, p. 45.

56. See, for example, Américo Pinto Barreto, "Discurso," *O Atheneu Pernambucano* (April 1863): p. 6.

57. See, for example, Bispo Tomás, "Relatório, 20/September/1844," 1E368, MI, Curso Jurídico de Olinda, Arquivo Nacional.

58. See Antonio Vasconcellos Menezes de Drummond, "Memória Histórica," (Recife: Typographia Manuel Figueiroa de Faria e Filho, 1864), p. 6. This can be found in the Recife Law School Library.

59. Bevilaqua, *Faculdade do Recife*, pp. 41–42; See also Vampré, *Memórias*, 1:162–63. See director Vergeuiro's complaints in 2 December 1837 report in 1E354, MI, Curso Jurídico de São Paulo, Arquivo Nacional. See also the 12 October 1830 report by Toledo Rendon in 1E351, MI, Curso Jurídico de São Paulo, Arquivo Nacional. See also Pedro Autran's complaints in a 3 February 1837 report in 1E367, MI, Curso Jurídico de Olinda, Arquivo Nacional.

60. See the 8 April 1873 and 10 May 1873 reports in 1E363, MI, Curso Jurídico de São Paulo, Arquivo Nacional.

61. See, for example, Avellar Brotero, "Relatório 20/May and 25/May/ 1844" in 1E355, MI, Curso Jurídico de São Paulo, Arquivo Nacional. See also Vampré, *Memórias*, 1:348.

62. Vampré, *Memórias*, 1:174–75; Almeida Nogueira, *Academia de São Paulo*, 8, p. 135.

63. Almeida Nogueira, *Academia de São Paulo*, 1:272.

64. Almeida Nogueira, *Academia de São Paulo*, 2:179.

65. See, for example, "Mappa das Faltas dos Estudantes em 1873," 1E363, Curso Jurídico de São Paulo, Arquivo Nacional; see director Vergueiro's complaints in 1E354, MI, Curso Jurídico de São Paulo, Arquivo Nacional.

66. See, for example, the 17 August 1869 issue of *Correio Paulistano*.

67. Vampré, *Memórias*, 1:339–40.

68. Cachoeira, "Projecto ou Estatutos," p. 19.

69. "Curso Jurídico," *O Olindense*, 31 May 1831, pp. 40–41.

70. "Correspondência," *O Olindense*, 3 June 1831, p. 46. The letter is from Marcos Antonio de Araujo Abreu.

71. Almeida Nogueira, *Academia de São Paulo*, 8, p. 265.

72. See particularly the "Memórias Históricas," written by João Capistrano de Mello in 1861, pp. 15 and 16, as well as the Jansen Pereira pamphlet cited in note 52. This publication is available in the Recife Law School Library. For more information on censorship of student speeches, see Almeida Nogueira, *Academia de São Paulo*, 8, p. 265.

73. Almeida Nogueira, *Academia de São Paulo*, 4:74–76.

74. See package 1473 in the Pernambuco law school archive, which includes a typed manuscript summarizing material in the *Diario de Pernambuco* from 1 June 1833 and 5 September 1833. See also Bevilaqua, *Faculdade do Recife*, p. 36.

75. Vampré, *Memórias*, 2:141.

76. Almeida Nogueira, *Academia de São Paulo*, 1:266–69, 2:176.

77. Vampré, *Memórias*, 2:142.

78. Bandeira de Mello, "Memória Histórica Acadêmica" (Recife: Typographia Universal, 1861), p. 15. This publication is available in the Recife Law School Library.

79. Bevilaqua, *Faculdade do Recife*, pp. 41–42; Vampré, *Memórias*, 1:162–

63; See director Vergeuiro's complaints in the 12 October 1830 report in 1E354, MI, Curso Jurídico de Olinda, Arquivo Nacional. See Autran's complaints from 3 February 1837 report in 1E367, MI, Curso Jurídico de Olinda, Arquivo Nacional.

80. "Continuado do N. Antecedente," *Argos Olindense*, 18 August 1838, p. 4. The editors also suggested that their teachers were immoral idiots. See also "Boletim Acadêmico: Ordem do Dia," 22 September 1838, p. 4, and 6 October 1838, p. 2.

81. Miguel do Sacramento Lopes Gama, "Relatório: 6/September/1838," 1E368, MI, Curso Jurídico de Olinda, 1838–1848, Arquivo Nacional.

82. Bevilaqua, *Faculdade do Recife*, pp. 48–49; Vampré describes the grades as "unjust." See *Memorias*, 2:314–15.

83. For a collection of these types of letters, see package 1494 in the Recife law school archives.

84. João José Pinto Junior, "Memória Histórica Acadêmica, 1865 (Recife)" (Rio de Janeiro: Typographia Nacional, 1866), p. 41 (available in the Recife Law School Library); Carvalho, *Cantor dos Escravos*, p. 73.

85. Almeida Nogueira, *Academia de São Paulo*, 7:92–100.

86. See the discussion by Maciel Monteiro, quoted in Bevilaqua, *Faculdade do Recife*, pp. 54, 57.

87. Bevilaqua, *Faculdade do Recife*, p. 66.

88. J. Campos, "Sabbatina," *O Clarim Litterário* (July 1856): 8.

89. See, for example, José Antonio de Figueiredo, "Memória Histórica Acadêmica" (Recife: n. p., 1857), pp. 3–4. This publication is available in the Recife Law School Library.

90. Antonio de Vasconcellos Menezes de Drummond, "Memória Histórica Acadêmica, 1864," pp. 87–88.

91. Bevilaqua, *Faculdade do Recife*, pp. 85–86. For an example of student complaints regarding this rule, see *Imprensa Acadêmica*, 28 April 1864. For an example of a student who was a "devotee of 39 absences," see Almeida Nogueira, *Academia de São Paulo*, 8:186; See also 4:206–7.

92. Vampré, *Memórias*, 2:207–8, 215. See also the coverage in the Rio-based newspaper, *A República*, particularly the 8 November, 12 November, and 14 November 1871 issues.

93. Bevilaqua, *Faculdade do Recife*, p. 41. For a description of another similar incident, see the 12 April 1837 report in 1E367, MI, Curso Jurídico de Olinda, Arquivo Nacional.

94. Almeida Nogueira, *Academia de São Paulo*, 4:163–66. See Prudente de Morais's complaints about his teachers in Debes, "Alguns Aspectos," p. 338.

95. Almeida Nogueira, *Academia de São Paulo*, 7:123.

96. J. J. Monte Junior, "Relatório," *O Atheneu Pernambucano* (April 1863): p. 4.

97. Quoted in Vampré, *Memórias*, 1:388.

98. Almeida Nogueira, *Academia de São Paulo*, 2:66.

99. Bevilaqua, *Faculdade do Recife*, p. 26.

100. Joaquim Vilella de Castro Tavares, "Discurso," *Atheneu Pernambucano* (August 1856): p. 76.

101. See, for example, Vampré, *Memórias*, 1:411; "Sessão Magna," *Atheneu Pernambucano* (August 1856): p. 33, and A. Muniz, "Chrônica," *O Atheneu Pernambucano*, 19 July 1860, pp. 63–64.

102. *O Atheneu Pernambucano* (August 1856): p. 33.

103. Nemo, "As Associações Litterárias na Academia," *Imprensa Acadêmica*, 28 April 1864, p. 3.

104. Debes, *Campos Salles*, p. 33.

105. Maximiano Bueno, "Chrônica da Academia," *Memórias da Associação Culto á Sciencia*, April 1860, p. 36.

106. João Antonio de Figueiredo, "Memória-Histórica Acadêmica Apresentada a Congregação dos Lentes da Faculdade de Direito," (Recife: n.p., 1857), p. 8. This publication is available in the Recife Law School Library.

107. Author unknown, "Memória Histórica Acadêmica" (Recife: n.p., 1864): p. 4. Note the way Joaquim Vilella de Castro Tavares disparages the associations' importance in the "Memória Histórica" for 1856: "Two student associations I must mention (not that I think them important) . . .". For the students themselves, as I have argued, these associations were at the heart of the law school experience.

108. Francisco de Paula Baptista, "Memória Histórica dos Aconteci-

mentos mais Notáveis do Anno Finado" (Recife: n. p., 1858), pp. 6–7. This publication is available in the Recife Law School Library.

109. Author unknown, "Memórias Históricas Acadêmicas" (Recife: Typographia Universal, 1864), p. 4. This publication is available in the Recife Law School Library.

110. For information on student opinions of Autran, see F. J. de Sampião, "Sôbre a Divisão do Trabalho, e vantagens, que d'ahi, podem resultar," *O Lidador Acadêmico*, 30 August 1860, p. 134. See also Maciel de Barros, *Ilustração Brasileira*, p. 20.

111. For descriptions of Autran, see Bevilaqua, *Faculdade do Recife*, pp. 73 and 305; Nestor, *Faculdade do Recife*, pp. 37–38. The professor Paula Baptista, according to Bevilaqua the best teacher before the arrival of Bevilaqua's own mentor, Tobias Barreto, was the one whose work was said to have been adopted in Germany. See pp. 309–11.

112. See, for example, *O Lidador Acadêmico*, published in 1861, and *Faculdade do Recife*, particularly the 15 May 1863 issue.

113. Nestor, *Faculdade do Recife*, p. 38, and Bevilaqua, *Faculdade do Recife*, p. 325.

114. Carolina Nabuco, *Life of Joaquim Nabuco*, p. 17.

115. See Antonio Vasconcellos Menezes de Drummond, "Memória Histórica, 1864," p. 97.

116. The only full-length biography is Faria, *José Bonifácio*. Regarding his years as a teacher, see particularly pp. 76–86. On faculty recruitment of students in Mexico, see Camp, *Political Recruitment*, pp. 20–23, 83–111.

117. Quoted in Carolina Nabuco, *Life of Joaquim Nabuco*, p. 15.

118. For descriptions of his teaching style, see Almeida Nogueira, *Academia de São Paulo*, 2:178–79, 4:271–72, and Lins, *Rio-Branco*, pp. 35–36. For a discussion of his activities as honorary president of the Culto á Sciencia association, see *Memórias da Associação Culto á Sciencia* (August 1859): p. 53, and (August 1861): p. 203.

5: STATUS QUO LIBERALISM AND ITS DISCONTENTS

1. Barman, *Citizen Emperor*, pp. 118–21, 165–67, 170–72.

2. See, for example, Viana Filho, *Vida de Rui Barbosa*, p. 8.

3. Latin American historians who study liberalism often ignore imperial Brazil. Witness the collection of essays edited by Peloso and Tenenbaum, *Liberals, Politics, and Power.*

4. Pimenta Bueno, *Direito Público Brasileiro,* p. 49.

5. Pimenta Bueno, *Direito Público Brasileiro,* p. 52; see also Mattos, *Tempo Saquarema,* pp. 159–61.

6. Pimenta Bueno, *Direito Público Brasileiro,* p. 22.

7. See Manoel Pereira de Sousa Arouca, "Melhor Forma de Governo," *Memórias da Associação Culto á Sciencia,* 10 November 1859, pp. 76–79; Identical sentiments are expressed by A. A. de Souza Carvalho in "A Centralisação no Brasil," *Aurora* (May 1849): 45–49.

8. José Antonio de Figueiredo, "Memória Histórica Acadêmica" (Recife: n.p., 1859), p. 9. This publication is available in the Recife Law School Library.

9. Pimenta Bueno, *Direito Público Brasileiro,* pp. 27, 28, 30.

10. Pimenta Bueno, *Direito Público Brasileiro,* pp. 27, 28, 30. Maria de Lourdes Monaco Janotti denies, however, that true monarchists existed in Brazil prior to the very end of the imperial period. See her article, "Monarchist Response."

11. Sousa Arouca, "Qual a Melhor Forma de Governo?" *Memórias da Associação Culto á Sciencia,* 10 November 1859, pp. 76–79. See also the discussion in A. A. de Souza Carvalho, "A Centralisação no Brasil," *Aurora* (May 1849): 45–49, 85–90.

12. Nabuco, *Minha Formação,* pp. 36–41; see also Needell, "Liberal Embraces Monarchy," 166, and Graham, *Britain and the Onset of Modernization,* pp. 263–64. For a twentieth-century celebration of Brazil's imperial political system, see Oliveira Torres, *Democracia Coroada,* particularly pp. 18, 85, 472, 476.

13. See, for example, one student's tribute to the Emperor in Affonso Guimarães Junior, "Relatório," *Revista Acadêmica Recréio e Instructivo* (July 1861): p. 5. For more direct, if rather limited, information on his role as patron, see Auler, *Os Bolsistas,* particularly pp. 20–24.

14. Williams, *Dom Pedro the Magnanimous,* pp. 214–27.

15. Rio-Branco, *Reminiscências,* p. 29.

16. On the reintroduction of the *beija-mão* ceremony, see Williams, *Dom*

Pedro the Magnanimous, p. 48, and Barman, *Brazil: Forging of a Nation*, p. 197.

17. Rangel Pestana, "As Lettras, Sciencias e Artes no Brasil," *Memórias da Associação Culto á Sciencia* (April 1860): p. 42.

18. J. R. Coelho de Macedo, "Direito Público Constitucional," *Ensaios da Sociedade Brazília*, 15 October 1859, pp. 2–4.

19. Burns, *Nationalism in Brazil*, pp. 30, 31; Barman, *Brazil: Forging of a Nation*, pp. 34, 239; Freyre, *Mansions and Shanties*, pp. 68–69.

20. Barman, *Brazil: Forging of a Nation*, pp. 34, 239. See also Peter H. Smith's thoughtful discussion of these issues in "Political Legitimacy," particularly pp. 230–33.

21. Rangel Pestana, "As Lettras, Sciencias, e Artes no Brasil," *Memórias da Associação Culto á Sciencia* (April 1860): p. 43.

22. A. F. Vianna, "Discurso," *Ensaios Litterários do Atheneu Pernambucano* (September 1852): p. 28.

23. Francisco Gomes dos Santos Lopes, "Discurso," *Ensaios Litterários do Atheneu Pernambucano* (September 1852): p. 27.

24. Coelho Duarte, *Ensaios Litterários*, 11 August 1849, p. 28.

25. The phrase *liberty and order*, borrowed from the French thinker Guizot, perfectly illustrated the elite political consensus during this time. See de Mattos, *Tempo Saquarema*, p. 154. See also Barman, "Late Brazilian Empire," p. 250.

26. Da Costa, *Brazilian Empire*, pp. 55–56, 76.

27. Graham, *Patronage and Politics*, p. 156.

28. Adorno, *Os Aprendizes do Poder*, p. 234. See also Rama, *Lettered City*, p. 41.

29. Ayres de A. Gama, "Liberdade Política," *Atheneu Pernambucano* (July 1856): p. 3.

30. Francisco Gomes dos Santos Lopes, "Discurso," and Manoel Antonio Duarte de Azevedo, "Discurso," *Ensaios Litterários do Atheneu Paulistano* (September 1852): 26–27, 35.

31. M. P. de Lacerda Werneck, *O Atheneu Pernambucano* (August 1856): p. 81.

32. Moreira Brandão, "Introducção," *Aurora* (May 1849): p. 4.

33. *A Legenda*, 1 July 1860, p. 1.

34. "Direito Público – Algumas Idéias Sobre a Liberdade Política," *Memórias da Associação Culto á Sciencia*, 31 May 1859, pp. 17–19, and the 30 July 1859 edition of the same newspaper, pp. 33–34.

35. Macedo Soares, *Forum Litterário* (July 1860): p. 1.

36. "Da Ordem Social," *Memórias da Associação Culto á Sciencia* (May 1860): 83–84.

37. Adorno, *Os Aprendizes do Poder*, p. 159.

38. Francisco Carlos de A. Reis, "Ligeiras Considerações sobre a Revolução de 1842, em Minas Gerais," *Memórias da Associação Culto á Sciencia* (June 1861): 164–66.

39. Adorno, *Os Aprendizes do Poder*, pp. 75, 12–134, 234.

40. Mallon, *Peasant and Nation*, p. 311.

41. Adorno, *Os Aprendizes do Poder*, pp. 21–25.

42. "Da Soberania do Povo," *Aurora* (May 1849): 10–12.

43. "Boletim," *A Legenda*, 21 August 1860, p. 47.

44. *A Legenda*, 1 October 1860, p. 73.

45. "Idéias para o Povo" and "Carta ao meu Amigo," *O Tymbira*, 5 May 1860, p. 2.

46. Vieira, *Nabuco*, p. 28.

47. Graham, *Patronage and Politics*, p. 74. See also Malerba, *Os Brancos da Lei*, pp. 15–23.

48. Letter from João Ferreira de Moura (3 January 1869) to Rui Barbosa in Barbosa, *Correspondência*, p. 73.

49. "A Civilisação do Brasil," *O Album dos Acadêmicos Olindenses*, 30 June 1850, pp. 118–120.

50. Melo Franco, *Rodrigues Alves*, pp. 21–22.

51. "O que pensamos e o que queremos," *O Tymbira*, 5 May 1860, p. 1.

52. Nabuco, *Minha Formação*, p. 37.

53. For a new and challenging interpretation of the Conservative Party's beginnings, see Needell, "Party Formation and State-Making."

54. Da Costa, *Brazilian Empire*, p. 72; see also Barman, "Politics on the Stage," p. 253.

55. Carvalho, *Construção da Ordem*, p. 165.

56. Carvalho, *Construção da Ordem*, p. 159.

57. Da Costa, *Brazilian Empire*, pp. 71–72.

58. See the discussion of Joaquim Nabuco's restatement of these traditional Liberal ideals in the late 1860s in Vieira, *Nabuco*, p. 29.

59. Graham, *Patronage and Politics*, pp. 159–66, 167, 169–70, 175; J. Campos, "Sabbatina," *O Clarim Litterário* (May 1856): p. 8.

60. Bevilaqua, *Faculdade do Recife*, p. 120; Almeida Nogueira, *Academia de São Paulo*, 1:163–64, 3:158.

61. J. Campos, "Sabbatina," *O Clarim Litterário* (May 1856): p. 8.

62. Bieber, *Power, Patronage, and Political Violence*, p. 153.

63. Needell, "Provincial Origins."

64. Calmon, *Vida e Amores*, p. 68; see also J. M. Vaz Pinto, "Carta ao Meu Amigo T.," *O Tymbira*, 25 June 1860, p. 2.

65. Bevilaqua, *Faculdade do Recife*, p. 428.

66. Hoffnagel, "From Monarchy to Republic," pp. 21, 23, 24, 27. The Sousa Leão family, according to Hoffnagel, had forty-eight sugar plantations in 1857 and seventy by 1880. For information on the Baron of Vila Bela, see Gouvêa, *O Partido Liberal*. For a description of the impact of the Praieira revolt on the Olinda school, see Bevilaqua, *Faculdade do Recife*, p. 61. See also Nabuco, *Estadista do Império*, p. 114.

67. Antonio de Vasconcellos Menezes de Drummond, "Memórias Históricas Acadêmicas, 1864," p. 97.

68. Hoffnagel, "From Monarchy to Republic," pp. 27–29.

69. See, for example, Almeida Nogueira's comments in *Academia de São Paulo*, 7:293, 8:125.

70. "Conservadores," *O Tymbira*, 21 July 1860, p. 2. The student was quoting a French thinker, Elias Regnault.

71. See, for example, the description of Diogo Luiz de Almeida Pereira de Vasconcellos, the nephew of Bernardo Pereira de Vasconcellos, in Almeida Nogueira, *Academia de São Paulo*, 8:169–70.

72. Morse, *Community to Metropolis*, pp. 170–71.

73. Barman, *Citizen Emperor*, pp. 189–91.

74. *A Legenda*, 11 October 1860, p. 74; 11 August 1860, p. 47; 1 July 1860, p. 1.

75. *O Futuro*, 30 August 1862, p. 65.

76. Joaquim Nabuco (writing as Juvenal), *Povo e Throno*, p. 4.

77. Nabuco, *Povo e Throno*, pp. 13–14.

78. Da Costa, *Brazilian Empire*, pp. 69–70, 72. Arinos de Melo Franco, *Apogeu e Declínio*, pp. 19–22.

79. Barman, *Citizen Emperor*, pp. 219–24.

80. See Rui Barbosa's description of the event in Vampré, *Memórias*, 2:p. 156, as well as Joaquim Nabuco's in *Povo e Throno*, p. 11. See also Joaquim Nabuco, "Ao Público," *Independência* (July 1868). See also Barman, *Citizen Emperor*, pp. 219–24.

81. Nabuco, *Povo e Throno*, p. 16.

82. Viana Filho, *Vida de Rui Barbosa*, p. 22.

83. 15 April 1870 letter for Albino José Barbosa de Oliveira to Rui Barbosa in *Correspondência*, p. 113.

84. Letter from Rui Barbosa (11 April 1870) to Albino José Barbosa de Oliveira in *Correspondência*, p. 112. (There probably is an error in the dating of this letter; otherwise, Rui would be responding to a letter he had not yet received.)

85. Almeida Nogueira, *Academia de São Paulo*, 2:p. 187.

86. See, for example, the 9 May 1869 letter in *Correspondência*, p. 81.

87. Letter from João Barbosa to Rui Barbosa (27 September 1869) in *Correspondência*, pp. 92, 121–23.

88. Lelbo, "A Onde Sóbe," and "O Brasil e a Monarchia," in *A Propaganda*, 14 April 1871 and 28 April 1871, respectively.

89. Hoffnagel, "From Monarchy to Republic," p. 137.

90. See the discussion in Mendonça, "Lúcio de Mendonça," 86, and Azevedo, *Vida e Obra*, pp. 33, 50–51, 54.

91. For an example of a student republican in the 1860s who was not involved in politics during the imperial period, see Almeida Nogueira's description of Paulo de Souza Queiros in *Academia de São Paulo*, 2: 333. Antônio Antunes Ribas, on the other hand, became a member of the General Assembly as a Liberal and did not join the Republican Party until 1887. He went on to be a member of Júlio de Castilhos's government in Rio Grande do Sul in the 1890s. See Almeida Nogueira, 2:201–2.

92. See Toplin, *Abolition of Slavery*, pp. 41–43.

93. Pimenta Bueno, *Direito Público Brasileiro*, pp. 29, 32.

94. M. P. S. Arouca, "Sete de Setembro," *Memórias da Associação Culto á Sciencia*, 10 November 1859, p. 79.

95. Joaquim Nabuco, "A Escravidão," p. 79.

96. *Revista da Academia* (May 1859): p. 205.

97. Gomes, *Negro e Romantismo Brasileiro*, pp. 1, 3.

98. R. B. L. Castello-Branco, "A Escravidão no Brasil," *O Clarim Litterário* (July 1856): 2–3.

99. See *O Futuro*, 24 May 1862, p. 9; J. A. Fernandes discussed the Civil War in "A Guerra Civil dos Estados Unidos," *O Lidador Acadêmico*, 20 August 1861, pp. 124–26. See also Conrad, *Destruction of Brazilian Slavery*, pp. 57–58.

100. "Chrônica," *Atheneu Pernambucano* (April 1863): p. 20.

101. Toplin, *Abolition of Slavery*, pp. 44–45; see Bevilaqua, *Faculdade do Recife*, pp. 298–99, for information on students who fought. See also Morse, *Community to Metropolis*, pp. 146–50.

102. Luis F. Maciel Pinheiro, "A Escravidão," *O Futuro*, 30 June 1864, p. 17.

103. For a bilingual edition of his abolitionist poetry, see Castro Alves, *Major Abolitionist Poems*. "The Slave Ship" is on pp. 20–22.

104. Luis F. Maciel Pinheiro, "A Escravidão," *O Futuro*, 30 June 1864, p. 17.

105. Ribeiro da Cunha, "Estudo Político — A Escravidão," *O Atheneu Pernambucano* (August 1856): 56–59.

106. Nabuco, "A Escravidão," pp. 10, 13.

107. Viana Filho, *Vida de Rui Barbosa*, p. 18; Bevilaqua, *Faculdade do Recife*, p. 118.

108. Nabuco, "A Escravidão," pp. 10, 13.

109. Vieira, *Nabuco*, p. 27.

110. See the 9 September 1869 letter from Charles Sumner in Fundação Joaquim Nabuco, CPp306 doc. 6234, 1a7g2.

111. Toplin, *Abolition of Slavery*, pp. 9, 17.

112. Vampré, *Memórias*, 1:p. 482.

113. Melo Franco, *Rodrigues Alves*, p. 24; Vampré, *Memórias*, 2:p. 132.

114. "Misérias da Escravidão — Scenas Verídicas," *O Kaleidoscópio*, 14 April 1860.

115. 15 April 1870 letter from Albino José Barbosa de Oliveira, *Correspondência*, p. 113. For a discussion of Rui's father's relationship with Albino, see Viana Filho, *Vida de Rui Barbosa*, p. 4.

116. See "A Mocidade e os Retrogrados," *O Futuro*, 12 July 1862, p. 38.

117. See, for example, Da Costa, *Brazilian Empire*, p. 197; Burns, *Nationalism in Brazil*, p. 38; Freyre, *Order and Progress*, p. 185; Hermes Lima, *Tobias Barreto*, p. 21. Judy Bieber has suggested that the graduates of the law schools helped transform "local judicial norms" in remote areas of the empire as a result of their openness to new ideas. See her "Slavery and Social Life," 619.

118. Magalhães Junior, *Vida Turbulenta*, p. 159.

119. Orico, *Silviera Martins*, pp. 186–88. I am grateful to Roger Kittleson for this citation.

120. Pedro do Amaral, "Actualidades: O Movimento Acadêmico em São Paulo," *Revista Acadêmica de Sciencias e Lettras* (June-July 1876): 148–52.

6: REFORM, REDEFINITION, AND DECLINE

1. For a review of this argument and a partial critique of it, see Carvalho, "Brazil, 1870–1914." For an outdated, but nevertheless useful, review of historiographical arguments surrounding the fall of the empire, see Boehrer, "Brazilian Republican Revolution." An earlier version of this chapter was published as Kirkendall, "From 'Liberty and Order.' "

2. Maciel de Barros, *Ilustração Brasileira*, p. 7.

3. Barman, *Citizen Emperor*, pp. 150–53, 240–47, 261–69, 318–21. On the exhaustion of the political system, see also Pang, *In Pursuit of Honor and Power*, pp. 228–31.

4. Monaco Janotti's phrase refers primarily to the late 1880s, but I find it useful for understanding the broader changes already taking place by the late 1870s. See her article, "Monarchist Response," pp. 223–43.

5. For a discussion of the transformation of education in a society undergoing a similar transition, see Leloudis, *Schooling the New South*, pp. 38–39.

6. "By 1890, almost 10,000 kilometers of track had been laid," according to Colson, "On Expectations," 270.

7. Coelho dos Reis, "A Actualidade," *A República*, 5 June 1882, p. 2.

8. Da Costa, *Brazilian Empire*, p. 217.

9. For a discussion of a similar society's attempt to create a more technically trained elite by fostering the development of engineering schools, see Safford, *Ideal of the Practical*.

10. Dias, *Power and Everyday Life*, p. 94.

11. Da Costa, "1870–1889," pp. 164, 201–2.

12. Da Costa, *Brazilian Empire*, p. 219.

13. Mattoon Jr., "Railroads, Coffee."

14. Morse, *Community to Metropolis*, p. 175.

15. Morse, *Community to Metropolis*, p. 173.

16. Morse, *Community to Metropolis*, p. 195.

17. For a contemporary traveler's comments on the greater visibility of women in São Paulo, see Junius, *Notas de Viagem* (São Paulo: Jorge Seckler, 1882), p. 49. See also Borges, *Family in Bahia*, p. 37; Besse, *Restructuring Patriarchy*, p. 17.

18. Bessie, *Restructuring Patriarchy*, pp. 17, 113.

19. For a general discussion of women in the professions, see Hahner, *Mulher Brasileira*, 68–70. She notes that Myrthes de Campos was "authorized to defend a client in court in 1899"; see pp. 77–78. See also Bevilaqua, *Faculdade do Recife*, p. 198. For information on the marriage of Orlando and Fragoso, see Delgado, "Centenário do Nascimento," particularly pp. 12–13. Fragoso was the first woman invited to join a Brazilian Academy of letters. See Chacon, *Da Escola do Recife*, p. 114. A good example of her writing is "A Questão da Mulher," *A Cultura Acadêmica* (November-December 1904): 233–39.

20. Da Costa, "1870–1889," p. 166.

21. See Felix Bocayuva in *A República*, 17 September 1886.

22. Besse, *Restructuring Patriarchy*, p. 14.

23. See E. A. Caldas Britto, "Uma Resposta em Tempo," *Revista Acadêmica*, 5 May 1886, pp. 5–7. Flory notes criticisms of the law schools beginning as early as the 1840s and suggests that the law degree was already devalued. See *Judge and Jury*, pp. 198–99. While some were critical prior to the late 1870s, these critics did not have a major impact on the self-image of the law students and they did not prompt a major reevaluation of their role or an attempt to define a new identity for themselves.

24. Da Costa, "1870–1889," p. 168.

25. Joaquim José de França's play "Caiu o Ministério" is quoted in Barman, "Politics on the Stage," p. 253.

26. Da Costa, "1870–1889," pp. 163, 168–69.

27. Luz, "Papel das Classes Médias."

28. See Maciel de Barros's analysis of the debate over higher education reform in *Ilustração Brasileira*, pp. 207–339. See also Venâncio Filho, *Arcadas ao Bacharelismo*, pp. 85–91, and Hendricks, "Education and Maintenance of the Social Structure," pp. 49–53 and 74–75 (although, here as elsewhere, Hendricks overstates the novelty of developments after 1870).

29. Morse, *Community to Metropolis*, p. 155.

30. Complaints regarding the requirement to use what many thought were outdated textbooks had been heard before, but this problem was clearly not resolved as quickly as the reformers had hoped. See Joaquim de Albuquerque Barros Guimarães in "Memória Histórica Acadêmica do Anno de 1882," 1E396, MI, Curso Jurídico do Recife, Arquivo Nacional.

31. Vampré, *Memórias*, 2:256–58. See also Bevilaqua, *Faculdade do Recife*, pp. 162, 180.

32. Vicente Mamede de Freitas, "Memória Histórica do Anno de 1882," (São Paulo: Typographia do Comércio, 1883), p. 19 in 1E3123, MI, Faculdade de Direito de São Paulo, Arquivo Nacional.

33. Mamede de Frietas, "Memória Histórica 1882," pp. 15–16 in 1E3123, MI, FDSP, Arquivo Nacional; see also "Notas, August 1888," in 1E399, MI, CJR, Arquivo Nacional.

34. Mamede de Freitas, "Memória Histórica 1882," pp. 15–16 in 1E3123, MI, FDSP, Arquivo Nacional.

35. Bevilaqua, *Faculdade do Recife*, p. 180.

36. Vicente Pires da Motta, "Relatório 20/December/1881" in 1E3122, MI, Faculdade do Direito de São Paulo, Arquivo Nacional.

37. Mamede de Freitas, "Memória Histórica 1882," pp. 17 and 19 in 1E3123, MI, FDSP, Arquivo Nacional.

38. João Capistrano Bandeiro de Mello's comments in 1E396, MI, Curso Jurídico do Recife, and similar comments in 1E395, MI, FDR, Arquivo Nacional.

39. Bevilaqua, *Faculdade do Recife*, p. 157.

40. Mamede de Freitas, "Memória Histórica 1882," pp. 17–18 in 1E3123, MI, FDSP, Arquivo Nacional.

41. C. B. Monteiro, "O Ensino Livre na Academia de São Paulo," *A União*, 15 October 1884; see also Bevilaqua, *Faculdade do Recife*, p. 299.

42. Bevilaqua, *Faculdade do Recife*, p. 302.

43. See C. B. Monteiro, "O Ensino Livre na Academia de São Paulo," *A União*, 15 October 1884; J. Dias da Rocha, *A União*, 18 August 1884; Francisco Paiva *A Ordem*, 28 May 1883.

44. E. A. de Caldas Britto, "Uma Resposta em Tempo," *Revista Acadêmica*, 5 May 1886, p. 6.

45. Morse, *Community to Metropolis*, p. 154.

46. Silva Jardim, *A Gente no Monsteiro (no Anno Passado)* (São Paulo: Typographia da 'Tribuna Liberal': 1879), pp. 7–8.

47. Laurentina A. Cesario d'Azevedo, "Ensino Livre," *Revista Acadêmica*, 5 May 1886, p. 3.

48. Morse, *Community to Metropolis*, p. 193. On the decline of repúblicas, see Pedro Affonso Junior, *O Evolucionista*, 28 May 1887.

49. Almeida Nogueira, *Academia de São Paulo*, 9:211. For descriptions of various republican student newspapers, see Vampré, *Memórias*, 2:316, 322–23. 325, 330.

50. Quoted in Amaral, "Jornalismo Acadêmico," p. 62.

51. *Aurora* in 1E397, MI, FDR, Arquivo Nacional.

52. For the numbers of students passing the 1885 exams, see *O País*, 18 November 1885 in 1E397, MI, FDR, Arquivo Nacional. For information on secondary education during the imperial period, see Haidar, *Ensino Secundário*, particularly pp. 22, 53, 62, 95, 262.

53. Silva Jardim, *Memórias e Viagens*, pp. 24–25, 70–71. See also *Gente do Mosteiro*, pp. 27–28, 31–32.

54. Vampré, *Memórias*, 2:277.

55. Bevilaqua, *Faculdade do Recife*, pp. 156, 342–43. On Rodrigues dos Santos, see Vampré, *Memórias*, 2:307.

56. Maciel de Barros argues that the reform of the law schools is largely responsible for the new intellectual and political efflorescence at the law schools. See *Ilustração Brasileira*, pp. 335–37.

57. Barman and Barman, "Role of the Law Graduate," pp. 441–44. For data on the number of graduates per year, see Almeida Nogueira, *Academia de São Paulo*, 2:152–53. See also Graham's discussion of the glut of law graduates in *Patronage and Politics*, pp. 226, 266–67. For a humorous if jaundiced view of this situation, see Valentim Magalhães, "Cá Fóra," in *Quadros e Contos* (São Paulo: Dolivaes Nunes, 1882): 29–37.

58. For information on the number of Recife graduates, see Martins, *Lista Geral dos Bacharéis.* For a discussion of the weakness of republicanism in the northeast even after the establishment of the Republic, see Levine, *Pernambuco in the Brazilian Federation.*

59. Da Costa, "1870–1889," pp. 174–76. See also her discussion in *Brazilian Empire*, pp. 220–22.

60. Borges, "A República," p. 56.

61. Quoted in Amaral, "Jornalismo Acadêmico," p. 66.

62. E. A. de Caldas Britto, "Uma Resposta em Tempo," *Revista Acadêmica*, 5 May 1886, p. 6.

63. See Paixão Liau's unpublished master's thesis, "A Lucta," pp. 47–48.

64. Phaelante da Camara, "A Monarchia e os seus Sectários," *A República*, 5 June 1882, p. 4.

65. Colson, "Crisis of 1889," p. 276.

66. The quotation is from Borges, "Um Jornal Acadêmico," p. 156. See also Nilo Peçanha, "Princesa Isabel," *Era Nova*, 15 June 1887.

67. Pang and Seckinger, "Mandarins of Imperial Brazil," pp. 215–18.

68. See, for example, the "Homenagem do Club Vinte de Setembro a Venâncio Ayres, do trigésimo dia de sua Morte," (São Paulo: Baurel, Pauperio e Comp., 1885).

69. Assis Brasil, *História da República*, pp. vii, 45–47.

70. Arthur Ribeiro, *A Onda*, 16 June 1887.

71. "O Que Somos e O Que Queremos," *O Federalista*, 5 April 1880, p. 3.

72. Colson, "Crisis of 1889," pp. 272–74.

73. F. Pennaforte Mendes de Almeida, *O Constitucional*, 27 July 1882.

74. Fonseca Portella, "Os Republicanos e a Monarchia," *A Ordem*, 16 July 1884.

75. Alcides Lima, *O Federalista*, 3 May 1880, pp. 11–12.

76. Quoted in Lins, *História do Positivismo*, p. 146.

77. Quoted in Amaral, "Jornalismo Acadêmico," p. 66.

78. Carvalho e Morães, "Ordem e Progresso," *O Constitucional*, 11 August 1882.

79. Borja da Almeida, *A Ordem*, 25 June 1884.

80. See, for example, Assis Brasil's poem "Danton" in *O Federalista*, 11 August 1880, p. 32.

81. "Durante o Mez," *Revista Republicana*, 5 August 1885, p. 3.

82. Izidora Martins Junior, "Á Memória de José Joaquim da Silva Xavier," on the front page of *A República*, 15 May 1882. See also Cassiano Lopes, "Vinte e Um de April," *Revista Acadêmica*, 5 May 1886, pp. 4–5.

83. Silva Jardim in 1878, quoted in Amaral, "Jornalismo Acadêmico," p. 75.

84. Gastão da Cunha, *A Ordem*, 6 June 1883; see also F. Pennaforte Mendes de Almeida, *O Constitucional*, 16 July 1883, and similar comments in *O Constitucional*, 19 May 1883; Francisco Paiva, "Os Nossos Adversários," *A Ordem*, 10 May 1883.

85. J. Canuto de Figueiredo Junior, "A Revolução e o Progresso," *A Reacção*, 8 July 1881.

86. F. de Campos Junior, *A República*, 31 December 1885. See also Borges, "Um Jornal Acadêmico," p. 154.

87. Adorno, *Os Aprendizes do Poder*, pp. 119–20.

88. Bevilaqua, *Faculdade do Recife*, pp. 395–96.

89. Barman, *Citizen Emperor*, pp. 242–43.

90. Lauderdale Graham, "Vintem Riot."

91. See Phaelante Da Câmara, "Martins Junior, O Jornalista," *A Cultura Acadêmica* (September 1904): 108.

92. L. de Piza e Almeida, quoted in Liau, "Dimensões de um Jornal Acadêmico," pp. 47–48.

93. Luiz Gonzago Bacellar, *Era Nova*, 22 May 1887; see also Borges, "Um Jornal Acadêmico," p. 152.

94. Alcides Lima, *A Lucta*, 5 May 1880.

95. Quoted in Barman, "Politics on the Stage," pp. 253–54.

96. Borja da Almeida *A Ordem*, 25 June 1884; J. P. da Veiga Filho, *A Ordem*, 18 May 1884; A. O. Viveiros de Castro, "O Republicanismo," *Era Nova*, 15 June 1887; J. P. Veiga Filho *A Ordem*, 7 September 1884.

97. See the discussion in Boehrer, "Republican Revolution," pp. 47–48.

98. Coelho dos Reis, "A Actualidade," *A República*, 5 June 1882, p. 2; Alberto Salles, quoted in Liau, "Dimensões de um Jornal Acadêmico," p. 101.

99. *A Onda*, 17 August 1884; *Ça Irá*, 19 August 1882; V. Silva Ayrosa, *A Onda*, 16 June 1887.

100. Quoted in Colson, "Crisis of 1889," p. 276.

234

101. Franco, *Júlio de Castilhos*, pp. 18–29.

102. "O Que Somos e o que Queremos," *O Federalista*, 5 April 1880, p. 3.

103. Da Costa, "1870–1889," p. 181; See Rama's discussion of the rise of realism in Brazil in the late 1870s in *Lettered City*, pp. 64–65. See also Cândido, *Formação da Literatura Brasileira*, 2:295.

104. Quoted in Gervasio Fioravanti, "Martins Junior (O Poeta)," *A Cultura Acadêmica* (September 1904): 19.

105. See *A União*, 5 September 1883; See also Amâncio de Souza, "Algumas Considerações," *Revista Acadêmica*, 5 May 1886. For further discussion of student calls for literary reform, see Liau, "Dimensões de um Jornal Acadêmico," p. 64; Alcides Peçanha, *Era Nova*, 15 June 1887, and Amâncio de Souza, "Monomania Poetica," *Revista Acadêmica*, 22 May 1886, pp. 3–4. In addressing his poetry to a Spanish actress, Martins Junior warned her that his poetic gifts were not lyrical but scientific. See Fioravanti, "Martins Junior (O Poeta)," p. 19.

106. Eakin, "Race and Identity," pp. 154–55. For the pronouncement of the "end of subjectivity," see "O Que Somos e o que Queremos," and Alcides Lima, "Rocha Lima (Crítica e Literatura)–Maranhão–1878," *O Federalista*, 5 April 1880, p. 3. See also Maciel de Barros, *Ilustração Brasileira*, pp. 138–44, on "scientific poetry." For a discussion of the growth of what Lilia Moritz Schwarcz calls a "diffuse scientism" in the late imperial period, see her *Spectacle of the Races*, pp. 29–35.

107. See, for example, Alberto Salles, "Effeitos da Escravidão Sobre a Mentalidade do Povo Brasileiro," in *O Federalista*, 11 August 1880.

108. Daniel Machado, "Culto ao Poeta," in "Castro Alves: Homanegem da Academia de São Paulo," 10 July 1881, in Biblioteca Nacional, Seção de Obras Raras.

109. See Francisco Paiva's comments in *A Ordem*, 28 May 1883.

110. Gil Amora, "A Actualidade," *Ensaios Jurídicos e Litterários*, 1 June 1888, p. 41.

111. Silva Jardim, *Gente do Mosteiro*, p. 15.

112. See, for example, Jeronymo Muniz, "Da Leis da Evolução," *Revista Acadêmica de Sciencias e Lettras* (June-July 1876): 138–43.

113. Morse, *Community to Metropolis*, pp. 163–64; Filinto Bastos, *A Reacção*, 8 July 1881.

114. Graham, *Britain and the Onset of Modernization*, pp. 232–51.

115. Castilhos, *A Evolução*, 15 May 1879, p. 17.

116. See Liau's discussion in "Dimensões de um Jornal Acadêmico," p. 23.

117. Da Costa, "1870–1889," pp. 185–86; Nachman, "Positivism, Modernization," p. 7.

118. Vampré, *Memórias*, 2:274–75.

119. Quoted in Da Costa, *Brazilian Empire*, p. 223. For a discussion of industry, see, for example, A. Pedro de Mello, "O Industrialismo Moderno," *A República*, 15 May 1882, pp. 3–4.

120. Quoted in Lins, *História do Positivismo*, p. 146. The Brazilian elite's model country, France, was itself undergoing "the replacement of a liberalism based on metaphysical philosophy by a liberalism based on sociology." See Logue, *From Philosophy to Sociology*, p. 2.

121. Jernonymo Muniz, "Economic Política," *Revista Acadêmica de Sciencias e Lettras* (June-July 1865): p. 65. See Rama's discussion of the rise of sociology in *Lettered City*, p. 78, and Cândido's discussion of the "deification" of sociology in *Formação da Literatura Brasileira*, 2:288–89. For examples of law graduates who continued to study sociological issues after graduation, see Bevilaqua, *Faculdade do Recife*, pp. 174, 176.

122. Izidoro Martins Junior, *A República*, 5 June 1882, p. 1.

123. *O Federalista*, 5 September 1880, p. 43.

124. Gil Amora, "A Actualidade," *Ensaios Jurídicos e Litterários*, 1 June 1878, p. 41.

125. Alberto Salles, "O Ensino Superior no Império," *O Federalista*, 11 August 1880, pp. 36–37; Graciano de Almeida, writing in *A Lucta*, 20 April 1882.

126. Quoted in Chacon, *Da Escola do Recife*, p. 203.

127. There is no adequate study of Tobias Barreto's life or his ideas. The best source of information on him available in English is Medina, "Tobias Barreto." See also Maciel de Barros, *Ilustração Brasileira*, pp. 131–33, 149–61, Hendricks, "Education and Maintenance of the Social Structure," pp. 75–88, and Araujo, *Escola no Rio Grande do Sul*, pp. 97–125.

128. Quoted in Bevilaqua (himself a follower), *Faculdade do Recife*, p. 373.

129. See Medina, "Tobias Barreto," p. 221.

130. Izidoro Martins Junior, "O Dr. Tobias Barreto," *A República*, 5 June 1882, p. 2. See also Amâncio de Souza, "Algumas Considerações," *Revista Acadêmica*, 5 May 1886, p. 3.

131. See Bevilaqua, *Faculdade do Recife*, p. 340, and Paim, "Artur Orlando," pp. 5, 7.

132. Medina, "Tobias Barreto," pp. 128, 221, 234; Bevilaqua, *Faculdade do Recife*, p. 192.

133. Hinckmar, *Cinco Annos*, p. 96. His real name was João Tomás de Melo Alves.

134. Celso, *Oito Anos no Parlamento*, pp. 9–14. For other examples of republicans turned Liberals who gained seats due to family influence, see Almeida Nogueira, *Academia de São Paulo* 9:253.

135. See Liau's discussion in "Dimensões de um Jornal Acadêmico," pp. 127, 132–33.

136. Júlio de Castilhos, *A Evolução*, 15 May 1879, p. 17.

137. Almeida Nogueira, *Academia de São Paulo*, 9:255

138. Vampré, *Memórias*, 2:132.

139. Fontoura, *Memórias*, 1:6. See also Almeida Nogueira's discussion of Antônio Augusto Bittencourt in *Academia de São Paulo*, 4:161–62. Bittencourt, the republican son of a Conservative father, founded a republican newspaper in Amparo in the province of São Paulo in 1879.

140. For information on republicans in Rio Grande do Sul and São Paulo, see Da Costa, "1870–1889," pp. 204–6.

141. "Centro Republicano," *Revista Acadêmica*, 22 May 1886, p. 4.

142. According to Oliveira Vianna, 79 percent of the republican newspapers and 89 percent of the republican clubs were in these three provinces. See da Costa, *Brazilian Empire*, pp. 226–27.

143. Morse, *Community to Metropolis*, pp. 162–63.

CONCLUSION

1. Dudley, "Professionalization and Politicization." See also Beattie, "Transforming Enlisted Army Service," pp. 53–55, 66–68.

2. Dudley, "Professionalization and Politicization," pp. 107, 110.

3. See William Sheldon Dudley's discussion of the military schools in "Reform and Radicalism in the Brazilian Army, 1870–1889," Unpublished doctoral dissertation, Columbia University, 1972, pp. 32–35; John Schulz, *O*

Exército na Política: Origens da Intervenção Militar, 1850–1894 (São Paulo: Editora da Universidade de São Paulo, 1994), p. 29.

4. See Dudley, "Reform and Radicalism," p. 193; Schulz, *Exército na Política*, pp. 24, 26–32, 40–42, 205–16. Castro, *Militares e República*, pp. 19–20, 27–28, 140–43.

5. The most complete study of this reform movement is Dudley, "Reform and Radicalism in the Brazilian Army, 1870–1889." See particularly pp. 6–10, 89–101.

6. Mattoon, "Railroads, Coffee, and Big Business," pp. 289–90. See also Pedro Carlos da Silva Telles, *História da Engenharia no Brasil*, pp. 65, 68, 83–84, 379–83, 469.

7. Dudley, "Professionalization and Politicization," pp. 114–15, 119, 123, and his "Reform and Radicalism," pp. 160–62, 189–90. Colombia's *Colegio Militar* was also the center of technical training in that country. See Safford, *Ideal of the Practical*, pp. 166–84. Beattie, "Transforming Enlisted Army Service," p. 68.

8. Rama, *Lettered City*, p. 76.

9. Dudley, "Professionalization and Politicization," pp. 116–17, 121, 124, and his "Reform and Radicalism," pp. 201, 266–71, 470–72, 534–35.

10. Dudley, "Professionalization and Politicization," pp. 115–16, 120–22; Castro, *Militares e República*, pp. 85–103.

11. Da Costa, *Brazilian Empire*, p. 229. Beattie, "Transforming Enlisted Army Service," pp. 189–91; Castro, *Militares e República*, pp. 48–76.

12. Castro, *Militares e República*, pp. 7–9, 17–18, 29–51, 112–23, 136–42, 166–91, 194–95. Castro argues that the junior officers and students influenced Constant as much as, if not more than, he influenced them.

13. Quoted in Castro, *Militares e República*, p. 190.

14. Lewin, *Parentela*, p. 117.

15. Vargas, *Contribuições para a História*, pp. 11–16.

16. See Sevcenko, *Literatura como Missão*, pp. 119–54, and Needell, *Tropical Belle Époque*, pp. 218–21.

17. Carvalho, "Forces of Tradition," p. 157; Moritz Schwarcz, *Spectacle of the Races*, pp. 249, 253, 256–310; Coelho, however, suggests that the new authority of public health officials has been exaggerated. See *Profissões Imperiais*, pp. 139–44, 216–21. See p. 268 for the number of students enrolled in various areas of study from 1907 to 1934.

18. Nachman, "Positivism, Modernization," pp. 14–15.

19. Carvalho, *Formação das Almas*. See also Carvalho, *Construção da Ordem*, p. 45.

20. Castro, *Militares e República*, pp. 196–200.

21. Hahner, *Civilian-Military Relations*, p. 199.

22. Carvalho, *Construção da Ordem*, p. 182. On the decline of the Recife law school after 1889, see Hendricks, "Education and Maintenance of the Social Structure," pp. 88–104, 122–26.

23. Bevilaqua, *Faculdade do Recife*, p. 212. Bevilaqua himself was the first editor-in-chief of the new publication.

24. Vampré, *Memórias*, 2:338.

25. Almeida Nogueira, *Academia de São Paulo*, 4:270.

26. 1e8125, mi, fdsp, Arquivo Nacional, particularly the letters of 27 November 1889 and 5 December 1889. In the same folder, see the telegram from 24 August 1888, for the proclamation celebrating Dom Pedro II's recovery. See also Vampré, *Memórias*, 2:333–34, 340–341, and Bevilaqua, *Faculdade do Recife*, pp. 201–2 and 207, for a discussion of responses to the declaration of the republic.

27. Martins, *Patriarca e Bacharel*, pp. 150–55; Carolina Nabuco, *Life of Joaquim Nabuco*, p. 249.

28. Monaco Janotti, "Monarchist Response," pp. 224–25, 228.

29. Debes, *Campos Sales*, pp. 48, 52–53, 78. Afonso Arinos de Melo Franco, *Rodrigues Alves*.

30. Love, *São Paulo*, pp. xiii–xx; Graham, *Patronage and Politics*, p. 219.

31. Levine, *Pernambuco in the Brazilian Federation*, pp. 124–40; Pang, *Bahia in the First Brazilian Republic*, pp. 18–19, 22, 443–44, 446.

32. Wirth, *Minas Gerais in the Brazilian Federation*, pp. 96–139, 140–70; Love, *São Paulo*, pp. 102–10.

33. Love, *Rio Grande do Sul*, pp. 28–29, 34–36, 60–76, 78.

34. See Dávila, " 'Perfecting the Race,' " particularly pp. 3–11, 13–18, 22–29, 64–67, 74–100, 121–46, 184–202, 308–13.

35. See Stepan, *Military in Politics*. For a discussion of the greater complexity of the elite in modern Brazil, see Conniff and McCann, *Modern Brazil*, pp. xv–xvii, 3–46, 103–20.

36. Camp, *Political Recruitment*, p. 36. On the military period, see Skidmore, *Politics of Military Rule*, pp. 185–87, 200–203.

BIBLIOGRAPHY

MANUSCRIPT MATERIALS

Bastos, Tavares, Coleção. Biblioteca Nacional, Seção dos Manuscritos, Rio de Janeiro.

Curso Jurídico no Brazil. "Criação do Curso Jurídico no Brazil." 006.0-076, Arquivo Nacional Microfilm.

Garcez, Henrique, Coleção. Instituto Histórico e Geográfico Brasileiro, Rio de Janeiro.

Ministério do Império (MI). Curso Jurídico de São Paulo, Recife, e Olinda. Relatórios e Ofícios do Diretor. Arquivo Nacional, Rio de Janeiro.

Nabuco, Joaquim, letters of. Fundação Joaquim Nabuco, Instituto de Documentação, CEHIBRA-DOTEX, Pernambuco (Recife).

Pereira, Antônio Baptista. "Crônica." Arquivo Histórico do Rio Grande do Sul, Arquivos Particulares. Lata 40, maço 1.

BOOKS, ARTICLES, AND DISSERTATIONS

Addy, George M. *The Enlightenment in the University of Salamanca.* Durham: Duke University Press, 1966.

Adelman, Jeremy. *The Republic of Capital: Buenos Aires and the Transformation of the Atlantic World.* Stanford: Stanford University Press, 1999.

Adorno, Sérgio. *Os Aprendizes do Poder: O Bacharelismo Liberal na Política Brasileira.* Rio de Janeiro: Paz e Terra, 1988.

Alencastro, Luiz Felipe de, ed. *História da Vida Privada no Brasil, Volume II: Império: a Corte e a Modernidade Nacional.* São Paulo: Companhia das Letras, 1997.

Almeida, Joaquim Angêlico Bessoni de. *Neste Caso Eu Me Caso; ou Os Estudantes do Recife.* Recife: Typographia Universal, 1862.

Almeida Nogueira, José Almeida. *A Academia de São Paulo: Tradições e*

Reminiscências, Estudantes, Estudantões, Estudantadas. 9 volumes. São Paulo: Vanorden and A Editora, 1907–1912.

Álvares de Azevedo, Manuel Antônio. *Cartas de Álvares de Azevedo.* São Paulo: Biblioteca Academia Paulista de Letras, 1976.

Amaral, Antônio Barreto do. "Jornalismo Acadêmico," *Revista do Arquivo Municipal (São Paulo)* (July–December 1977): 11–293.

Anderson, Benedict. *Imagined Communities: Reflections on the Origins and Spread of Nationalism.* London: Verso, 1983.

Anderson, Perry. *Lineages of the Absolutist State.* London: Verso, 1980.

Andrade, Manuel Correia de. *Movimentos Nativistas em Pernambuco: Setembrizada e Novembrada.* Recife: Universidade Federal de Pernambuco, 1971.

Antunes, José Leopoldo Ferreira. *Medicina, Leis e Moral: Pensamento Médico e Comportamento no Brasil (1870–1930).* São Paulo: Fundação Editora da UNESP, 1999.

Araujo, José Francelino de. *A Escola do Recife no Rio Grande do Sul: Influência dos Nordestinos na Magistratura, no Magistério e nas Letras Jurídicas do Rio Grande do Sul.* Porto Alegre: Sagra; D.C. Luzzato; Instituto dos Advogados do Rio Grande do Sul; Faculdades Integradas Ritter dos Reis, 1996.

Aron, Raymund. "Social Class, Political Class, Ruling Class." In *Power, Modernity, and Sociology: Selected Sociological Writings.* Aldershot, England: Edward Elgar, 1988.

Assis Brasil, Joaquim Francisco de. *História da República Rio-Grandense.* Facsimile edition. Porto Alegre: Estante Rio-Grandense União de Seguros, 1982.

Auler, Guilherme. "Dom Pedro II—Viagem a Pernambuco (em 1859)," *Revista do Arquivo Público (Pernambuco)* 12 (December 1975): 52–122.

———. *Os Bolsistas do Imperador.* Petrópolis: Tribuna de Petrópolis, 1956.

Azevedo, Fernando de. *Brazilian Culture: An Introduction to the Study of Culture in Brazil.* Translated by William Rex Crawford. New York: Macmillan and Company, 1950.

Azevedo, José Afonso Mendonça. *Vida e Obra de Salvador de Mendonça.* Brasília: Ministério das Relações Exteriores, 1971.

Bandecchi, Pedro Brasil. "Libero Badaró, Júlio Frank, e o Liberalism em

São Paulo," *Revista do Instituto Histórico e Geográfico Brasileiro* (April–June 1985): 103–18.

Barbosa, Rui. *Correspondência: Primeiros Tempos: Curso Jurídico. Colegas e Parentes*. Rio de Janeiro: Fundação Casa de Rui Barbosa, 1973.

Barbosa Lima Sobrinho, Alexandré José. *A Lingua Portuguesa e a Unidade do Brasil*. Rio de Janeiro: Livraria José Olympio, 1977.

Barman, Roderick J. *Brazil, The Forging of a Nation, 1798–1850*. Stanford: Stanford University Press, 1988.

———. "Brazilians in France, 1822–1872: Doubly Outsiders." In *Strange Pilgrimages: Exile, Travel, and National Identity in Latin America, 1800–1990s*, edited by Ingrid E. Fey and Karen Racine. Wilmington DE: Scholarly Resources, 2000.

———. *Citizen Emperor: Pedro II and the Making of Brazil, 1825–1891*. Stanford: Stanford University Press, 1999.

———. "Politics on the Stage: The Late Brazilian Empire as Dramatized by França Junior," *Luso-Brazilian Review* 13, no. 2 (winter 1976): 244–60.

Barman, Roderick J., and Jean Barman. "The Role of the Law Graduate in the Political Elite in Imperial Brazil," *Journal of Inter-American Studies and World Affairs* 18 (November 1976): 423–48.

Barreto, José Feliciano de Castilhos. *A Questão Acadêmica em 1871*. Rio de Janeiro: Imparcial, 1871.

Barreto, Vicente. *A Ideologia Liberal no Processo da Independência no Brasil (1798–1824)*. Brasília: Câmara dos Deputados, Centro de Documentação e Informação, 1973.

Beattie, Peter M. "The House, the Street, and the Barracks: Reform and Honorable Masculine Social Space in Brazil, 1864–1945," *Hispanic American Historical Review* 76, no. 3 (August 1996): 439–73.

———. "Transforming Enlisted Army Service in Brazil, 1864–1940): Penal Servitude versus Conscription and Changing Conceptions of Honor, Race, and Nation." Ph.D. diss., University of Miami, 1994.

Besse, Susan K. *Restructuring Patriarchy: The Modernization of Gender Inequality in Brazil,1914–1940*. Chapel Hill: University of North Carolina Press, 1996.

Bethell, Leslie, and José Murilo de Carvalho. "1822–1850." In *Brazil:*

Empire and Republic, 1822–1930, edited by Leslie Bethell. Cambridge: Cambridge University Press, 1989.

Bevilaqua, Clovis. *História da Faculdade de Direito do Recife*. 1927. Reprint, São Paulo: Instituto Nacional do Livro, 1977.

Bezarra Máriz, Zélia Maria. *Nísia Floresta Brasileira Augusta*. Natal: Editora Universitária, 1982.

Bieber, Judy. *Power, Patronage, and Political Violence: State Building on a Brazilian Frontier, 1822–1889*. Lincoln: University of Nebraska Press, 1999.

Bieber Freitas, Judy. "Slavery and Social Life: Attempts to Reduce Free People to Slavery in the Sertão Mineiro, Brazil, 1850–1871," *Journal of Latin American Studies* 26, no. 3 (October 1994): 597–619.

Bledstein, Burton. *The Culture of Professionalism: The Middle Class and the Development of Higher Education in America*. New York: W. W. Norton, 1976.

Bloom, Harold. *The Ringer in the Tower: Studies in the Romantic Tradition*. Chicago: University of Chicago Press, 1971.

Boehrer, George C. A. "The Brazilian Republican Revolution: Old and New Views," *Luso-Brazilian Review* 3, no. 2 (December 1966): 43–57.

Borges, Dain. *The Family in Bahia, 1870–1945*. Stanford: Stanford University Press, 1992.

———. " 'Puffy, Ugly, Slothful, and Inert': Degeneration in Brazilian Social Thought, 1880–1940," *Journal of Latin American Studies* 25, no. 2 (Jay 1993): 235–56.

Borges, Urquiza Maria. "*A República*: Um Jornal Acadêmico." *História* (1982): 149–62.

Borroul, Estevão Leão. *Não: Simples Resposta a uma Consulta*. São Paulo: Estereotypia King, 1890.

———. *O Partido Conservador da Franca: Breves Considerações sobre Política Hodierna*. São Paulo: Jorge Seckler, 1883.

Bourdieu, Pierre. *Homo Academicus*. Translated by Peter Collier. Stanford: Stanford University Press, 1988.

———. *Language and Symbolic Power*. Edited and introduced by John B. Thompson. Translated by Gino Raymond and Matthew Adamson. Cambridge MA: Harvard University Press, 1991.

———. *The State Nobility: Elite Schools in the Field of Power.* Translated by Lauretta C. Clough. Stanford: Stanford University Press, 1996.

Brandão, Maria, and M. Lopes d'Almeida. *A Universidade de Coimbra: Esboço da sua História.* Coimbra: Universidade de Coimbra, 1937.

Buarque de Holanda, Sérgio. *Raizes do Brasil.* Rio de Janeiro: Livraria José Olympio Editora, 1969.

Burkholder, Mark A. "Honor and Honors in Colonial Spanish America." In Lyman L. Johnson and Sonya Lipsett-Rivera, *The Faces of Honor: Sex, Shame, and Violence in Colonial Latin America.* Albuquerque: University of New Mexico Press, 1998.

Burns, E. Bradford. *Nationalism in Brazil: A Historical Survey.* New York: Frederick A. Praeger, 1968.

Bushnell, David, and Neill Macaulay. *The Emergence of Latin America in the Nineteenth Century.* New York: Oxford University Press, 1994.

Calmon, Pedro. *Vidas e Amores de Castro Alves.* Rio de Janeiro: A Noite, 1937.

Camp, Roderic Ai. *Political Recruitment across Two Centuries: Mexico, 1884–1991.* Austin: University of Texas Press, 1995.

Cândido, Antônio. *Formação da Literatura Brasileira (Momentos Decisivos) 1836–1880.* Volume 2. São Paulo: Livraria Martins Editora, 1971.

Cardoso de Oliveira. *Dois Metros e Cinco.* Rio de Janeiro: H. Garnier, 1905.

Carvalho, João de. *O Cantor dos Escravos: Castro Alves.* São Paulo: T. A. Queroz, 1989.

Carvalho, José Murilo de. "Brazil, 1870–1914 — The Force of Tradition," *Journal of Latin American Studies* 24 (1992): 146–62.

———. *A Construção da Ordem: A Elite Política Imperial.* Rio de Janeiro: Campus, 1980.

———. *A Formação das Almas: O Imáginario da República no Brasil.* São Paulo: Companhia das Letras, 1990.

———. "Elite and State Building in Imperial Brazil." Ph.D. diss., Stanford University, 1975.

———. "Political Elites and State-Building: The Case of Nineteenth-Century Brazil," *Comparative Studies in Society and History* 24 (July 1982): 378–99.

———. *Teatro de Sombras: A Política Imperial.* São Paulo: Edições Vértice, 1988.

Castelo Branco, Vitorino Prata. *Um Esteio da Liberdade na Corte do Segundo Império: A Vida e a Obra de José Antônio Pimenta Bueno, Marques de San Vicente, Jurista e Parlamentar Brasileiro (1803–1878)*. São Paulo: Sugestões Literárias, 1973.

Castro, Celso. *O Espírito Militar: Um Estudo de Antropologia na Academia Militar das Agulhas Negras*. Rio de Janeiro: Jorge Zahar Editora Ltda., 1990.

———. *Os Militares e a República: Um Estudo Sobre Cultura e Ação Política*. Rio de Janeiro: Jorge Zahar Editora Ltda., 1995.

Castro Alves, Antônio de. *The Major Abolitionist Poems*. Edited and translated by Amy A. Peterson. New York: Garland Publishing, 1990.

———. *Poesias Completas de Castro Alves*. Rio de Janeiro: Ediouro, 1980.

"Castro Alves: Homanegem da Academia de São Paulo" (special issue of newspaper). In Biblioteca Nacional, Seção de Obras Raras, 10 July 1881.

Celso, Afonso. *Oitos Anos no Parlamento*. Brasília: Editora Universidade de Brasília, 1981.

Chacon, Wamireh. *Da Escola do Recife ao Código Civil: Arthur Orlando e sua Época*. Rio de Janeiro: Organização Simões, 1969.

Chasteen, John Charles. "*Cabanos* and *Farrapos*: Brazilian Nativism in Comparative Perspective," *Locus* 7, no. 1 (fall 1994): 31–46.

———. *Heroes on Horseback: A Life and Times of the Last Gaucho Caudillos*. Albuquerque: University of New Mexico Press, 1995.

Coelho, Eduardo Campos. *Os Profissões Imperiais: Medicina, Engenharia, e Advocacia no Rio de Janeiro, 1822–1930*. Rio de Janeiro: Editora Record, 1999.

Colson, Frank. "On Expectations — Perspectives on the Crisis of 1889 in Brazil," *Journal of Latin American Studies* 13, no. 2 (November 1981): 265–92.

Connell, R. W. *Masculinities*. Berkeley: University of California Press, 1995.

Conniff, Michael L., and Frank D. McCann, eds. *Modern Brazil: Elites and Masses in Historical Perspective*. Lincoln: University of Nebraska Press, 1989.

Conrad, Robert Edgar. *The Destruction of Brazilian Slavery, 1850–1888*. Malabar FL: Krieger Publishing, 1993.

Cunha, Celso. *Lingua, Nação Alienação*. Rio de Janeiro: Editora Nova
   Fronteira, 1981.

Da Costa, Emília Viotti. "1870–1889." In *Brazil: Empire and Republic,
   1822–1930*, edited by Leslie Bethell. Cambridge: Cambridge University
   Press, 1989.

————. *The Brazilian Empire: Myths and Histories*. Chicago: University of
   Chicago Press, 1985.

Da Matta, Roberto. *A Casa e a Rua: Espaço, Cidadania, Mulher e Morte no
   Brasil*. São Paulo: Editora Brasiliense, 1985.

Davidson, Theresa. "The Brazilian Heritage of Roman Law." In *Brazil,
   Papers Presented in the Institute for Brazilian Studies*. Nashville:
   Vanderbilt University Press, 1953.

Dávila, Walter J. J. " 'Perfecting the Race': Education and Social Discipline
   in Brazil's Vargas Era (1930–1945)." Ph.D. diss., Brown University,
   1998.

Dealy, Glen Caudill. *The Public Man: An Interpretation of Latin American
   and Other Catholic Cultures*. Amherst: University of Massachusetts
   Press, 1977.

Deas, Malcolm. "Miguel Antonio Caro and Friends: Grammar and Power
   in Colombia," *History Workshop* 34 (fall 1992): 47–71.

Debes, Celio. "Alguns Aspectos da Vida Acadêmica Através da
   Correspondência de um Estudante," *Revista do Arquivo Municipal* (São
   Paulo) (July–December 1977): 321–50.

————. *Campos Sales: Perfil de um Estadista: Volume I: Na Propaganda*. Rio
   de Janeiro: Livraria Francisco Alves, 1978.

DeFreitas, Affonso A. *Tradições e Reminiscências Paulistas*. São Paulo:
   Livraria Martins Editora, 1955.

Delgado, Luiz. "Centenário do Nascimento de Artur Orlando," special
   publication published by Faculdade de Direito de Caruarú, Caderno
   No. 10, 1961.

Dias, Maria Odila Silva. *Power and Everyday Life: The Lives of Working
   Women in Nineteenth-Century Brazil*. Translated by Ann Frost. New
   Brunswick NJ: Rutgers University Press, 1995.

Dornas Filho, João. *Silva Jardim*. São Paulo: Companhia Editora Nacional,
   1936.

Dudley, William S. "Professionalization and Politicization as Motivational Factors in the Brazilian Army Coup of 15 November 1889," *Journal of Latin American Studies* 8, no. 1 (1976): 101–25.

———. "Reform and Radicalism in the Brazilian Army, 1870–1889." Ph.D. diss., Columbia University, 1972.

Dulles, John W. F. *The São Paulo Law School and the Anti-Vargas Resistance (1938–1945)*. Austin: University of Texas Press, 1986.

Eakin, Marshall C. "Race and Identity: Sílvio Romero, Science and Social Thought in Late Nineteenth-century Brazil," *Luso-Brazilian Review* 22, no. 2 (winter 1985): 151–74.

Elazaria, Judith Mader. "Lazer e Vida Urbana em São Paulo, 1850–1910." Master's thesis, Universidade de São Paulo, 1979.

Erikson, Erik H. *Identity: Youth and Crisis*. New York: W. W. Norton, 1968.

Fairclough, Norman. *Language and Power*. London: Longman, 1989.

Faoro, Raymundo. *Os Donos do Poder: Formação do Patronato Político Brasileiro*. Rio de Janeiro: Editora Globo, 1958.

Faria, Júlio Cezar de. *José Bonifácio (O Moço)*. Rio de Janeiro: Companhia Editora Nacional, 1944.

Farnham, Christine Anne. *The Education of the Southern Belle: Higher Education and Student Socialization in the Antebellum South*. New York: New York University Press, 1994.

Faust, Drew Gilpin. *James Henry Hammond and the Old South: A Design for Mastery*. Baton Rouge: Louisiana State University Press, 1982.

Fioravanti, Gervásio. "Martins Junior (O Poeta)," *A Cultura Acadêmica* (September 1904).

Fitzsimmons, Michael P. *The Parisian Order of Barristers and the French Revolution*. Cambridge MA: Harvard University Press, 1987.

Flory, Thomas. *Judge and Jury in Imperial Brazil, 1808–1871: Social Control and Political Stability in the New State*. Austin: University of Texas Press, 1981.

Fontoura, João Neves da. *Memórias, Volume I: Borges de Medeiros e seu Tempo*. Rio de Janeiro: Editora Globo, 1958.

Fragoso, Maria. "A Questão da Mulher." *A Cultura Acadêmica* (November–December 1904): 233–39.

Franco, Sérgio da Costa. *Júlio de Castilhos e sua Época*. Porto Alegre: Editora Globo, 1977.

Freyre, Gilberto. *The Mansions and the Shanties*. Translated and edited by Harriet de Onis. New York: Alfred A. Knopf, 1963.

———. *Olinda: Segunda Guía Prática, Histórica, e Sentimental de Cidade Brasileira*. Rio de Janeiro: Livraria José Olympio Editora, 1968.

———. *Order and Progress: Brazil from Monarchy to Republic*. New York: Alfred A. Knopf, 1970.

———. *O Recife, Sim! Recife, Não*. São Paulo: Imprensa Gráfica Carioca, 1969.

Gilmore, David D. *Manhood in the Making: Cultural Concepts of Masculinity*. New Haven: Yale University Press, 1990.

Gleason, Abbott. *Young Russia: The Genesis of Russian Radicalism in the 1860s*. New York: Viking Press, 1980.

Gomes, Heloisa Toller. *O Negro e o Romantismo Brasileiro*. São Paulo: Atual Editora Ltda., 1988.

Gonçalaves de Magalhães, Domingos José. *Suspíros Poéticos e Saudades*. Paris: Dauvin et Fontaine, 1836.

Goody, Jack. *The Logic of Writing and the Organization of Society*. Cambridge: Cambridge University Press, 1986.

Gouvêa, Fernando da Cruz. *O Partido Liberal no Império: O Barão de Vila Bela e sua Época*. Brasília: Senado Federal, 1986.

Graff, Harvey J. *The Labyrinths of Literacy: Reflections on Literacy Past and Present*. Pittsburgh: University of Pittsburgh Press, 1995.

Graham, Richard. *Britain and the Onset of Modernization in Brazil, 1850–1914*. Cambridge: Cambridge University Press, 1966.

———. *Patronage and Politics in Nineteenth-century Brazil*. Stanford: Stanford University Press, 1990.

Grossberg, Michael. "Institutionalizing Masculinity: The Law as a Masculine Profession." In *Meanings for Masculinity: Constructions of Masculinity in Victorian America*, edited by Mark Carnes and Clyde Griffens. Chicago: University of Chicago Press, 1990.

Guimarães, Bernardo. *Rosaura, A Engeitada*. Rio de Janeiro: Editora Moderna, 1944.

Haber, Samuel. *The Quest for Authority and Honor in the American Professions, 1750–1900*. Chicago: University of Chicago Press, 1991.

Haberly, David T. "Eugênia Câmara: The Life and Verse of an Actress," *Luso-Brazilian Review* 12, no. 2 (winter 1975): 162–74.

———. "The Mystery of the Bailiff's List, or What Fagundes Varela Read," *Luso-Brazilian Review* 24, no. 2 (winter 1987): 1–13.

Haddad, Jamil Almansur. *O Romantismo Brasileiro e as Sociedades Secretas do Tempo*. São Paulo: Gráfica Siqueira, 1945.

———, ed. *Poemas de Amor de Álvares de Azevedo*. Rio de Janeiro: Civilização Brasileira, 1970.

Hahner, June. *Civilian-Military Relations in Brazil, 1889–1898*. Columbia: University of South Carolina Press, 1969.

———. *A Mulher Brasileira e Suas Lutas Sociais e Políticas*. São Paulo: Editora Brasiliense, 1981.

Haidar, Maria de Lourdes Mariotto. *O Ensino Secundário no Império Brasileiro*. São Paulo: Editorial Grijalba Ltda., 1972.

Hale, Charles A. *Mexican Liberalism in the Age of Mora, 1821–1853*. New Haven: Yale University Press, 1968.

Hemming, John. *Red Gold: The Conquest of the Brazilian Indians*. London: Macmillan, 1978.

Hendricks, Howard Craig. "Education and Maintenance of the Social Structure: The Faculdade de Direito do Recife and the Brazilian Northeast, 1870–1930." Ph.D. diss., State University of New York, Stony Brook, 1977.

———. "The Role of Brazilian Law Schools in Elite Development," *South Eastern Latin Americanist* 27, no. 1 (June 1983): 10–18.

Hinckmar [João Tomás de Melo Alves]. *Cinco Annos n'uma Academia, 1878–1882*. São Paulo: J. Seckler, 1882.

Hite, Katherine. "The Formation and Transformation of Political Identity: Leaders of the Chilean Left, 1968–1990," *Journal of Latin American Studies* 28 (May 1996): 299–328.

Hoffnagel, Marc Jay. "From Monarchy to Republic in Northeastern Brazil: The Case of Pernambuco, 1868–1895." Ph.D. diss., Indiana University, 1975.

Holland, Dorothy, and Margaret A. Eisenhart. *Educated in Romance:*

Women, Achievement, and College Culture. Chicago: University of
Chicago Press, 1990.

Horowitz, Helen Lefkowitz. *Campus Life: Undergraduate Cultures from the
End of the Eighteenth Century to the Present.* New York: Alfred A. Knopf,
1987.

Jaksić, Iván, and Sol Serrano. "In the Service of the Nation: The
Establishment and Consolidation of the Universidad de Chile, 1842–
79," *Hispanic American Historical Review* 70, no. 1 (February 1990):
139–71.

Janotti, Maria de Lourdes Monaco. "The Monarchist Response to the
Beginnings of the Brazilian Republic," *Americas* 48, no. 2 (October
1991): 223–43.

Jansen Perreira, Bruno. *Duas Palavras ao meus Collegas por Occasião da
Collecão do Grau de Bacharel no Dia 1 de Dezembro de 1865* (pamphlet).
Recife: Typografia Commercial de Gerald Henrique de Mira, 1866.

Junius. *Em São Paulo: Notas de Viagem.* São Paulo: Jorge Seckler, 1882.

Kagan, Richard K. *Student and Society in Early Modern Spain.* Baltimore:
Johns Hopkins University Press, 1974.

Kelsall, Malcolm. *Byron's Politics.* Sussex NJ: Harvester Press, 1987.

Kett, Joseph F. *Rites of Passage: Adolescence in America, 1790 to the Present.*
New York: Basic Books, 1977.

Kimball, Bruce A. *Orators and Philosophers: A History of the Idea of Liberal
Education.* New York: College Entrance Examination Board, 1995.

———. *The 'True Professional Idea' in America: A History.* 2d ed. Lanham
MD: Rowman & Littlefield, 1995.

Kirkendall, Andrew J. "From 'Liberty and Order' to 'Order and Progress':
Republican Discourse among São Paulo Law Students, 1878–1889,"
SECOLAS Annals 27 (March 1996): 91–96.

———. "Orators and Poets: Language and Elite Male Identity at the São
Paulo Law School,1850–1889," *South Eastern Latin Americanist* 38,
no. 4 (spring 1995): 43–48.

Lamy, Alberto Sousa. *A Academia de Coimbra, 1537–1990.* Lisbon: Reis dos
Livros, 1990.

Lanning, John Tate. *Academic Culture in the Spanish Colonies.* 1940.
Reprint, Port Washington NY: Kennikat Press, 1971.

Lauderdale Graham, Sandra. *House and Street: The Domestic World of Servants and Masters in Nineteenth-Century Rio de Janeiro.* Cambridge: Cambridge University Press, 1988.

————. "The Vintem Riot and Political Culture: Rio de Janeiro, 1880," *Hispanic American Historical Review* 60, no. 3 (August 1980): 431–49.

Lears, T. J. Jackson. "The Concept of Cultural Hegemony: Problems and Possibilities," *American Historical Review* 90, no. 3 (June 1985): 567–93.

Leeds, Anthony. "Brazilian Careers and Social Structure: An Evolutionary Model and Case History," *American Anthropologist* 66, no. 6 (December 1964): 1321–47.

Leloudis, James L. *Schooling the New South: Pedagogy, Self, and Society in North Carolina,1880–1920.* Chapel Hill: University of North Carolina Press, 1996.

Lemos, Francisco de. *Relação Geral do Estado da Universidade de Coimbra.* Facsimile edition. 1777. Reprint, Coimbra: University of Coimbra, 1980.

Levine, Robert. *Pernambuco in the Brazilian Federation.* Stanford: Stanford University Press, 1978.

Levinson, Bradley Adam. " 'Todos Somos Iguales': Cultural Production and Social Difference at a Mexican Secondary School." Ph.D. diss., University of North Carolina at Chapel Hill, 1993.

Levinson, Bradley Adam, Douglas Foley, and Dorothy Holland. *The Cultural Production of the Educated Person: Critical Ethnographies of Schooling and Local Practice.* Albany: State University of New York Press, 1996.

Lewin, Linda. *Politics and Parentela in Paraiba: A Case Study of Family-based Oligarchy in Brazil.* Princeton: Princeton University Press, 1987.

Lima, Hermes. *Introdução Geral: Tobias Barreto: A Época e o Homem.* São Paulo: Instituto Nacional do Livro, 1963.

Lincoln, W. Bruce. *In the Vanguard of Reform: Russia's Enlightened Bureaucrats, 1825–1861.* DeKalb: Northern Illinois University Press, 1982.

Lins, Álvaro. *Rio-Branco (O Barão do Rio Branco), 1845–1912*. Rio de Janeiro: Livraria José Olympio Editora, 1945.

Lins, Ivan. *Histório do Positivismo*. São Paulo: Companhia Editora Nacional, 1967.

Logue, William. *From Philosophy to Sociology: The Evolution of French Liberalism, 1870–1914*. DeKalb: Northern Illinois University Press, 1983.

López-Alves, Fernando. *State Formation and Democracy in Latin America, 1810–1900*. Durham: Duke University Press, 2000.

Love, Joseph. *Rio Grande do Sul and Brazilian Regionalism, 1889–1930*. Stanford: Stanford University Press, 1971.

———. *São Paulo in the Brazilian Federation, 1889–1937*. Stanford: Stanford University Press, 1980.

Loveman, Brian. *For la Patria: Politics and the Armed Forces in Latin America*. Wilmington DE: Scholarly Resources, 1999.

Luz, Nícia Villela. "O Papel dos Classes Médias no Movimento Republicano," *Revista de História* (January–March 1964): 13–27.

Lynch, John. *Caudillos in Spanish America*. New York: Clarendon Press, 1992.

Macaulay, Neill. *Dom Pedro I: The Struggle for Freedom and Liberty in Brazil and Portugal*. Durham: Duke University Press, 1986.

Macedo, Ubiritan Borges de. *A Liberdade no Império: O Pensamento sobre a Liberdade no Império Brasileiro*. São Paulo: Editora Convivo, 1977.

Maciel de Barros, Spencer. *A Ilustração Brasileira e a Idéia da Universidade*. São Paulo: Editora da Universidade de São Paulo, 1986.

———. *A Significação Educativa do Romantismo: Gonçalves de Magalhães*. São Paulo: Editora da Universidade de São Paulo, 1973.

Magalhães Junior, R. *José de Alencar e sua Época*. Rio de Janeiro: Civilização Brasileira, 1977.

———. *A Vida Turbulenta de José do Patrocínio*. São Paulo: LISA, 1972.

Magalhães, Valentim. *Quadros e Contos*. São Palo: Dolivaes Nunes, 1882.

Malerba, Jurandir. *Os Brancos da Lei: Liberalismo, Escravidão e Mentalidade Patriarcal no Império do Brasil* (Maringá, Paraná: Editora da Universidade Estadual de Maringá, 1994).

Mallon, Florencia. *Peasant and Nation: The Making of Postcolonial Mexico and Peru*. Berkeley: University of California Press, 1995.

Marson, Izabel Andrade. *Movimento Praieiro, 1842–1849: Imprensa, Ideologia, e Poder*. São Paulo: Editora Moderna, 1980.

Martin, Denis-Constant. "The Choices of Identity," *Social Identities* 1, no. 1 (1995): 5–20.

Martins, Heitor. "Byron e *O Guaraní*," *Luso-Brazilian Review* 2 (December 1965): 69–74.

Martins, Henrique. *Lista Geral dos Bacharéis e Doutores que Tem Obtido o Respectivo Grao na Faculdade de Direito do Recife*. Recife: Imprensa Industrial, 1923.

✓ Martins, Luís. *O Patriarca e o Bacharel*. São Paulo: Editora Livraria Martins, 1949.

Mattos, Ilmar Rohloff de. *O Tempo Saquarema: A Formação do Estado Imperial*. São Paulo: Editora Hucitec, 1990.

Mattoon Jr., Robert H. "Railroads, Coffee, and the Growth of Big Business in São Paulo, Brazil," *Hispanic American Historical Review* 57, no. 2 (1977): 273–95.

Maxwell, Kenneth. *Pombal: Paradox of the Enlightenment*. Cambridge: Cambridge University Press, 1995.

McLachlan, James. "The Choice of Hercules: American Student Societies in the Early Nineteenth Century." In *The University in Society*, edited by Lawrence Stone. Volume 2. Princeton: Princeton University Press, 1976.

Medina, Maricela. "Tobias Barreto (1838–1889): Odyssey of a Nineteenth-Century Brazilian." Ph.D. diss., University of Michigan at Ann Arbor, 1986.

Melo Franco, Afonso Arinos de. *Rodrigues Alves: Apogeu e Declínio do Presidencialismo*. Volume 1. Rio de Janeiro: Livraria José Olympio, 1973.

Mendonça, Carlos Süssekind de. "Lúcio de Mendonça: Anos de Formação," *Revista do Livro* 1, no. 3–4 (December 1956): 93–103.

———. "Lúcio de Mendonça: Últimos Anos de Estudante," *Revista do Livro* 4, no. 16 (December 1959): 83–97.

Mendonça, Lúcio de. *Horas do Bom Tempo: Memórias e Phantasias.* Rio de Janeiro: Laemmert e C., Editoras, 1901.

Mendonça, Renato. *Um Diplomata na Corte de Inglaterra: O Barão do Penedo e sua Época.* São Paulo: Companhia Editora Nacional, 1942.

Metcalf, Alida. *Family and Frontier in Colonial Brazil: Santana de Parnaiba, 1580–1822.* Berkeley: University of California Press, 1992.

Morse, Richard. *O Espelho do Próspero: Cultura e Idéias nas Americas.* São Paulo: Companhia das Letras, 1988.

———. *From Community to Metropolis: A Biography of São Paulo, Brazil.* New York: Octagon Books, 1974.

———. *New World Soundings: Culture and Ideology in the Americas.* Baltimore: Johns Hopkins University Press, 1989.

Mosher, Jeffrey Carl. "Pernambuco and the Construction of the Brazilian Nation-State, 1831–1850." Ph.D. diss., University of Florida, 1996.

Murray, Pamela. *Dreams of Development: Colombia's National School of Mines and its Engineers, 1887–1970.* Tuscaloosa: University of Alabama Press, 1997.

Nabuco, Carolina. *The Life of Joaquim Nabuco.* Translated and edited by Ronald Hilton. Stanford: Stanford University Press, 1950.

Nabuco, Joaquim. "A Escravidão," *Revista do Instituto Histórico e Geográfico Brasileiro* 204 (July–September 1949): 3–126.

———. *Minha Formação.* Rio de Janeiro: Edições de Ouro, 1966.

———. *O Povo e o Throno.* Rio de Janeiro: n. p., 1869.

———. *Um Estadista do Império.* Rio de Janeiro: Editora Nova Aguilar S.A., 1975.

Nachman, Robert G. "Positivism, Modernization, and the Middle Class in Brazil," *Hispanic American Historical Review* 57, no. 1 (February 1977): 1–23.

Naldi, Mildred Reina Gonçalves. "O Barão e o Bacharel: Um Estudo de Política Local no Segundo Reinado (O Caso da Franca)." Ph.D. diss., Universidade de São Paulo, 1988.

Nascimento, Luíz do. *História da Imprensa de Pernambuco (1821–1954).* 4 volumes. Recife: Universidade Federal de Pernambuco, 1970.

Nazarri, Muriel. *Disappearance of the Dowry: Women, Family, and Social change in São Paulo, Brazil (1600–1900)*. Stanford: Stanford University Press, 1991.

Needell, Jeffrey. "A Liberal Embraces Monarchy: Joaquim Nabuco and Conservative Historiography," *Americas* 48, no. 2 (October 1991): 159–79.

————. "Party Formation and State-Making: The Conservative Party and the Reconstruction of the Brazilian State, 1831–1850," *Hispanic American Historical Review* (forthcoming).

————. "Provincial Origins of the Brazilian State: The Province of Rio de Janeiro, the Monarchy, and National Political Organization, 1808–1853," *Latin American Research Review* (forthcoming).

————. *A Tropical Belle Époque: Elite Culture and Society in Turn-of-the-Century Rio de Janeiro*. Cambridge: Cambridge University Press, 1987.

Nestor, Odilon. *Faculdade de Direito do Recife: Traços da sua História*. Recife: Imprensa Industrial, 1976.

Novak, Steven J. *The Rights of Youth: American Colleges and Student Revolt, 1798–1815*. Cambridge MA: Harvard University Press, 1977.

Ong, Walter J. *Orality and Literacy: The Technologizing of the Word*. London: Methuen, 1982.

Orico, Osvaldo. *Silveira Martins e sua Época*. Porto Alegre: Livraria do Globo, 1935.

Paim, Artur. "Artur Orlando e a Escola do Recife," *Estudos Universitários (Universidade Federal de Pernambuco)* 3–4 (July–December 1975).

Paixão Liau, Wilma. "*A Lucta*: Dimensões de um Jornal Acadêmico (1882)." Master's thesis, Universidade de São Paulo, 1979.

Pang, Eul-Soo. *Bahia in the First Brazilian Republic, 1889–1934*. Gainesville: University Press of Florida, 1978.

————. *In Pursuit of Honor and Power: Noblemen of the Southern Cross in Nineteenth-Century Brazil*. Tuscaloosa: University of Alabama Press, 1988.

Pang, Eul-Soo, and Ron Seckinger. "The Mandarins of Imperial Brazil," *Comparative Studies in Society and History* 14 (March 1972): 215–44.

Peloso, Vincent C., and Barbara A. Tenenbaum, eds. *Liberals, Politics, and*

Power: State Formation in Nineteenth-Century Latin America. Athens: University of Georgia Press, 1996.

Pessanha Povoa. *Annos Acadêmicos: São Paulo, 1860–1864*. Rio de Janeiro: Typographia Perserverança, 1870.

Pimenta Bueno, José Antônio. *Direito Público Brasileiro e Análise da Constituição do Império*. Rio de Janeiro: Ministério da Justiça e Negócios Interiores, Serviço da Documentação, 1958.

Prado, Paulo. *Retrato do Brasil: Ensaio sôbre a Tristeza Brasileira*. Rio de Janeiro: Livraria José Olympio Editora, 1962.

Rama, Angel. *The Lettered City*. Translated by John Charles Chasteen. Durham: Duke University Press, 1996.

Reddy, William M. *The Invisible Code: Honor and Sentiment in Postrevolutionary France, 1814–1848*. Berkeley: University of California Press, 1997.

Reinhart, Helen Katherine. "A Political History of the Brazilian Regency, 1831–1840." Ph.D. diss., University of Illinois at Urbana, 1960.

Rio-Branco, Raul do. *Reminiscências do Barão do Rio-Branco*. Rio de Janeiro: Livraria José Olympio Editora, 1942.

Robson, David W. *Educating Republicans: The College in the Era of the American Revolution, 1750–1800*. Westport CT: Greenwood Press, 1985.

Rocha, Hildon. *Álvares de Azevedo: Anjo e Demônio do Romantismo*. Rio de Janeiro: Livraria José Olympio Editora, 1982.

Roeber, A. G. *Faithful Magistrates and Republican Lawyers: Creators of Virginia Legal Culture, 1680–1810*. Chapel Hill: University of North Carolina Press, 1981.

Rothblatt, Sheldon. "How 'Professional' Are the Professions? A Review Article." *Comparative Studies in Society and History* 37, no. 1 (January 1995): 194–204.

————. *The Revolution of the Dons: Cambridge and Society in Victorian England*. New York: Basic Books, 1968.

Rotundo, E. Anthony. *American Manhood: Transformations in Masculinity from the American Revolution to the Modern Era*. New York: Basic Books, 1993.

Rozbick, Michael J. *The Complete Colonial Gentleman: Cultural Legitimacy in Plantation Virginia*. Charlottesville: University of Virginia Press, 1998.

Russell-Wood, A. J. R. "Antônio Álvares Pereira: A Brazilian Student at the University of Coimbra in the Seventeenth Century." In *Society and Government in Colonial Brazil, 1500–1822*. Aldershot, England: Variorum, 1992.

Safford, Frank. *The Ideal of the Practical: Colombia's Struggle to Form a Technical Elite*. Austin: University of Texas Press, 1976.

——. "Politics, Ideology, and Society in Post-Independence Spanish America." In *The Cambridge History of Latin America*. Edited by Leslie Bethell. Volume 3. Cambridge: Cambridge University Press, 1984.

Santos, Wanderly Guilherme dos. "Liberalism in Brazil: Ideology and Praxis." In *Terms of Conflict: Ideology in Latin American Politics*, edited by Morris J. Blackman and Ronald G. Hellman. Philadelphia: Institute for the Study of Human Values, 1977, pp. 1–38.

Santos Filho, Lyçurgo de Castro. "Martim Cabral," *Revista do Arquivo Municipal (São Paulo)* 40 (July–December 1977): 397–400.

Sarmiento, Domingo. *Life in the Argentine Republic in the Days of the Tyrants; or Civilization and Barbarism*. Translated by Mrs. Horace Mann. New York: Hafner, 1868.

Schamber, Ellie Nower. *The Artist as Politician: The Relationship between the Art and the Politics of the French Romantics*. Lanham MD: University Press of America, 1984.

Schmitt, Carl. *Political Romanticism*. Translated by Guy Oakes. Cambridge MA: MIT Press, 1986.

Schulz, John. *O Exército na Política: Origens da Intervenção Militar, 1850–1894*. São Paulo: Editora da Universidade de São Paulo, 1994.

Schwarcz, Lilia Moritz. *As Barbas do Imperador: D. Pedro II, um Monarca no Trópicos*. São Paulo: Companhia das Letras, 1998.

——. *The Spectacle of the Races: Scientists, Institutions, and the Race Question in Brazil, 1870–1930*. Translated by Leland Guyer. New York: Hill and Wang, 1999.

Schwarcz, Roberto. *Misplaced Ideas: Essays on Brazilian Culture*. London: Verso, 1992.

Schwartz, Stuart. *Sovereignty and Society in Colonial Brazil: The High Court of Bahia and Its Judges, 1609–1751*. Berkeley: University of California Press, 1973.

Serbin, Kenneth. "Priests, Celibacy, and Social Conflict: A History of Brazil's Clergy and Seminaries." Ph.D. diss., University of California at San Diego, 1993.

Sette, Mario. *Arruar, História Pitoresca do Recife Antigo*. Rio de Janeiro: Livraria Editora da Casa dos Estudantes do Brasil, 1952.

Sevcenko, Nicolau. *Literatura como Missão: Tensões Sociais e Criação Cultural na Primeira República*. São Paulo: Brasiliense, 1983.

Silva Jardim. *A Gente do Mosteiro (no Anno Passado)*. São Paulo: Typographia da 'Tribuna Liberal,' 1879.

———. *Memórias e Viagens: Campanha de um Propagandista (1887–1890)*. Lisbon, n. p., 1891.

Simmel, Georg. *The Web of Group Affiliations*. Glencoe IL: Free Press, 1955.

Skidmore, Thomas. "Eduardo Prado: A Conservative Nationalist Critic of the Early Brazilian Republic," *Luso-Brazilian Review* 12, no. 2 (winter 1975): 149–61.

———. *The Politics of Military Rule in Brazil, 1964–85*. New York: Oxford University Press, 1988.

Smith, Peter H. "Political Legitimacy in Spanish America." In *New Approaches in Latin American History*, edited by Richard Graham and Peter H. Smith. Austin: University of Texas Press, 1974.

Smith-Rosenberg, Carroll. "The Female World of Love and Ritual," *Signs* 1, no. 1 (fall 1975): 1–29.

Soares, Angêlica. *Ressonâncias Veladas da Lira: Álvares de Azevedo e o Poema Romântico-Intimista*. Rio de Janeiro: Tempo Brasileiro, 1989.

Sommer, Doris. *Foundational Fictions: The National Romances of Latin America*. Berkeley: University of California Press, 1991.

Souza, Roberto Acízelo de. *O Império da Eloqüencia: Retórica e Poesia no Brasil Oitocentista*. Rio de Janeiro: EdUERJ e EdUFF, 1999.

Spitzer, Alan B. *The French Generation of 1820*. Princeton: Princeton University Press, 1987.

Stepan, Alfred. *The Military in Politics*. Princeton: Princeton University Press, 1971.

Stowe, Steven M. *Intimacy and Power in the Old South: Ritual in the Lives of the Planters.* Baltimore: Johns Hopkins University Press, 1987.

Suleiman, Ezra N. *Elites in French Society: The Politics of Survival.* Princeton: Princeton University Press, 1978.

Szuchman, Mark D. "The Middle Period in Latin American History: Values in Search of Explanations." In *The Middle Period in Latin American History,* edited by Mark Szuchman. Boulder CO: Westview Press, 1989.

———. *Order, Family, and Community in Buenos Aires, 1810–1860.* Stanford: Stanford University Press, 1988.

Telles, Pedro Carlos da Silva. *História da Engenharia no Brasil Séculos XVI a XIX).* Rio de Janeiro: Livros Técnicos e Científicos Editora S.A., 1984.

Tolman, Jon. "Castro Alves, Poeto Amoroso," *Luso-Brazilian Review* 12, no. 2 (winter 1975): 241–62.

Toplin, Robert Brent. *The Abolition of Slavery in Brazil.* New York: Atheneum, 1972.

Tôrres, João Camilo de Oliveira. *A Democracia Coroada: Teoria Política do Império do Brasil.* Petropolis: Vozes, 1964.

Turner, Victor W. *The Ritual Process: Structure and Anti-Structure.* New York: Aldine, 1969.

———, and Edward M. Burner. *The Anthropology of Experience.* Urbana: University of Illinois Press, 1986.

Uribe, Victor. "Rebellion of the Young 'Mandarins': Lawyers, Political Parties, and the State in Colombia, 1780–1850." Ph.D. diss., University of Pittsburgh, 1993.

Uribe-Uran, Victor. "Changing Meanings of Honor, Status, and Class: The Letrados and Bureaucrats of New Granada in the Late Colonial and Early Post-Colonial Periods." Unpublished paper, Latin American Studies Association, 1995.

———. *Honorable Lives: Lawyers, Family, and Politics in Colombia, 1780–1850.* Pittsburgh: University of Pittsburgh Press, 2000.

———. "The Lawyers and New Granada's Late Colonial State," *Journal of Latin American Studies* 27, no. 3 (October 1995): 517–49.

Uricoechea, Victor. *The Patrimonial Foundations of the Brazilian Bureaucratic State.* Berkeley: University of California Press, 1980.

Vampré. Spencer. *Memórias para a História da Academia de São Paulo.*
  2 vols. São Paulo: Livraria Acadêmica, 1924.
Vargas, M. *Contribuições para a História da Engenharia no Brasil.* São Paulo:
  EDUSP, 1994.
Veiga, Gláucio. *História das Idéias da Faculdade de Direito do Recife.*
  7 volumes. Recife: Universidade Federal de Pernambuco and
  Artegrafi, 1980–1993.
Venâncio Filho, Alberto. *Das Arcadas ao Bacharelismo: 150 Anos de Ensino
  Jurídico no Brasil.* São Paulo: Editora Perspectiva, 1977.
———. *Notícia Histórica da Ordem dos Advogados do Brasil (1930–1980)*
  Rio de Janeiro: Ordem dos Advogados do Brasil, 1979.
Viana Filho, Luís. *A Vida de Rui Barbosa.* Rio de Janeiro: Instituto Nacional
  do Livro, 1977.
Weffort, Francisco. *Por Que Democracia?* São Paulo: Editora Brasiliense,
  1984.
Werneck Sodré, Nelson. *A História da Imprensa no Brasil.* Rio de Janeiro:
  Editora Civilisação Brasileira, 1960.
Williams, Mary Wilhelmine. *Dom Pedro the Magnanimous: Second Emperor
  of Brazil.* New York: Octagon Books, 1966.
Willis, Paul. *Learning to Labor: How Working-class Kids Get Working-class
  Jobs.* New York: Columbia University Press, 1977.
Wirth, John D. *Minas Gerais in the Brazilian Federation.* Stanford: Stanford
  University Press, 1977.
Wyatt-Brown, Bertram. *Southern Honor: Ethics and Behavior in the Old
  South.* New York: Oxford University Press, 1982.
Yeager, Gertrude M. "Elite Education in Nineteenth-Century Chile,"
  Hispanic American Historical Review 71, no. 1 (February 1991): 73–105.
Zaluar, Augusto Emílio. *Peregrinação Pela Provincia de São Paulo (1860–
  1861).* São Paulo: Universidade de São Paulo, 1975.
Zilbermann, Regina. "Mulher Educável, Depois Educadora, Enfim Leitora
  Infiel: O Público Feminino no Brasil do Século XIX," *Luso-Brazilian
  Review* 26, no. 2 (winter 1989): 131–43.

NEWSPAPERS

Unless otherwise noted, the following newspapers are student newspapers and are available at the Biblioteca Nacional, Seção de Obras Raras, Rio de Janeiro.

A Actualidade (nonstudent)
O Album dos Academicos Olindenses
O Amigos das Letras
O Argos Olindense
O Atheneu Pernambucano
Aurora
O Bello Sexo
O Brado da Indignação
Ça Irá
O Clarim Litterário
O Constitucional (Library of the Faculdade de Direito de São Paulo)
Corréio Paulistano (nonstudent)
O Eco D'Olinda
Ensaios da Sociedade Brazilia
Ensaios Jurídicos e Litterários
Ensaios Litterários
Ensaios Litterários do Atheneu Pernambucano
Era Nova (Library of the Faculdade de Direito de São Paulo).
A Estréa
A Evolução
O Evolucionista
Faculdade do Recife
O Federalista
Forum Litterário
O Futuro (1862)
O Futuro (1864)
A Ganganelli
Imprensa Acadêmica
Independência (Library of the Faculdade de Direito de São Paulo)
O Kaleidoscópio

A Legenda
O Lidador Acadêmico
A Lucta
Memórias da Associação Culto á Sciencia
O Olindense
A Onda
A Ordem
O País (nonstudent)
A Propaganda
O Publicador Paulistano (nonstudent)
A Reacção
A República (1871; nonstudent)
A República (1882)
A República (1886)
Revista Acadêmica
Revista Acadêmica de Sciencias e Lettras
Revista da Academia
Revista da Academia Litterária
Revista da Associação Recréeio Instructivo
Revista do Club Acadêmico
Revista Republicana (nonstudent)
O Sete de Setembro
Tribuna Acadêmica
O Tymbira
A União
O Ypiranga (nonstudent)

Index